The Play of Terror
in Nineteenth-Century
France

The Play of Terror in Nineteenth-Century France

Edited by

John T. Booker

and

Allan H. Pasco

DELAWARE

Newark: University of Delaware Press
London: Associated University Presses

Associated University Presses
440 Forsgate Drive
Cranbury, NJ 08512

Associated University Presses
16 Barter Street
London WC1A 2AH, England

Associated University Presses
P.O. Box 338, Port Credit
Mississauga, Ontario
Canada L5G 4L8

The paper used in this publication meets the requirements
of the American National Standard for Permanence of Paper
for Printed Library Materials Z39.48–1984.

Library of Congress Cataloging-in-Publication Data

The play of terror in nineteenth-century France / edited by John T. Booker and Allan H. Pasco.
    p.   cm.
Includes bibliographical references and index.
ISBN 0-87413-589-3 (alk. paper)
    1. French literature—19th century—History and criticism.
2. Terror in literature.   3. France—History—Reign of Terror, 1793–1794.   I. Booker, John T., 1942–   . II. Pasco, Allan H.
PQ283.P555   1997
840.9'16—dc20   96-12771
                                                  CIP

PRINTED IN THE UNITED STATES OF AMERICA

Contents

Part Three: Resolution?

Contributors

JOHN T. BOOKER is Associate Professor of French at the University of Kansas. He has published articles on Constant, Balzac, Stendhal, Gide, and Mauriac, and is interested in particular in first-person narration.

CATHARINE SAVAGE BROSMAN is the Kathryn B. Gore Professor of French at Tulane University. Her most recent book is *French Culture 1900–1975* (1995). The author of books on Beauvoir, Gide, Martin du Gard, Roy, and Sartre, she has also edited five volumes in the *Dictionary of Literary Biography* series, including the two devoted to French fiction of the nineteenth century.

FRÉDÉRIC CANOVAS, Visiting Assistant Professor of French at Reed College, has published articles on André Gide, René Crevel, Julien Gracq, and Vercors. He is currently completing a collection of essays on literary dreams from Baudelaire to surrealism.

HOPE CHRISTIANSEN is Assistant Professor of French at the University of Arkansas. Her publications include articles on Crébillon fils, Balzac, Flaubert, and Colette. She is presently working on a study of the waltz scenes in *Madame Bovary* and Daniel Stern's *Nélida*.

MARY JANE COWLES is Associate Professor of French at Kenyon College. She has published on Anatole France and is currently completing a project on the Absent Mother in French Literature, 1770–1850.

PAMELA GENOVA, Assistant Professor of French at the University of Oklahoma, has a recent book, *André Gide dans le labyrinthe de la mythotextualité* (1995). She has also published articles on Decadence, Symbolist poetics, Modernism and Surrealism, and the interrelationship among the arts in fin-de-siècle France.

RICHARD E. GOODKIN is Professor of French at the University of Wisconsin-Madison. He has published books on Mallarmé, Proust, and Racine, and is at present working on the question of family relations in French classical theater.

RICHARD B. GRANT is Professor of French Language and Literature at the University of Texas in Austin. He is the author of numerous books and articles on nineteenth-century French fiction.

KATHLEEN HART is Assistant Professor of French at Vassar College. She is currently exploring the relations between pre-Marxist socialism and women's autobiography in nineteenth-century France.

OWEN HEATHCOTE is Senior Lecturer in French Studies at the University of Bradford, U.K. His scholarly interests include Balzac, as well as twentieth-century authors such as Marguerite Duras, Hervé Guibert, Eric Jourdan, and Monique Wittig. He is a member of the Research Unit in Violence, Abuse and Gender Relations at the University of Bradford.

J. A. HIDDLESTON is Fellow in French at Exeter College in the University of Oxford. His research interests lie especially in nineteenth- and twentieth-century poetry and in the relationship between literature and the visual arts.

RENÉE KINGCAID, Associate Professor of French at Saint Mary's College, is the author of *Neurosis and Narrative: The Decadent Short Fiction of Proust, Lorrain, and Rachilde.* She has published a number of articles on nineteenth- and twentieth-century French literature and is editing a collection of essays on mothers' deaths in French literature.

ARMINE KOTIN MORTIMER is Professor of French Literature and of Criticism and Interpretive Theory at the University of Illinois in Urbana-Champaign. She is the author of *La clôture narrative, The Gentlest Law: Roland Barthes's The Pleasure of the Text,* and *Plotting to Kill.* She is working at present on the *écriture* of realism in several key texts.

CHARLES NUNLEY is Assistant Professor of French at Middlebury College and has written articles on Francis Ponge and the nineteenth-century French prose poem tradition. His current research interests include the journalistic writings of French poets during World War II.

ALLAN H. PASCO is the Hall Distinguished Professor of Nineteenth-Century Literature at the University of Kansas. His most recent books are on Balzac's *La comédie humaine* and on allusion as a literary device.

WILLIAM PAULSON is Professor of French at the University of Michigan, Ann Arbor. He has published a number of articles on Ballanche and Balzac. His most recent book is *Sentimental Education: The Complexity of Disenchantment* (1992).

JONATHAN P. RIBNER is Associate Professor of Art History at Boston University. Pursuing interdisciplinary research in French art of the late eighteenth and nineteenth centuries and in Victorian art, he is the author of *Broken Tablets: The Cult of the Law in French Art from David to Delacroix* (1993).

PATRICIA A. WARD, Professor of French at Vanderbilt University, is the author of *The Medievalism of Victor Hugo, Joseph Joubert and the Critical Tradition: Platonism and Romanticism,* and *Carnet bibliographique Victor Hugo: 1978–1980* and *1981–1983,* the latter with Bernadette Lintz Murphy. She has published several essays dealing with the rhetoric and mythology of the French Revolution.

PAULINE WAHL WILLIS is Associate Professor of French Language and Literature at the University of Calgary. She is the coauthor of two textbooks in the field of French as a second language and has published a number of articles on Stendhal.

The Play of Terror
in Nineteenth-Century
France

Introduction

JOHN T. BOOKER

THIS volume brings together a number of studies that were originally presented as papers at the nineteenth annual Colloquium
in Nineteenth-Century French Studies, held at the University of
Kansas in October, 1993. Organized around the theme of "Terror
and Terrorism," that conference featured work that was both excellent in quality and very diverse in terms of subject matter and
approach. The present volume, the result of a careful process of
selection, reflects that general excellence and diversity.

The term "terror" evokes a range of connotations, from the
historical Terror of the French Revolution to the more common
acceptation of fear or intense anxiety experienced in the face of
violence, coercion, or intimidation. The Terror itself remains the
most striking image of a Revolution which not only altered the
immediate course of French history, but was to have an impact,
directly or indirectly, on virtually every facet of life in
nineteenth-century France. A number of articles in this collection do in fact bear on the representation—historical, fictional,
or artistic—of some aspect of that turbulent revolutionary period. In most cases, however, the "terror" in question here is of
a more general, at times even figurative nature, resulting from a
fundamental imbalance of power between opposing factions. It
is that broader sense of a "play of terror" between uneven and
antagonistic forces that the title and organization of the present
volume are intended to convey.

Grouped together in a first section are essays that deal in one
way or another with the apparent domination of one party
(whether individual, group, or sex) over another. The articles
of the central section, by contrast, highlight a more open and
unresolved tension, without either side being able to establish
dominance. The studies of the third section address a series of
different situations which seem to lead to a degree of resolution,
the working out of an ostensibly stable order. In fact, however, the
"resolution" of Part 3 is revealed to be every bit as problematic as

13

the "domination" of Part 1; in each instance, there remains that underlying play of terror, literal or figurative, which is the unifying theme of this collection.

I

Catharine Savage Brosman's overview of nineteenth-century attitudes toward the large-scale violence of warfare provides an appropriate opening, not only for the first section, but for the volume as a whole. While armed combat between states had frequently been justified on philosophical grounds, the changing nature of military campaigns as they were waged during the Revolutionary and Napoleonic periods prompted a reconsideration of the issue. On what grounds (if any) might it be possible to justify the organized terror of this new, more modern face of warfare? Among those under the Restoration and July Monarchy who reflected on that question, Brosman focuses on the contrasting positions articulated by Joseph de Maistre and Alfred de Vigny.

With Charles Nunley's essay on *Quatrevingt-treize*, we move from a more abstract consideration of the terror of warfare to Victor Hugo's dramatic evocation of the historical Terror itself. The role of the central female character, Michelle Fléchard, calls attention to the interplay of gender, language, and terror (a subject treated, in different ways, by a number of the authors in this volume). In the often terrifying world of Hugo's novel, to speak— and especially to write—is to exercise power, and that power lies predominantly in the hands of men. Defined above all by her maternity, Michelle Fléchard would seem to be effectively "silenced" by the men with whom she comes into contact, and yet her situation, Nunley suggests, is perhaps less clearcut in that respect than it might at first appear.

Like Nunley, Kathleen Hart looks at the gendered nature of language and terror, but from the perspective of a woman writer. Flora Tristan's autobiographical text, *Pérégrinations d'une paria*, invokes a geological terror associated with the oppression of women. Relegated to the role of pariah by paternal law, the excluded female becomes, in Tristan's unsettling vision, the source of cataclysmic events—earthquakes and volcanic eruptions— which threaten to undermine the patriarchal order itself.

The haunting specter of the historical Terror is highlighted by Jonathan P. Ribner in his treatment of the Salon of 1827–28, where the state-sponsored paintings revealed a continuing struggle for ascendancy between Monarchists and those who sought to undo the Restoration. The selection of works to be exhibited can be viewed in one sense as an attempt to "paint over" the Terror. At the same time, the depiction of that struggle, the decision to display edifying examples of courage in the face of revolutionary violence, serves to keep alive an image of the very sort of upheaval so feared by those in power.

The first section of the volume comes to a close in a much lighter vein, with Pamela A. Genova's look at the seemingly incongruous "terror" of dandyism. Often dismissed as bizarre and pointless behavior not only by nineteenth-century society, but by much of modern criticism, dandyism, argues Genova, might be assessed more appropriately as a subtle, indirect—and perhaps thereby all the more effective—means of calling into question the foundations of the dominant order which would seek to dismiss it out of hand.

II

Setting the tone for the second section, Richard E. Goodkin brings together, in a rich, suggestive reading, two texts quite dissimilar in appearance, Mallarmé's early poem, "Brise marine," and Maupassant's short story, "Sur l'eau." In each case, the presence of a female figure stands in a particular relationship to the unknown, longed for by Mallarmé's restless poet, but a source of indefinable and gripping terror for Maupassant's protagonist. Goodkin's own text effectively traces through these two works the play of desire between the familiar and the unknown.

In an analogous manner, Mary Jane Cowles explores the shifting boundaries between truth and fiction, reason and insanity, historical fact and supernatural vision, in two very different works, Nodier's *conte*, "Jean-François les Bas-Bleus," and Nerval's biography of Jacques Cazotte. What seems striking in both instances, as Cowles points out, is what is missing: any precise representation of the period of revolutionary terror, the historical backdrop in each case, has been curiously elided.

Stendhal's *Lamiel* provides an equally fertile field of inquiry for Pauline Wahl Willis, who takes as her point of departure the novel's unfinished status. Following the interplay of recurrent motifs, notably those of fire and blood, Willis is able to identify terror as the primary textual principle at work in each version of the novel; it is responsible, she argues, not only for the existence of the fiction in the first place, but, paradoxically, for its ultimately incomplete state.

With his analysis of Balzac's *Une ténébreuse affaire*, Owen Heathcote brings us back to a more direct consideration of the Revolutionary period. His essay, like a number of others in this collection, raises basic questions about the fictional representation of terror. To what extent can a coherent narration capture (and still faithfully convey) the disorder and chaos of a violent era? Can such a representation serve to critique that violence, or must it inevitably remain in complicity with it? For Heathcote, *Une ténébreuse affaire* is especially interesting in this context, since it does not appear to propose a clear resolution of these issues.

The representation of a very different sort of terror—that of the nightmare—is taken up by Frédéric Canovas. The text in question is an intriguing piece by Huysmans which seems to defy easy classification: published initially as a "review" of new work by the artist, Odilon Redon, it then appeared a year later, with only slight modifications, as a prose poem in its own right. Focusing on the differences between the two versions of that problematic text, Canovas explores the relationship between writing and art, on the one hand, and between writing and dream, on the other.

Huysmans is also the subject of the following essay by Renée Kingcaid, who looks at three rather disparate works—*En ménage* (1881), *La cathédrale* (1898), and *Sainte Lydwine de Schiedam* (1901)—in which women are depicted, from a masculine point of view, as "sexual terrorists." In a manner which is playful on occasion and consistently convincing, Kingcaid uncovers the strategies (semantic as well as spatial) by which the male characters of Huysmans attempt—in vain—to confine and control a female sexuality perceived as threatening.

The final essay of the second section, by William Paulson, draws on the notion of "literary terrorism" formulated by Jean Paulhan early in this century. Paulson's own point of departure is a little-known text by Pierre-Simon Ballanche, *L'homme sans nom*, in which the central character, *le Régicide*, figures as a "proto-terrorist," one who denounces the tyranny of revolutionary rhetoric while ultimately yielding, in spite of himself, to its seductive power. The dilemma of Ballanche's protagonist allows Paulson to expose more generally the ambivalent situation of the writer at that moment in history when the culture of the printed word was being firmly established.

III

In the first of the studies to explore the possibility of a stable resolution of tensions, Hope Christiansen traces the shifting roles of master and slave in *Le rouge et le noir* and *Indiana*. Christiansen underlines the interdependence of those roles— there can be no master without slave, and vice versa—as well as the surprising ease with which they come to be exchanged by Julien and Mathilde, in Stendhal's novel, and by Indiana and Raymon de Ramière, in that of George Sand. While the ending of each work suggests that true happiness is possible only when individuals move beyond the symbiotic master/slave relationship to one of equality, the particular circumstances of each dénouement call into question the realistic possibility of any such resolution.

The endings of *Le rouge et le noir* and *Indiana* provide an appropriate transition to J. A. Hiddleston's wide-ranging survey of suicide as a recurring feature in nineteenth-century French fiction. Hiddleston looks closely at *Atala* and *René*, which were to have an inordinate impact on later writers, before going on to consider more briefly novels by Stendhal, Flaubert, Zola, and others. The recourse to suicide as a "solution" in the work of so many major writers of the century indicates for Hiddleston a fundamental—and troubling—shift in Western consciousness.

With her essay on Prosper de Barante, Patricia A. Ward shifts our attention from fiction back to history, although one of her principal points is that the distinction between those two genres, at least in the case of Barante, is often problematic. In undertaking his *Histoire de la Convention Nationale*, published in mid-century, Barante set himself the ambitious goal—one that would prove to be unattainable, in Ward's view—of recording the reality of a turbulent period in a narrative mode that would itself remain objective and impartial.

That same historical period had already furnished much of the material for Balzac's *Histoire des Treize*. In his study of that work, Richard B. Grant draws attention to the terror experienced by the Balzacian character in the face of events which can no longer be understood according to accepted laws of behavior; the result, not surprisingly, is an overriding desire to find—or to invent, if need be—a logical explanation which will once again permit a reassuring view of the world. For Grant, Balzac's characters reflect the collective psyche of France at a time when the Terror was still recent enough, in terms of the nation's cultural memory, to be perceived as a real threat.

In the final essay of the volume, Armine Kotin Mortimer turns to *Une ténébreuse affaire* for a probing analysis of the principles of "tenebrosity" and "explication" in Balzac. On the one hand, Balzac obviously claims to penetrate mysteries and reveal historical truth; on the other hand, he adopts a narrative strategy which allows the reader to see that "truth"—to move, figuratively speaking, from darkness to light—only little by little, in the course of the reading experience. In that respect, *Une ténébreuse affaire* illustrates a fundamental tension at the heart of the realist enterprise as a whole, which aspires to reveal objective reality, while conspiring to keep readers "in the dark" long enough to ensure that they do, after all, keep reading.

✳   ✳   ✳

This brief introduction will serve as something of an Ariadne's thread tendered to prospective readers. As editors of similar volumes in the past have been prompted to note, the nineteenth century is a remarkably fertile and complex period, one that resists any attempt at classification in a simple and categorical manner. Those so inclined will have every opportunity to "read across" the formal divisions proposed here and to make their own way through this rich body of material. In the final analysis, a collection such as this one is offered most appropriately as one more testimony to the continuing vitality of nineteenth-century French studies.

Part 1
Domination?

1

Violence Justified?
Raison d'armée in Early Nineteenth-Century France

CATHARINE SAVAGE BROSMAN

HAVING observed that war "has something sublime in it," Immanuel Kant went on to assert, in his *Critique of Judgment* (1790): "Although war is an undesigned enterprise of men (stirred up by their unbridled passions), yet it is perhaps a deephidden and designed enterprise of supreme wisdom for preparing . . . a morally grounded system of those states. In spite of the dreadful afflictions with which it visits the human race . . . [war] is . . . a motive for developing all talents serviceable for culture to the highest possible pitch" (Kant 1951, 282–83). In France, a parallel can be found in the early eighteenth-century writer Vauvenargues, who viewed *gloire*—honor and military achievement—as the source of human virtue, the proof of merit, the highest reward, and wrote that peace, which "restricts talent and weakens the people," is not a good, either in morals or politics (Vauvenargues 128–37, 187–88). "There is no perfect glory without that of arms" (Vauvenargues 446).

These views, while foreign to today's thinking, at least in the Occident, belong to a long-standing philosophic tradition that stresses the positive value of warfare, a tradition going back to Heraclitus, who called war "father of all and king of all,"[1] and stretching through Nietzsche, who wrote that "It is the good war that hallows any cause," and "You should love peace as a means to new wars."[2] The strand of thought reaches to our century, when more than one society has regarded war, as Modris Eksteins put it (in reference to Germany prior to 1914), as "the supreme test of spirit . . . a test of vitality, and culture, and life" (Eksteins 90). War is seen as the school of civic virtue, the test

of a man. Henry de Montherlant, while acknowledging that the
Great War had been worse than most, argued in *Le songe*, which
John Fletcher calls a "rather tasteless panegyric of war" (Fletcher
279), that one should "reintroduce into peace the virtues of war."
As Jules Roy, who has nothing of the fascist in him, said in 1969,
"Even just . . . war is humanity's curse. And yet it is there that
men reveal their true selves."[3]

As background to an examination of early nineteenth-century
attitudes, it is useful to survey briefly the views on warfare of
certain eighteenth-century thinkers.[4] At the same time that there
was an upsurge in military literature (Gat 25), the Enlightenment
witnessed considerable criticism of war and the policies that led
to it. Even Vauvenargues deplored a petty and disastrous war of
alliances in which a young friend was killed (Vauvenargues 146),
and in his *Traité sur le libre arbitre* (1737), spoke of the "epi-
demic diseases which ravage the human species everywhere,"
seeing that "men destroy each other through wars, that the weak
are the prey of the strong," and denying that the "désordres" are
really useful and beneficial (Merlant 362). Kant, whose qualifi-
cation of war as an "enterprise of supreme wisdom" arrests attention, nevertheless considered armed conflict as one of the
greatest of human evils, the source of all moral corruption (Kant
1970, 183), at least by 1795, the date when he published his
pamphlet, *Perpetual Peace.*[5]

In opposition to the principle of the divine right of kings, with
its implied right to make war, Enlightenment thought generally
identified, as the foundation of sovereignty, social contracts and
natural law, or what Montesquieu calls in *Les lettres persanes*
"the right of people or, rather, that of reason."[6] Departing from
the *compétence de guerre* principle, Montesquieu, who de-
nounced holy or religious wars, which spring from the spirit of
intolerance (Montesquieu 1:174, 259), asserted in letter ninety-
five that justice among nations is no different from justice among
individuals, and, in a step toward a rationalization of war that
departed from his predecessors' and emphasized the *relations*
among social and physical factors, he asserted that there were
only two cases of justice in warfare: self-defense against the aggression of an enemy (based, as he wrote in *L'esprit des lois*, on
the analogy of the right to self-defense in nature [Montesquieu
2:377]), and assistance to an ally who has been attacked; all dec-
larations of war should be acts of justice.[7] Conquest in itself
confers no rights, but only obligations; peace treaties are sacred
(Montesquieu 2:272).

Voltaire's statements on warfare indicate contrasting views, in a pattern of oscillation between politically motivated militancy and pacifism. In various early poems, including *La Henriade* (1723, 1728), and in "Poème de Fontenoy" (1745) he enthusiastically describes combats at length and evokes heroism and martial achievements—signs of his attachment to the classical tradition and to individual commanders. And he clearly understood dynastic wars as a political phenomenon, a deplorable one, but one that could at best be controlled, not eliminated, in the Europe that he knew; he took toward the notion of international law, as set forth by Grotius and Pufendorf, a very cynical position (Meyer, chapter 3). After the publication of the comte de Guibert's *Essai général de tactique* (1772), Voltaire wrote a poem, "La tactique," in which he acknowledged that the art of war was, unfortunately, a necessary one; wars of defense, he argued often, were legitimate (see Gay 160–61). Yet he viewed most armed conflict as a foolish and burdensome expenditure for the state, undertaken "for very trivial interests and often for petty whims,"[8] an undertaking for which those least responsible often bore the heaviest responsibility; or, worse, they were the product of religious intolerance, and thus totally unacceptable.[9] What reader of *Candide* does not remember his satire of the wars of the Bulgares (that is, the Seven Years' War), an "heroic slaughter," and of the so-called "laws of public right" that purport to justify violence? (Voltaire 1984, 126–27). Only those wars having freedom as their object and result can be justified (Voltaire 1961, 22).

The question of war engaged Rousseau repeatedly; he wrote a "Jugement sur le projet de paix perpétuelle" of l'abbé Saint-Pierre and took a stand elsewhere against Hobbes, the Western philosopher whose writings are most fundamentally concerned with war, and to whom, of course, Rousseau was thoroughly opposed, arguing, as his title puts it, "That the state of war arises from the social state."[10] According to his view of history, in the prolapsarian world, war was the result of the institution of property and civil society, not (as in Hobbes's view) of the state of nature. As he indicates in *Discours sur l'origine de l'inégalité*, "The nascent society gave way to the most horrifying state of war" (Rousseau 176), a warfare both domestic—between the haves and have-nots—and national, as the relationships between nations, constituting a sort of *degraded* state of nature, corrupted by the desires introduced by property and without the counterbalancing forces existing *within* society, produced "National Wars, Battles, murders, reprisals which make Nature shiver and

go against reason . . . The most honorable people learned to consider the massacre of their fellow man as one of their duties"
(Rousseau 178–79). Denying the validity of conquest as a foundation of law ("The Right of conquest not being a Right was unable
to establish any other"), Rousseau denies in effect the right to
self-defense of all modern nations, as based upon such con-
quests, while recognizing that as soon as one state was formed,
others were obliged to constitute themselves similarly.[11]

The Revolutionary and Napoleonic Wars transformed military
realities and attitudes toward armed conflict. "Eighteenth-
century warfare, which, because of the political and social structure of the ancien régime, had been relatively limited in aims
and scope, was now increasingly discredited and perceived as
inadequate, if not absurd" (Gat 200). This does not mean, to be
sure, the disappearance of war. From dynastic, it became national
and popular, the purpose of arming being no longer to support
altar and throne, but—in France, that is—principally to defend
a people and a political philosophy that, to some degree at least,
sprang from them. This attitude represents a synthesis of certain
philosophic positions on war displayed in the previous century.
"According to the legacy of the Enlightenment," writes Michel
Delon, "militant action is fully justified by [the] gap between
progress proposed and the vicissitudes of chance" (Gutwirth
1991, 26). Universal military service was a sign of the change of
warfare from dynastic to nationalistic; soldiers were no longer
just hirelings.[12] Military commanders of the nobility were replaced in some cases by self-made men, of whom the Little Cor-
poral is the most striking example. Revolutionaries came to see
war as a *civic* undertaking, necessarily an extension of revolution, to which the military code no longer applied. Robespierre
stated the view in the extreme when he wrote, in articles to be
appended to the Declaration of Rights, that "those who make
war on a people to arrest the progress of liberty, and to destroy
the rights of man, deserve to be attacked by all, not as ordinary
enemies, but as brigands, rebels, and assassins" (Thompson 353).
Warfare within the state, whether against individual or collective
enemies of the Revolution (such as the royalists in the Vendée),
was of a piece with that waged against enemies beyond French
borders.[13]

Similarly, for *émigrés* and other royalists, war turned into a
desperate battle against not a territorial rival but an enemy at
home, sacrilegious, destructive—thus a battle of and for the soul.
In *Considérations sur les principaux événemens de la Révolu-*

tion française (1818), Germaine de Staël, speaking from both the tradition of Enlightenment thought and from the experience of an observer of the Revolution, considered the revolutionary conflicts that she witnessed and numerous previous wars to spring from both religious and political fanaticism, but especially from the need to dominate and the desire for property (Staël 1987, 363–64); Napoleon, she was convinced, needed and used war as a means to extend his tyranny and rally support through military glory (Staël 1964, 107).

It is less the *political* attitudes toward armed conflict in the aftermath of the Revolutionary and Napoleonic Wars that interest me, however, but, to the degree that they can be separated, moral and philosophic ones. In the previous century the *philosophes* could condemn dynastic violence easily, in the name of liberal principles, since it was chiefly a phenomenon of rival monarchies, and bore little positive relationship to what they considered the national welfare; they had no conception of how violence would be installed, at the center of their nation and of a "liberal" society, by the Revolution and its subsequent wars.[14] Moreover, in Rousseau's case at least, no consideration was given to the value of the moral energies associated with military achievement. The thinkers of the nineteenth century, by contrast, had to deal with what Jeanne Bem calls "the chain of violence" (Bem 43) from 1789–93 to mid-century—a nationalized, institutionalized violence—which in its Napoleonic form represented a new heroism, a noble counterpart to the military cult of the Roman Empire.[15] To what use did writers of the period propose putting organized violence? Could it be rationalized and justified in post-Revolutionary terms? Could it be made more tolerable or should it, as Clausewitz was to suggest when he was composing his work in the 1820s, be pushed *à outrance* by its own logic? These questions must be seen of course in the context of the Restoration and the July Monarchy, especially in light of the repression of revolutionary movements in the 1820s and 1830s.[16]

For Joseph de Maistre, violence is a necessary arm of the state, whether in the form of the executioner or that of the army, both "executions" of the monarch's will, expressing divine will. This ultraconservative position, expressed in the first and seventh "Entretiens" of the *Soirées de Saint-Petersbourg* (1821), reflects of course the rabid fear of Jacobinism that characterized many French governments after the First Republic, and singularly the extreme reactionism of the Bourbon Restoration.[17] But de Maistre was not satisfied with adopting violence as a political tool; for him, it had to be rationalized in opposition to the liberal Enlightenment tradition, which, although it did not cause the Revolution, underlay it—a tradition by which, as I noted earlier, authority for government was recognized as coming from the governed, implying that the use of armed force was a prerogative only of the latter.[18] While de Maistre has recourse to terminology and notions from the ancien régime, his view of the state has a great deal in common with that of Hegel and other thinkers of the German school, for whom the state—not the individual— is the supreme expression of rationality and morality, the true masterpiece of man, of which force is a necessary and justified arm, which cannot be evaluated according to humanistic ethics.[19]

De Maistre's rationalization went farther than that of some earlier thinkers in the direction of divine determination. While in the sixteenth century Blaise de Monluc, for instance, held that God willed the conflicts of his age—that is, war was necessarily justified because it was either decreed or allowed by God (a position that left open the question of theodicy)—de Maistre stated bluntly that "war is divine" (de Maistre 26). One can also suggest that it is not divine because God wills it, but rather God wills it because it is divine—violence hypostatized to the level of a manifestation of the Omnipotent, or, as de Maistre calls him, following the Old Testament, the DIEU DES ARMEES (de Maistre 21).

De Maistre's dialectic on this topic bears examination. When, in the Septième entretien, the Sénateur claims that war cannot be explained humanly, the Chevalier retorts by using Monluc's argument, in its pragmatic form: "Kings command you, and . . . you must go" (de Maistre 2). The Sénateur objects that such explanations are simplistic; even the supposed love of glory does not suffice to explain war, since military renown is available only to leaders, not the ordinary soldier, and anyway such an explanation merely pushes back the question. Rather, says the Sénateur, the soldier's functions are by their nature spiritual, part of a divine scheme both in the world and beyond it. Man, the creature "who kills for the sake of killing," is part of a chain of being, similar to that envisioned by the Enlightenment thinkers, but without the same implications. "It is man who is responsible for slaughtering man . . . In this way is carried out endlessly, from insects to men, the great law of the violent destruction of living beings" (de Maistre 23, 25). This is a sacrificial, religious destruction, part of an eschatological vision, for which de Maistre cites the authority of St. Paul (Cor. I: 15, 26), but which is, rather, Hegelian. "The entire world, continually soaked with blood, is nothing more than an immense altar where all living creatures must be sacrificed, endlessly, immoderately, continually, until the extinction of evil, until the death of death" (de Maistre 25). Man as a species is particularly marked out by the exterminating angel, who circulates around the globe, raising nation against nation everywhere, but especially where unspecified crimes have been committed. War is divine, in short, for transcendent reasons, as its results "are absolutely beyond the scope of human reason" (de Maistre 27). De Maistre concludes by asking at what period of time the *moral power* of war has played a more crucial role than his own (de Maistre 35)—a question that reveals his understanding of the integral role of the Napoleonic Wars and others in modern history. (Thus, in his *Considérations sur la France*, 1796, he treated the Revolution as divine purification.)[20]

De Maistre's reflections on armed conflict are directed only toward wars between states, not civil unrest; he does not need to consider the army as an instrument of social order, since the *bourreau* (executioner) functions in that way. His view of the army is, moreover, static: recognizing no legitimacy in the revolutionary upheavals and liberal institutions of his age, he sees warfare as a timeless undertaking, not one whose nature has been modified by historical change; it is a manifestation of divine law like those seen in the past.[21]

The position of Alfred de Vigny vis-à-vis the historical situation around him is exactly the opposite; he could have agreed with the statement of Terrence Des Pres that "after 1789 the individual knows no armistice with history" (Des Pres 12), changes in kind having taken place from the Revolution onwards. After having served as a career officer for a restored Bourbon government concerned with *reacting* against the Napoleonic legacy, Vigny saw all too well that the role of the army had been radically changed. His own dream of military glory was dashed by the peace that followed the Congress of Vienna and the end to French expansionism in Europe;[22] "Destiny has refused me the war I loved" (Vigny 1935, 2:1050). Like his liberal opposite Stendhal, he continued nonetheless to admire the moral energies associated with military achievement and to nurture nostalgic visions of war; after his resignation, he harbored great disappointment, although he spoke of his "cure for this disease of military enthusiasm" (Vigny 1955, 93). He called his *Servitude et grandeur militaires* part of "a sort of epic poem on disillusionment" (Vigny 1935, 2:1037), a companion piece to the tragedy of the writer as portrayed in *Stello*—"two theses on disenchantment" (Vigny 1955, 334).

What is more significant, he saw that the moral foundations of the army were threatened by the political uses to which military power was being put in the post-Napoleonic period and by lack of fiber in the army itself. He observed what his later editor Baldensperger termed "passive obedience often submitted to an inept command, deterioration of officers, because of the progressive assimilation of bourgeois values by societies, favoritism in high places and, among intellectuals, consequent deprecation of the 'paid' profession of soldiering" (Vigny 1948, 517). From the military point of view, Vigny belongs thus less to what Isaiah Berlin calls the "Counter-Enlightenment" (Gat 142) than to the Enlightenment itself, with its ideal of orderly battles as an expression of rational statecraft; one must not forget that his father told him about seeing Frederick the Great on the battlefield (Vigny 1955, 11–12). At the same time, he examined the relationship between military discipline and *le libre arbitre* or freedom of conscience—a notion that, in the form it takes for Vigny, is foreign to de Maistre's essentially theocratic view of the *polis*.[23] Vigny was, moreover, concerned with the problem of killing. Yet some of his views, especially on discipline and *gloire* and the contribution of military life to forming a man's character, are not dissimilar to those of the author of *Du Pape*, whose influence he denied, but which subsists in *Servitude et grandeur militaires* (Vigny 1948, 517; Haig 1987b, 47).

What, then, constitutes military right for Vigny? He denies explicitly the proposition of "un sophiste," that is, de Maistre—whom he had already combatted in connection with the same topic in *Stello* as a "falsifying . . . and menacing mind" (Vigny 1986, 180)—that war is divine. "War is cursed by God as well as by the very men who wage it and who secretly abhor it" (Vigny 1955, 100). Recognizing, however—in a view that anticipates the optimism of "La bouteille à la mer"—that while "the time of armies and war will be limited," their end has not yet come, he examines their principles and justification. The principles of operation are strict. The function of officers is to command, that of men, to obey; both demand discipline and sacrifice, *dévouement* and *abnégation*. This structure of authority makes of the army the creature of the supreme civil power that commands it. "The army is blind and mute. It strikes out from the spot at which it is placed. It wants nothing and acts by manipulation.

It is a thing that one moves and which kills; but it is also a thing that suffers" (Vigny 1955, 24–25). Soldiers are, morally speaking, slaves, since their freedom of conscience is subordinated to the will of others; Vigny compares them to Caesar's gladiators. As recognition, they receive scorn and malédiction.

The army, thus, is an encounter of two sorts of violence, that exercised by the state on its soldier-servants, and that exercised by one army against another. Justification of the first needs to conciliate the good of the state with freedom of conscience, a principle that Vigny strongly believed to be a natural right, whether influenced by the vein of Enlightenment thought that emphasized natural reason, or as a result of his personal (perhaps innate) moral vision. That is, ideally a soldier will renounce freely, in the name of a higher good, his right to exercise his own judgment, thus willing his abdication of will. Only then, if I read Vigny correctly, is the military condition less than tragic. But this can happen only when the army is truly at the service of the nation. It can no longer be a question of devotion to a man, as during the Napoleonic period and during the feudal wars up to the Revolution: rather, the army belongs "to Country and to Duty," and this duty is to "a Principle rather than to a Man."[24] What is the nation? Governments, in the post-Revolutionary period, change from one year to the next, and govern by caprice. Furthermore, they ask of the army tasks that are improper—for example, the absurd order to the ship's commander in "Laurette ou le cachet rouge" to execute a young man who had mocked the Directory, or the order in "La canne de jonc" to put down civil unrest—in short, to behave as a gendarmerie.[25] As the old commandant says, "Never will a ship's captain be forced to be an executioner, except when assassins and thieves take control of the government" (Vigny 1955, 75). Hence, "by looking closely at the life of these armed troops that, every day, all the succeeding Powers will impose on us, we will indeed find . . . that the existence of the soldier is . . . the most painful remnant of barbarity that subsists among men" (Vigny 1955, 100).

Even when properly seen in the context of the fatherland, the soldier's duty is to exert violence, a duty hard to reconcile with Vigny's horror of bloodshed, which had been reinforced by readings of Lammenais's Paroles d'un croyant and other authors (Haig 1987b, 51). "Laurette ou le cachet rouge" offers as a point of reconciliation the concepts of abnegation and honor ("the union of force and goodness" [Vigny 1935, 1:609]): obeying, the soldier, through honor, accepts what would be dishonor, renounces clean hands, and, like other victims, does expiation for the wrongs that he takes upon himself in the name of society. "The soldier is a glorious wretched man, victim and executioner, a scapegoat sacrificed daily to his people and for his people, who deceive him . . ."[26] One is struck by the word *bourreau* (executioner), the very term used by de Maistre to elevate to a sacred status the role of *civil* destruction. Vigny's solution opposes, to the dilemmas of violence, a position that does not eradicate them, much less the violence itself, but goes beyond them to a *mystique* of moral stoicism that allows the individual to achieve grandeur and redeems the individual *and* the army—as would be expected, an aristocratic position.[27]

If de Maistre rationalizes institutionalized violence in the name of divine reason, and Vigny does so, partially, in the name of honor, Stendhal, less concerned with the justification of war and the ideological questions involved, interests modern readers by treating war as a phenomenon that cannot be understood. I am referring of course to the conclusions one can draw from the Battle of Waterloo episode in *La chartreuse de Parme*.[28] It seems clear that the author accepts *raison d'armée* as a matter of course—for the imprinting of Napoleonic heroism in him was very strong, and to my knowledge he did not subsequently denounce the Romantic militarism that characterized his youth and appears in his two greatest novels as well as *Lucien Leuwen*. Nor would his *beylisme* have led him to the idealistic belief that conflict can be overcome or purified through honor and self-sacrifice, or ended through Utopian schemes. Moreover, one discerns in him a Romantic attraction to conflict and opposition— the antithetical forces within the self, and those within society, that call forth human energy and lead to self-surpassing; war is an illustration of these forces.[29] But at the same time Stendhal saw how the dynamics of experience escape from rational categories; and if what was meant by "war" posed no problem to him, the *experience* of battle, hence its meaning, was a different matter.

Perhaps the most extreme and original thinkers in early nineteenth-century France on *raison d'armée* are those radical socialists, in the wake of François-Emile (called Gracchus) Babeuf and Charles Fourier, who saw that militarism, being inexorably bound to, and an arm of, the state could not disappear until the state itself was remade from top to bottom, with the new social bond of *equality* replacing the primary republican value of *liberty*, and the organized oppression exercised by privileged governing classes (as in the scenes from "La canne de jonc") brought to an end.[30] This would be a product of class consciousness. But even remaking the state would not be enough, since, in practice, a *state* exists only in contradistinction and competition with other states; the very idea of statehood would need to be replaced by an international order, in which *raison d'état* would disappear. As a neo-Babouviste wrote in 1839, the French workers should cease expressing hostility toward foreign workers: "Blame privilege which is crushing you and not brothers who are suffering as much as you" (Dommanget 261). If one were to pursue this line of investigation, one would have to study the relationship between the Utopian dream of ending the state and the violence that, both in theory and in practice, accompanies it, from Rousseau through the Soviet Union, each time that "the people, arms in hand, will demand that their property be returned."[31]

Tulane University

NOTES

1. Heraclitus 37. For Heraclitus, the term *war* seems, however, at least partly metaphorical, indicating the universality of opposition and conflict in the cosmos. See Glenn.

2. Nietzsche 159. As with Heraclitus, however, the reference seems in part to refer to conflict in general, both that among human beings and that within the self.

3. Lhoste 1, 7. In both medieval and early modern times, prior to the period treated here, European dynastic wars were considered—by the ruling classes and the monarchies that engaged in them—inevitable and justifiable, willed by God. This conviction reflects the concept of divine omniscience and intervention in human affairs, and the belief in the divine right of kings. As Blaise de Monluc wrote, "God Almighty raised up these two great princes [Francis V and Charles I] sworn enemies to one another" (Monluc 1972, 37). Allegiance to the monarch and God required acceptance of the cause; *raison d'état* was the equivalent of *raison d'armée*. "Be full of the love and loyalty we all owe our prince," he wrote. "And in so doing although his quarrel should not be just, God will not for all that withdraw his assistance from you; for it is not for us to ask our King if his cause be good or evil, but only to obey him" (Monluc 231–32). This thinking reflects less the just war tradition in its classic form, which dates from the late Middle Ages—although antecedents existed in Aristotle (who makes the distinction between justifiable and unjustifiable participation in war) and Augustine—and includes the concepts of both *jus ad bellam* (just cause) and *jus in bello* (just conduct)—concepts worked out as an expression of Christendom's communal views—than the post-Reformation modification of *jus ad bellam* in the form of *compétence de guerre*—the doctrine that

"each sovereign had the right and authority to decide when just cause for war existed" (Johnson 8, 16; see also Glenn 6).

4. The following discussion centers on only the humanistic critique of war among the *philosophes*. Parallel to this philosophic line of thought there developed what Gat calls "the military school of the Enlightenment" (Gat ix and Part 1), including De Saxe, Puységur, Guibert, and numerous others, concerned with the rationalizing and systematizing of warfare according to universalist models. A counterpart in Prussia was Frederick the Great, toward whom, despite their friendship, Voltaire came to feel some coolness because of his cult of war as a political tool and an art.

5. In France, prior to Kant's publication, there were a number of other projects for perpetual peace, including those of the abbé Saint-Pierre, Rousseau, and Pierre André Gargas. See Meyer 53.

6. 1:272. Montesquieu calls peace treaties "the voice of Nature demanding its rights" (ibid.).

7. 1:271. He does allow, however, for preventive wars in self-defense. See *L'esprit des lois*, book 10, chapter 2. Moreover, as Voltaire points out, he asserts that it is acceptable to attack an enemy because he is becoming too strong (Meyer 86).

8. Voltaire 1963, 811. In the same passage, Voltaire praises "a new humanity that has been introduced into the scourge of war" (ibid., 811–12)—that is, increased scope of *jus in bello*.

9. In "La tactique," Voltaire praised the perpetual peace project of the abbé Saint-Pierre. See section on Rousseau below.

10. Hobbes rejected the Just War tradition, contending that in war, that is, the social state, "this war of every man against every man," "the notions of Right and Wrong, Justice and Injustice, have . . . no place" (Hobbes 188).

11. Rousseau 179, 603. In contrast to the *philosophes'* views on warfare, one can cite the positions adopted by the Prince de Ligne, who, observing that philosophy had not yet gained enough ground to put an end to war, concluded in his *Mélanges* (1795) that "one must look for practice where one can. If Russia is at war, one must ask permission to go there . . . If in another country there are camps, large-scale war reenactments, and especially sieges, one must try to go see them" (Ligne 42, 45).

12. David Thomson writes: "The *levée en masse*, or universal conscription for military service . . . revolutionized modern warfare. . . . The measures established a novel and far-reaching principle: that in time of emergency the state has the right to command the services of all its citizens. It enabled France to put into the field of battle massive formations . . . against which the older professional armies proved outmoded. . . . The system led eventually to the modern citizen-army, and helped to turn war from a battle between armies into a conflict between whole nations" (Thomson 22). As Céline wrote, with his usual cynicism, "By a few shouts, so deeply felt that they are still heard, [Danton] skillfully mobilized the good people! And that was the first departure of the first battalions of frenzied emancipated people! . . . The unpaid soldier, that was new . . . those ragged and impassioned cohorts who had just spontaneously been disembowelled by the King of Prussia in defense of the new patriotic fiction . . ." (Céline 93).

13. The implications of this position are too extensive to be examined here. Some of Robespierre's rhetoric on internal and external warfare can be found in his speeches on war in 1791.

14. Cf. Gallie 133: ". . . Such theorizing as had been attempted in the field of international relations had been based on the simple picture of peace and war as a seemingly endless alternation or ding-dong between rival political powers."

15. A striking example of the attempt to deal with the changes in patterns of war and their connection to political forces is the work of Carl von Clausewitz. See below, note 21.

16. The British Romantics were more widely concerned with the questions than were the French, however—a fact that can be attributed, perhaps, to the enormous magnetism of Napoleon and his successes, and also to the powerful hold of the *mal du siècle*. William Godwin, in *Political Justice* (1793), Shelley, in *Prometheus Unbound* (1820), Byron, Leigh Hunt, and Thomas Paine criticized variously the principle of war in general, dynastic wars as a result of the hereditary monarchy, and treatment of soldiers.

17. Among "many French governments after the First Republic" I am thinking especially of the early years of the Third Republic in the 1870s, the 1930s, and the period prior to the creation of the Fifth Republic.

18. De Maistre's opposition to Rousseau appears explicitly in his discussion on war.

19. Cf. Wilhelm von Humboldt, who said that war was "one of the most wholesome manifestations that play a role in the education of the human race" (quoted in Gat 243).

20. Robespierre had a similar view of violence as a necessary and indeed laudable instrument to bring about the consolidation of republican power and the salvation of the state. The "war of liberation against tyranny" was justified as long as needed. Similarly, Gracchus Babeuf exorted his followers to sweeping, indeed totalized violence as a means to an end. The oratory of these figures, Babeuf in particular, was of considerable importance in the formation of mid-nineteenth century socialism, including the thinking of Marx and his followers, whose eschatological communism offers obvious parallels with the eschatological Christian view of de Maistre.

21. Clausewitz, whose *On War* was written in the 1820s—thus dating from the same decade as *Les soirées de Saint-Petersbourg*—and was then published posthumously in three volumes (1832–34), emphasizes Absolute War as a possible—perhaps a necessary—instrument of politics; this is not without parallels in de Maistre's thinking, although for Clausewitz the context and rationale are entirely secular, based upon his readings of history and his observations of the Napoleonic Wars. Violence carried to its extreme point and conclusion, in the interest of statecraft, was to him the logic of history. See Gallie 37–65.

22. That is, until 1830. If Vigny had remained in the army, he might have participated in the conquest of Algeria. One cannot know whether he would have stayed there after the Bourbon flag was replaced by the *tricolore* of the July Monarchy. He seems sympathetic to those who left the army after the Trois Glorieuses, but does not criticize those who remained and "have again conquered citadels" for France (Vigny 1955, 194); moreover, as his journal shows, he himself became part of the Garde Nationale in August 1830 (Vigny 1955, 348–49).

23. Lebrun asserts that "despite his later reputation as an apologist of throne and altar, de Maistre would never advocate theocracy" (Lebrun 51). Perhaps, in the strictest sense, this is true; it seems to me, however, that his views imply it. Agreeing with me on this point is Arlette Michel (Ballanche 1981, 14).

24. Vigny 1955, 174, 284. Jules Roy made the same point in 1942 as he wrestled with the question of loyalty to Pétain under the circumstances of Operation Torch. See Roy and Davis; see also Brosman 1989 and 1996.

25. Haig (1987b, 46) points out the most appalling incident of such intervention, in April 1834, when the military attacked buildings on the rue Transnonain, butchering inhabitants. There were uprisings in 1832 also, put down by the army, although the regime was suspicious of it.

26. Vigny 1955, 22–23. Victor Hugo is another Romantic author who struggled with the implications of organized violence, but more in connection with revolutionary uprisings than in relation to warfare in general. His early views varied as his initial monarchism was replaced by enthusiasm for Napoleon and then evolved into a broadly-based social liberalism. Like Vigny, but along different lines, he wrestled with the dialectic of force wielded in the name of humanitarianism: revolution can serve the cause of social justice, at least initially, but its violent means undermine this same justice. A pertinent work in this connection is *Bug-Jargal* (1826).

27. Despite the ideological differences between them, Vigny can be compared with Charles Péguy with respect to the role of *mystique* as a redemption of *politique*.

28. See Brosman 1992.

29. This is a point of contact with Nietzsche, who, it is well known, admired Stendhal greatly. There is also some parallelism here with Hegel, for whom conflict was essential for the development of the human spirit and who saw in history a meaning to which the processes of war were not foreign. A third author who comes to mind in this connection is Henry de Montherlant (*Le songe*).

30. Cf. Tolstoy; see Gallie 126–27. On the other hand, socialists thought also that they must smash the "bureaucratic military machine . . . as the essential condition of every real revolution in the continent of Europe," as Engels put it (Gallie 80).

31. Dommanget 251. See Brosman 1985 and Popper. As G. D. H. Cole points out, for thinkers as various as Hegel, Comte, Saint-Simon and his followers, and the later Marx, "the eschatological end of human society was attained through the very conflict and imperfection which marked society" (*The Doctrine of Saint-Simon* xix).

2

(En)gendering Terror:
Women and Violence in *Quatrevingt-treize*

CHARLES NUNLEY

JUST a few months before he began work on *Quatrevingt-treize*, Hugo wrote a poem in praise of Louise Michel, recently captured, tried, and sentenced to six years of exile in New Caledonia for having been one of the leaders of the Paris Commune of 1871. In his poem—tellingly entitled "Stronger than a Man"—Hugo speaks highly of Louise Michel's contribution to the short-lived Commune, praising her for her abnegation, what he calls her "working-class woman's pride,"[1] and her heroic defense of the barricades (Hugo 1986, 199). Prior to becoming an anarchist, Louise Michel was not only a school teacher and poet, but also an avid reader of Hugo. It is thus hardly surprising that she should be hailed as an important woman revolutionary by Hugo, who had on several occasions expressed sympathy and support for women in their struggle for equality.

So why, one might ask, is the main female character of *Quatrevingt-treize*—unlike the novel's verbally assertive male protagonists—an inarticulate mother who depends solely upon her intuitions to see her and her children through some of the darkest days of *la Terreur*? Did Hugo mean to suggest that women like Louise Michel did not exist during the French Revolution, or that those like Charlotte Corday had transgressed sexual boundaries, making them unsuitable for the kind of maternal heroism he had in mind?[2] In a word, what could Louise Michel and Michelle Fléchard possibly have in common other than their homonymous names?[3] While Fléchard's role as woman-revolutionary in *Quatrevingt-treize* clearly differs from Louise Michel's intellectually motivated engagement with her fellow Communards of 1871, I will argue in the following that, despite her limitations, Fléchard is not belittled in Hugo's text.[4] In exam-

ining her place in the novel, it is possible to glimpse a vision of
the French Revolution according to which feminine values
would be recognized as an essential component of the revolutionary process.

In a particularly insightful passage of her recent study of the
role of women in the public sphere during the French Revolution, Joan Landes observes that, in his *Serment des Horaces*, "David removes his dutiful Roman matrons to the sidelines of
political life; still, they are there" (Landes 158). By situating
women in the margin of his painting, David underscores their
limited role as spectators to events in which they appear unable
to partake. According to Landes, the marginalization of women
in David's painting—as passive spectators of patriarchy—is emblematic of the fear of female subjectivity one often finds on the
part of male leadership during the French Revolution (Landes
158). On the contrary, critical allusion in *Quatrevingt-treize* to
Marat's well-known suspicion of women's clubs (156)[5] would
suggest a reluctance on Hugo's part to foreclose on possible
forms of feminine involvement in the revolutionary process. It
remains to be seen, however, what the exact nature of women's
contribution to revolution and specifically to *la Terreur* in
Hugo's novel actually is. For while the boudoir politics of the
Old Regime have been carefully filtered out of Hugo's epic tale,
women and mothers or women as mothers—in the novel, the two
are synonymous—continue to exercise a modicum of influence
within the public sphere. Like the Roman matrons of David's
painting, women in *Quatrevingt-treize* have perhaps been moved
by Hugo to the sidelines of political life; still, they are there.

Throughout *Quatrevingt-treize*, Michelle Fléchard's presence
reveals important aspects of Hugo's understanding of written
language as a strictly masculine form of Terror. Like the traces
left on the walls of La Tourgue's feudal *oubliette* by the instruments of torture previously used to tear victims limb from limb,
the traces of the Republican clerk's pen that writes out Gauvain's
death sentence toward the end of the novel (464) underscore
Hugo's equivocal view of written words as modern, abstract
agents of Terror that are as cutting as the guillotine's blade and—
I would argue—gendered in ways that preclude Fléchard's use
of them.[6] While able to bring men to act through the woeful cry
of her own private grief, Fléchard herself is unable to participate
verbally in the revolutionary process that Hugo's historical novel

portrays, trapped as it were for safe keeping within the author's gendered view of language, deprived of the instruments that might allow her to play a more reasoning role in Hugo's *épopée* of social change.

In the opening scene of the novel, Michelle Fléchard is found by the *batallion du Bonnet Rouge* on its way through the dark Saudraie forest in search of Vendée insurrectionists. Instead of the enemy, however, the soldiers find Michelle Fléchard and her three children housed within what Hugo calls "a kind of *chamber* of foliage, half open like an *alcove*" (9, emphasis added). There they see the mother nursing one child, with two others asleep at her side. From the beginning, Fléchard is portrayed as a consummate mother, one, to be sure, who has been forced to flee her home, but one that continues, nonetheless, even in the deepest thicket, to occupy what Victor Brombert has called an "unexpectedly feminine setting" (Brombert 210), a domestic space where Fléchard continues to perform her maternal duties.[7]

Throughout the scene, Fléchard is unable to comprehend sergeant Radoub as he aggressively attempts to determine her political opinions, while the battalion's *vivandière* plays the role of interpreter, translating the sergeant's formal discourse into terms the mother might comprehend. Indeed, if Fléchard speaks to the *vivandière*, it is because both fulfill similar functions: while Fléchard nurses her young, the *vivandière* "nurses" wounded soldiers. As she explains, "I give everybody and anybody a sip, yes ... Whites the same as Blues, though I am a Blue myself, and a good Blue too; but I serve them all alike" (16). Like the maternal statue of Nature, depicted as a female sphinx with huge breasts spouting the water of regeneration built in Paris in celebration of the Festival of Unity in August 1793 (Hunt 154), both the *vivandière* and Michelle Fléchard are cast as maternal agents of revolution through the biological act of nursing.[8] Although Fléchard is unable to comprehend what the soldiers want to know—is she royalist or republican?—she intuitively trusts them. The scene ends happily with the adoption of Fléchard and her children into the ranks of the battalion. The soldiers' initial suspicions give way to an overwhelming sense of paternal compassion as the sergeant cries out: "I conclude that the regiment is going to become a father" (20). Once a widow with three orphans at her side, Michelle Fléchard has miraculously become—in the closing line of the first chapter—*citoyenne*, a new member of that large family known as *la République*.

It would be possible to analyze the first chapter of Hugo's novel in terms of the ambivalence that surrounds Fléchard's initiation into the battalion's ranks and more generally into *la République*, an ambivalence specifically reinforced by the coercive way in which her new title of *citoyenne* is imposed upon her by the sergeant. Having replaced Fléchard's father and dead husband, sergeant Radoub's paternal control guarantees that the mother remain subordinate by granting her titular status as *citoyenne*. In her study, *The Family Romance of the French Revolution*, Lynn Hunt convincingly argues that "the shift toward the good father [in the late eighteenth century] fatally undermined absolutist royal authority" while safeguarding patriarchy as such (Hunt 25). In the opening scene of *Quatrevingt-treize*, the sympathetic image of a tear rolling down the sergeant's cheek as he looks into the eyes of Fléchard's daughter indeed confirms Radoub's dual vocation as leader and "good father" to the battalion. At a time when the king of France was about to lose his head— an event that bothered Hugo throughout his life—Radoub's benevolent paternal presence seals Fléchard's fate as mother, relegating her to the realm of domesticity and effectively silencing her in his very respect for her maternal function.

Shortly after Fléchard's assimilation into the battalion, the group is captured by Vendée insurrectionists under the leadership of the *ci-devant* marquis de Lantenac, who orders that the children be taken hostage and the mother shot along with the soldiers. After miraculously surviving execution, Fléchard sets out on the quest to find her children, who, she discovers, are held prisoner at La Tourgue, a feudal tower belonging to Lantenac. Here again, Hugo underscores the degree to which Michelle Fléchard enters *la République* as mother and not as a reasoning *citoyenne:* upon hearing the words "La Tourgue," the name begins to take on the mysterious air of an incantation: "Had there been any one near, he might have heard her ceaselessly murmur, half aloud, 'La Tourgue.' Except the names of her children, this word was all she knew" (350). With such a limited command of the French language, it is hardly surprising that Fléchard should have a difficult time finding her way not only through the unfamiliar woodlands she has been forced to inhabit but also through the thicket of a new, Republican lexicon. A few pages later, upon hearing the word "guillotine," her response is again intuitive: "This rude peasant, Michelle Fléchard, did not know what that was, but instinct warned her. She shivered *without being able to tell why*" (353, emphasis added). Once again, the lexical blinders Hugo has placed on the indigent mother keep her from becoming sidetracked on the quest to find her children, for anything other than Fléchard's intuitive comprehension of la Terreur's verbal trappings—the most emblematic of which is no doubt the word "guillotine" itself—would only lead her astray, distancing her even further from the domestic sphere to which she desperately seeks to return.

Fléchard's propensity to pop up every now and then in public settings without risk of opprobrium is directly related to her ability to remain silent and thus stay out of trouble. However, at least one scene in Quatrevingt-treize suggests that motherhood and citizenship are not always compatible. On her way to La Tourgue, Michelle Fléchard stumbles onto a village square in search of food, only to find a crowd standing before a public crier wearing a tricolored scarf over his peasant dress and holding a placard. To be sure, reference to the crier's revolutionary and pre-revolutionary dress aptly underscores the pointedly transitional stage of la Terreur, when new identities had not yet effaced older ones, but it also distinguishes the male peasant's eagerness and ease of assimilation from that of Michelle Fléchard, who carries no visible sign of her sympathy for the Republic, no phyrigian cap—no bonnet rouge. In ways reminiscent of her initial encounter with the bataillon du Bonnet Rouge, Fléchard is unable to comprehend the crier's message, and only hears him when he mentions La Tourgue, where Lantenac and his royalist sympathizers are holding Fléchard's children hostage. As in the first scene of the novel, in which the vivandière is the only member of the battalion able to communicate directly with the mother, another woman on the village square urges Fléchard to keep silent: "Listen, traveller. In times of revolution you mustn't say things that cannot be understood; you may get yourself taken up in that way" (361). By virtue of the fact that Fléchard is a stranger to the village and that she says things "that cannot be understood," she is viewed with mistrust, as a potential threat. As some of the suspicious male peasants observe: "She looks like a bandit" (357); and "She might easily be a spy" (359). Fléchard need only keep silent in order to maintain the modicum of respect necessary for her survival. Like the Roman matrons of David's painting, she must remain a passive spectator of the crier's address if she is to keep out of trouble. Ironically, however, it is precisely Fléchard's inability to keep still during the public crier's speech that testifies to her sincerity—her authentic expression of motherhood—while instilling the village people's mistrust of her as a potential spy. Here, as in the earlier scenes of the novel I have analyzed so far, Hugo imparts a keen awareness of the problematic, indeed dangerous place women held in the public sphere during the French Revolution.[9] As the concluding words to this chapter of *Quatrevingt-treize* make absolutely clear, there is no place on the village square for babbling mothers: "She plunged into the forest" (362).

Fléchard's most significant contribution to plot in *Quatrevingt-treize* no doubt occurs upon arriving at La Tourgue. When she realizes that the forms she sees through the library window are in fact her own children about to be swept up in the growing conflagration, the narrator tells us "She uttered a terrible cry" (413). Fléchard's cry—what Hugo calls "inarticulate, heart-rending; sobs rather than words" (415)—momentarily enables her to speak and be heard without being perceived suspiciously as a spy or a mad-woman as was the case on the village square, but as a mother whose exclusive concern is the welfare of her children. For this to occur, Fléchard has had to surrender articulate speech. While her words on the village square had included "They shot me;" "I am doing no harm. I am looking for my children;" "I must go to La Tourgue! Show me the way to La Tourgue" (359–60), here she is limited to "that cry of indescribable agony [that] is only given to mothers" (413). It is the force of what Hugo would like us to perceive as Fléchard's unequivocally maternal cry that sways the royalist Lantenac to return to La Tourgue after a narrow escape in order to free the children from the locked library to which he alone holds the key.

Indeed, had Lantenac not heard the mother's voice, Fléchard's role in *Quatrevingt-treize* would have remained isolated from the larger picture of Hugo's epic narrative as it depicts the Republican army's impending victory over the Vendée insurrectionists. Instead, Hugo uses Fléchard's cry to bolster his familial understanding of the French Revolution—"To abolish feudality is to found families" (438)—since her cry serves more than anything else to reunite the royalist Lantenac with his Republican nephew, Gauvain. In the final analysis, figures of patriarchy in *Quatrevingt-treize* are restored *because* Lantenac chooses to heed Fléchard's plea for mercy. Thanks to his ability to hear the mother's voice, the father figure is resurrected, if only temporarily, as progenitor of the newly engendered Republican family.[10]

Once Michelle Fléchard's scream is heard by the royalist Lantenac, she and her children all but disappear from the novel, swept up by the sea of Republicans who receive Fléchard's children from the hands of Lantenac as the library at la Tourgue goes up in flames. While it is not clear what Fléchard's personal fate as mother and *citoyenne* will be in post-revolutionary France, it is fair to assume that her early retreat from the novel—some fifty pages still remain—puts an end to her short-lived, intuitive engagement with Revolution. Indeed, Fléchard's absence at the end of the novel from Gauvain's public execution would appear to suggest the desire on Hugo's part to prevent Fléchard from witnessing Terror as an event that symbolically "beheads" the strictly familial nature of her role in the novel. Unlike the well-documented popularity of public executions among women in Paris during the French Revolution, Hugo's restricts his audience to four thousand *men*, who obediently look on as Gauvain is beheaded and Cimourdain shoots himself through the heart. In contrast to the chaotic, whimsical dynamics of non-gendered crowds evoked elsewhere in the novel, the movements of the male spectators in the closing scene of *Quatrevingt-treize* are rigidly regimented along lines that are in accordance with Cimourdain's heartlessly mathematical view of France's future: "They surrounded the guillotine on three sides in such a manner as to form about it the shape of a letter E; the battery placed in the center of the largest line made the notch of the E. The red machine was enclosed by these three battle fronts; a sort of wall of soldiers spread out on two sides of the edge of the plateau; the fourth side, left open, was the ravine, which seemed to frown at La Tourgue. These arrangements made a long square, in the center of which stood the scaffold" (487). Hugo's allusion to the shape of the *written* letter E in the above passage is not inconsequential. Not only is it the first letter of such words as "Echafaud" and "Egalité," it also testifies to the exclusively masculine nature—"l'E" evoking the definite article "le"—of those scenes in Hugo's novel where writing occurs in the absence of women and in the proximity of death: "Cimourdain was *writing—writing* these lines: 'Citizen Members of the Committee of Public Safety, Lantenac is taken. He will be executed tomorrow.' He dated and signed the dispatch" (459, emphasis added). Or, later, when Guéchamp votes in favor of Gauvain's execution: "'Gauvain is guilty. I vote—*death*.' 'Write, registrar,' said Cimourdain. The clerk *wrote*, 'Captain Guéchamp: *death*'" (464, emphasis added). In the end, writing as a silent and silencing agent of Terror unfolds in a strictly masculine space.[11]

Indeed, as *Quatrevingt-treize* draws to a close, all traces of feminine involvement are effaced, beheaded, as it were, like Gauvain himself, whose white neck—about to be severed—"reminded one of a woman" (490). Like his earlier description of the architectural coldness of the Convention—"these hard rectilinear angles, cold and sharp as steel; it was something like Boucher guillotined by David" (188)—the epitome of what Hugo perceives as Cimourdain's quintessential terrorist aesthetic precludes any feminine presence. There is simply no room for women in *Quatrevingt-treize* as the blade begins to fall.[12]

In Hugo's portrayal of *la Terreur*, women's roles are defined exclusively in terms of intuition, emotion, and biological function. One might say that Fléchard's sublime inability to comprehend revolution keeps her from indulging in intrigue and thus neglecting her duties as mother. Unlike Marie-Antoinette, whom Hunt calls the most celebrated "bad mother" (Hunt 99) of late eighteenth-century France, Michelle Fléchard is incapable of any kind of deception, verbal or otherwise. Moreover, it is her illiteracy that gives Hugo's archetypical mother the means to rise above the written word as an even greater emblem of truth. Although Hugo is careful to suggest in his novel that—to borrow a phrase from Lantenac—"[The Revolution] came from the scribblers and the rhymesters" (452), authorship as a means of precipitating the revolutionary process lies strictly in the hands of men.

Following the Commune and just prior to his 1872 retreat to Guernesey where he would write *Quatrevingt-treize*, Hugo sent a letter to the editor of *L'avenir des femmes*, a Paris newspaper voicing the opinions of the "Association pour le Droit de la Femme," of which Louise Michel was one of the founders. In his letter, Hugo expresses the following sympathetic position: "In our legislation as it is, woman does not own, she has no existence in courts of justice, she does not vote, she does not count, she does not exist. There are male citizens, there are no female citizens."—"Il n'y a pas de *citoyennes*." He concludes: "This is an extraordinary situation; it must cease" (Moses 194). One wonders whether Hugo might have thought back to this statement as Michelle Fléchard, *citoyenne*, began to emerge in his writing. While he imparts an ironic awareness of this predicament when he speaks of Fléchard's servile station in life—"She was indeed a slave. The slave of her lost children" (365)—Hugo does so without suggesting that Fléchard's slavery is perhaps more the result of her illiteracy than the result of her being a mother. But that would have entailed writing another novel, one whose author might have been Fléchard herself. And who knows what stories she might have told.

Middlebury College

NOTES

1. Unattributed translations are my own.

2. Charlotte Corday is briefly mentioned at one point in Hugo's novel: "Outside the door was stationed Marat's 'watch-dog'—a certain Laurent Basse, porter of number 18, Rue de Cordeliers, who, some fifteen days after this 28th of June, on the 13th of July, was to deal a blow with a chair on the head of a woman named Charlotte Corday, at this moment vaguely dreaming in Caen" (1963, 147). The fact, however, that Corday's assassination of Marat is only obliquely evoked and in a way that underscores the violence of Marat's "guard dog" and not that of Corday herself would suggest that Hugo saw no place for violent women in his novel.

3. In addition to echoing "Louise Michel," the name of Hugo's ficticious mother also contains resonances that suggest strong masculine characteristics including, but not limited to those of the sword-bearing archangel, Saint Michael, bolstered by the "virile" and indeed distinctly phallic patronym "Fléchard." Although such "manly" attributes clearly suggest that Hugo's peasant-heroine will have an important role in the novel, it remains to be seen to what degree the mother actually plays the part of peasant-revolutionary as the tale unfolds.

4. On the contrary, the only women who are belittled in Hugo's novel are those in Paris who, following Robespierre's execution, took pleasure in parodying revolution, seeing in the end of Robespierre's reign of Terror an opportunity for decadence and self-indulgence: "The artist Boze painted his daughters, innocent and charming heads of sixteen, 'en guillotinées;' that is to say, with bare necks and red shifts. . . . To grave citizenesses making lint succeeded sultanas, savages, nymphs; to the naked feet of the soldiers covered with blood, dust, and mud, succeeded the naked feet of women decorated with diamonds" (131). Hugo is quick, however, to counter such decadence with a reminder that his story has nothing to do with these latter days of the Revolution: "But in '93, where we are, the streets of Paris still wore the grandiose and savage aspect of beginnings" (132). We will see that Fléchard's archetypical status as mother remains spatially and temporally distant from the contagion of parody characteristic of Parisian street life after the fall of Robespierre as Hugo depicts it in his novel.

5. In Hugo's novel, Marat expresses his mistrust of women as follows: "Robespierre, Danton, the danger is in this heap of cafés, in this mass of gaming-houses, this crowd of clubs—Clubs of the Blacks, the Federals, the Women . . ." (Hugo 156).

6. To be sure, Hugo's choice of an illiterate peasant woman from the Vendée region was not the only one available to him. As Catherine Marand-Fouquet argues, there were peasant women from the Vendée who were able to read and write. We can assume therefore that Hugo's choice of an *illiterate* mother is

intentional. It is also significant, I believe, to note that Fléchard's male peasant counterpart in the novel, Halmalo—while also unable to write—has the ability to remember Lantenac's long message in a chapter entitled "The peasant's memory is as good as the captain's science" (74–86). While perhaps no better equipped than Michelle Fléchard to grasp the weighty implications of words, Halmalo's ease in assimilating Lantenac's discourse and accurately communicating it to others is unique in the novel and, I would argue, gender-specific.

7. In his engaging discussion of Quatrevingt-treize, Brombert's depiction of the batallion's ambush as "a trap of tenderness" (Brombert 210) aptly characterizes Fléchard's predicament throughout the novel, caught within a new form of patriarchy from which there appears to be no escape.

8. As Madelyn Gutwirth observes, "Women's biology . . . comes to the fore, defining their 'nature' and obscuring in them all else that might allow them to be perceived as civic beings" (1992, 161).

9. As Dorinda Outram observes, "the woman who refused to be respected but excluded [during the French Revolution] was faced with a series of difficult choices, in the actual act of speaking in public as much as in the choice of words to speak. If she was not respected, there was no way of being heard; if heard, the way was open for all sorts of attacks on a consequent loss of virtue— just the sort of attacks that were in fact made on the female activists of the political clubs and especially on the women's political club, the Société des républicaines révolutionnaires" (126). While Michelle Fléchard belongs to no club or organization, the dynamics Outram speaks of here closely resemble those operative in the scene that unfolds on the village square in Quatrevingt-treize (120–35).

10. For an interesting discussion of Lantenac's role as founder in Hugo's novel, see Aynesworth.

11. Needless to say, Hugo's own writing of Quatrevingt-treize, while safeguarding certain stereotypes that are gender-distinct, does little to uphold the qualities of Cimourdain's unfailingly terrorist rhetoric. On the contrary, it would be possible to argue that Hugo's discourse constitutes an attempt to legitimize Gauvain's egalitarian view of post-revolutionary France by assuming intentionally a-geometrical, protean, indeed, androgynous characteristics that are opposed to the angular, uncompromising regularity of Cimourdain's exclusively "male" agenda, according to which, as Cimourdain himself concedes, "Man is master. I admit only one royalty, that of the fireside. Man in his house is king" (475).

12. It is appropriate that Cimourdain's final gesture as nourrice (143) or wet-nurse to Gauvain should simultaneously entail the execution of his "offspring" and his own suicide. In confirmation of the gendered view of Terror played out in Quatrevingt-treize, Cimourdain is unable to engender anything other than his own destruction and that of his "son."

3

"There shall be earthquakes, in diverse places": Volcanic Terror in Flora Tristan's *Pérégrinations d'une paria*

KATHLEEN HART

THE nineteenth century might be called the golden age of volcano tourism. "Eager to see beautiful spectacles and experience powerful sensations," visitors flocked to Vesuvius and Etna, where an entire industry sprang up, providing coachmen, guides, donkeys and porters.[1] The Album of the Hermitage of Vesuvius bears the signature of many famous writers, including Goethe, Byron, Dumas, Malibran, Lamartine, and Flaubert, suggesting that the volcano pilgrimage may have had something in common with the voyage to the Orient. The treacherous climb to the summit of an active volcano appealed to those seeking to revivify their writing. Inspired, perhaps, by the stirring evocations of Vesuvius in Madame de Staël's *Corinne*, Chateaubriand most notably reinforced the association of volcanoes with a specifically romantic sensibility. In 1804, he described Vesuvius: "The kind of terror that it inspires is not diminished by the spectacle of a flourishing city at its feet. . . . I watch the abyss smoking around me. I reflect that a few fathoms below my feet I have a gulf of fire; I reflect that the volcano could open up and launch me into the air with shattered pieces of marble" (Chateaubriand 1969, 1469–70). Who can forget René, seated on the edge of Etna's crater, gazing at the panoramic view of Sicily, yet ever haunted by the abyss at his side? For romantic writers like Chateaubriand, volcanoes are the site of an ahistorical confrontation with the void.

Flora Tristan, however, attaches a new importance, at once religious and political, to the terrible force of the volcano. In the autobiographical *Pérégrinations d'une paria*,[2] published in 1838,

45

the pioneer socialist feminist describes with romantic reverence her first view of volcanoes. Yet her narrative invests with political meaning the powerful emotions induced by the volcano's presence. Drawing upon the socialist feminist doctrines of both the Saint-Simonians and Charles Fourier, Tristan transforms the volcano into a mysterious entity presiding over radical social change. Terror associated with revolution, including terror of the revolutionary woman, is converted by the autobiographer into a kind of sublime, volcanic terror.

Born in 1803, Flora Tristan was the illegitimate daughter of a plebeian French mother, Thérèse Laisnay, and an aristocratic Spanish-Peruvian father, Don Mariano de Tristan y Moscozo. When she was four years old, her father died, and, because her parents had not been legally married, her mother was obliged to vacate the family home, which was confiscated by the French government as "alien property."[3] The autobiographer professes not to have known about her illegitimate status until her teen years, when she was preparing to wed a young man, and was unable to produce a civil record of her birth. Upon discovering the irregularity of her parents' union, the man's father called off the engagement (1:47). Economic hardship compelled her to marry at the age of eighteen; after bearing three children, she left her abusive husband and reassumed the name "Tristan." As she observes in the autobiography, people instantly treated her as a pariah upon discovering that she was a married woman living apart from her husband (1:xxxvii).

Clearly, these personal experiences prompted Tristan's interest in socialist feminism. She attended a few meetings of the Saint-Simonian socialists, and, in 1830, was "exalted by the heroism of the people" during the July Revolution (1:197). However, neither the Revolution nor the birth of socialist feminism could provide her with an immediate solution to her troubles. In 1832 she undertook a desperate journey to the city of Arequipa, Peru, seeking emotional and financial support from her wealthy paternal uncle, Pio de Tristan. Pio's refusal to recognize her as a legitimate heir, an event accompanied by the outbreak of civil war in Peru, constitutes a climactic episode of the autobiography.

Tristan's capacity to dramatize this period of her life owes much to her familiarity with early socialist doctrines that linked women's emancipation to social progress. By affirming the connections between women's private experiences and a defective social order, both Fourierism and Saint-Simonian feminism permit her to assert the political import of her autobiography. However, it is also of note that in each of these doctrines, the transition to socialism is presided over by a deity which socialists reconceptualized in an effort to overcome the traditional Christian opposition of spirit to matter. Early socialist doctrines thus provide Tristan with important metaphysical support which, as I shall argue presently, is transmuted into the force within one of her most powerful rhetorical images: the volcano.

Charles Fourier posited an abstract deity regulating a universe in which natural catastrophes, including earthquakes and volcanic eruptions, are tangible manifestations of humanity's failure to achieve social harmony. "Harmony" is to be achieved when the extended family of the phalanstery replaces the tiny bourgeois family unit which constrains individuals, especially women, both sexually and vocationally. Fourier announced the general rule that social progress can be measured by the degree of women's progress towards liberty, a postulate restated by Tristan in her autobiographical preface.[4] Thus social harmony is the "pivot" around which revolves geological harmony, while women's freedom is the pivot around which revolves social harmony.

The Saint-Simonians also sought to build a new social order based on the principle of communal interdependency. Celebrating what they considered to be the more sentient qualities of women, they worshipped an androgynous divinity, "God, father and mother." In 1831, Saint-Simonian leader Prosper Enfantin made the famous "appel aux femmes," or call to women, to say what they want, and also announced the search for a Woman Messiah who would guide humanity into the socialist future. Ironically, the call for a Woman Messiah accompanied Enfantin's action of excluding real women from the religious hierarchy.[5] However, it served as a catalyst for the formation of "the first consciously separatist women's movement"[6] in France, and helps to account for the quasi-messianic status Tristan assumes in her narrative.

In Tristan's text, the figure of the volcano works in a special way to undo the spirit/matter opposition upheld by Christianity, an opposition which informs the structure of spiritual autobiography. Traditionally, the spiritual autobiographer recounts his or her progress towards a purely spiritual destiny, which requires abandoning a life of the flesh and worldly concerns. Early socialists, on the other hand, aspired to create a "heaven on earth" by "rehabilitating" the material realm with which women were culturally associated. In Pérégrinations, a text in which Tristan performs a rewriting of the genre of spiritual autobiography, volcanoes appear as agents of this divine revaluation of women and the material. Representing social change as a divine imperative, they also portend the terrible consequences of humanity's failure to live by the principle of association—a failure which revolves around women's oppression.

My discussion of Tristan's labyrinthian text will be confined to two important episodes involving volcanoes. In the first, the autobiographer hints at the ideological significance of what she describes as the volcanic "trinity" seen from a distance as she crosses the Peruvian desert on her way to her uncle's estate in Arequipa. In the second, the autobiographer describes an earthquake which occurs shortly after her arrival in Arequipa, and which is associated with the presence of an active volcano bordering the city. Together, these two episodes reinforce Tristan's messianic status, while displacing terror of the politically active woman onto other sources.

As the title suggests, *Pérégrinations d'une paria* develops the "perigrinatio" theme of religious autobiography; geographical displacements parallel phases in the autobiographer's spiritual development.[7] After a harrowing ocean voyage to Peru, Tristan discovers that in order to reach Arequipa, she must cross an immense desert, accompanied by two other travelers. This arduous journey across the desert resonates with Biblical connotations, the most obvious of which is Exodus: Moses leading his oppressed people across the desert to the promised land. However, the sign which the deity places in Tristan's path is neither a pillar of fire nor cloud, but rather the Cordillera mountain chain from which arise three enormous volcanoes. Tristan pauses to imagine that an unknown power leads her to contemplate the mountains, compared to the facade of a church, beyond which lies the promised land: "Was this the celestial court that an unknown power was having me contemplate, and was eternal paradise beyond this wall of high mountains which unite heaven and earth, beyond this ocean of shifting sand whose progress they impede?" (1:238) This vertical image of the mountain chain which momentarily inhibits linear progress across the desert may be construed as a metaphor for Tristan's autobiographical project. Her ability to progress as humanity's pathfinder by moving through figures of spiritual autobiography is occasionally impeded by the necessity to revise those figures.

In this episode, volcanoes provide her with a special opportunity to rewrite the Book of Exodus after which she patterns the narrative. First, she explicitly alludes to Exodus: "The infinite struck all my senses: my soul was penetrated and as he did before that shepherd on Mount Horeb, God appeared before me in all his power, in all his splendor." Yet hers is not the God who stood before Moses on a rock in Horeb. Rather, a mysterious "trinity" greets her eyes: "Then I turned my gaze toward those three volcanos of Arequipa joined at their base, presenting there chaos in all its confusion and extending to the heavens their three snow-covered summits which reflected the sun's rays and, at times, the flames of the earth, an immense torch with three branches which lights up for mysterious solemnities, *symbol of a trinity* which surpasses our understanding" (1:238, my emphasis). What could be the mystical significance of Tristan's volcanic trinity? Though unarticulated, it is confirmed by this heavily stylized description in which the number "three" is repeated three times.

Early socialists gave various new meanings to the Christian trinity, "translating" it in order to proclaim the new sanctification of matter (see Bowman 1974). Initially, the Saint-Simonians valorized the trinity of human faculties defined as the motor, the rational, and the emotive. However, this trinitarian formula eventually gave way to the androgynous divinity, "God, father and mother" ("Dieu, père et mère"), a shift which unfortunately allowed them to revert more frequently to the old binary logic opposing masculinity to femininity, mind to matter, and master to slave. (see Planté 1986). Specifically, Enfantin's announcement that God was both male and female was based on the belief in an essential difference between men and women: God was a dual being in which women's superior sentient faculties were combined with men's superior rational faculties. Such reasoning helps to explain why the Saint-Simonian hierarchy was overwhelmingly male-dominated even before women were excluded from it altogether. For Saint-Simonian men, the rhetoric of androgyny seems to have had less to do with actual women's emancipation than it did with the men's own pursuit of a "plenitudinous or androgynous power."[8]

Tristan, on the other hand, devised her own divinity, a plural "Gods Father-Mother-Embryo" ("Dieux Père-Mère-Embryon"), references to which appear in her 1844 journal, Le tour de France, as well as the posthumously published L'émancipation de la femme ou le testament de la paria.[9] Unlike other androgynous divinities inspired by the Saint-Simonian school,[10] Tristan's "Gods" offers in a variety of ways greater resistance to the

representation of sexual difference as a polar opposition. First,
the inclusion of the gender-neutral term, "Embryo," inhibits the
usual tendency to separate human beings according to sex, asso-
ciating women with passion, for instance, and men with intelligence. In Tristan's "Gods," the masculine and feminine
principles are joined in the material process of procreation signi-
fied by the term "Embryo." Traditionally, the ability to give birth
has aligned women with a base materiality, preventing them from
symbolically representing God. By contrast, Tristan's plural divinity, in which the feminine principle is "redoubled" by
woman's special role in procreation, permits women to assume
religious authority (see Desanti 1984). The word "Embryo,"
moreover, denotes an entity in the process of becoming, whose
indefinite traits might transcend the male/female opposition. It
is as if Tristan were signaling humanity's religious destiny to
move beyond the sexual dichotomy. Finally, the very plurality of
the word "Gods" is suggestive of a fundamentally shifting nature,
one that foils the attempt to attribute fixed traits either to the
divinity as a whole or to any of its constituent "parts."

In what ways, then, might the trinity of volcanoes described
in the autobiography prefigure Tristan's innovation of a plural
God? For one thing, the volcanic symbolism subverts the binary
logic subtending the traditional Christian myth of creation, according to which God, a purely spiritual, masculine intelligence,
endows inert matter with life and form. Such a view of creation
is undermined by the image of the volcano, whose apparently
fixed exterior is constantly subject to change by an interior brewing with energy. Volcanoes participate in a world of perpetual
self-transformation, breaking down distinctions between form
and formlessness, activity and passivity, creator and created.
"Presenting chaos in all its confusion" (1.238), they are emblematic of a dynamic and seemingly uncontrolled process of creation
taking place in an animistic universe.

The volcanic trinity, like the "Gods Father-Mother-Embryo,"
may also reflect back to Flora her own position in the family
constellation consisting of the plebeian mother, the aristocratic
father, and herself, the illegitimate child. Illegitimacy would
thereby acquire a special, almost divine signification—as it did
for many Saint-Simonian women.[11] From this perspective, the
volcanic symbolism would challenge at once the belief in a divine, masculine spirit, and a corollary belief in the primacy of
patrilineal descent.[12] Like the word "embryo," the illegitimate
child reminds us of the biological reality of procreation that ulti-

mately eludes paternal control. Tristan herself insistently reminds her readers of this reality both in the text of her autobiography, and through the gesture of publishing the work under her father's name. Though it may appear to respect the myth of patrilineal descent, Tristan's use of the patronymic actually subverts its function to the extent that her claim to this name rests on a relation to her father that is biological, not legal. By emphatically insisting on her own physical resemblance to her father, as evidenced by her strikingly dark hair and eyes,[13] the autobiographer in fact assigns primacy to the biological reality of procreation—a gesture that could as easily (if not more easily) justify the privileging of matrilineal descent.

Illegitimacy thus exposes what the paternal name would mask: the potential for women to have illicit sexual relations, and the absence of a natural link between a man's name, his property, and his progeny. It is this disturbing reality which, according to Catherine Gallagher, helps to explain why revolutionary violence is often emblematized in French literature and iconography as "the uncontrolled and luridly sexual woman": "Liberty, in the iconography of the age, often turns into a whore when she threatens the patriarchal family as such" (see Hertz 1985). The illegitimate child, like the volcano, may threaten society with chaos and confusion, that is, with creation uncontrolled by the paternal will. This is especially the case for the *woman* who is born illegitimate, for she has the power to reproduce in her turn, continuing to disrupt the "paternal fiction of absolute control."[14] However, Tristan's apocalyptic narrative, through its volcanic symbolism, suggests that the illegitimate female as pariah becomes the messiah, announcing a new law that defies the paternal law.

Tristan's arrival in Arequipa is closely followed by incidents of both geological upheaval and revolutionary violence. These turbulent events seem to validate her messianic status, especially if we recall the Biblical prophecy of the second coming, which was to be marked by political strife and "earthquakes, in diverse places."[15] In the Fourierist universe, however, such events are not the expression of a wrathful God; rather, they are a natural consequence of humanity's failure to live by the principle of interdependency. Oppression, particularly the oppression of women, is thus held to be the true source of geological and political terror. In *Pérégrinations*, a particularly close connection is made between social turmoil and Pio de Tristan's invocation of his niece's illegitimacy as an excuse for denying her a fair share of the family wealth.[16] Thus divine law disrupts the paternal law, while the paternal law in turn contributes to the conditions that terrorize the citizens of Arequipa.

Shortly after Tristan's arrival at the paternal family home in Arequipa, a massive earthquake occurs, described by the autobiographer in such a way as to condense the two events: "I had arrived in Arequipa September 13th; on the 18th of the same month I felt, for the first time, an earthquake" (1:292). Accustomed to the perpetual movement of her long ocean voyage, she is initially unafraid; later, when her cousin Carmen rushes into the room, terrified and exclaiming, Flora speaks calmly: "Cousin, I thought I was still on a ship: that is how one feels the movements of the waves, and I was frightened only when, in the courtyard, I saw the houses leaning towards me, the cobblestone streets moving, the sky swaying as when one is at sea. Then I understood all of the terror with which man's heart is gripped in the presence of a scourge which makes him feel so profoundly his powerlessness" (1:293). Tristan's choice of the biblical-sounding word "scourge" implies that the quake occurs in accordance with divine law, a law which, according to Fourier, is inseparable from the physical laws of the universe. The quake therefore has both negative and positive connotations: negative because it signifies humanity's failure to achieve social harmony, and positive because it confirms that the oppressive laws upheld by patriarchy are opposed to the divine law with which Tristan is allied. Tristan's composure during the upheaval reflects her privileged relation to the "truth" of humanity's presently impeded socialist destiny.

Yet Tristan is a also a victim of terror. When a second quake occurs, she watches transfixed as a barely noticeable crack in the ceiling vault of her father's mansion (which now belongs to her paternal uncle) is suddenly wrenched apart: "About seven o'clock, a muffled noise, which seemed to come from the bowels of the earth, was heard: it was its voice! My cousin cried out in fear and rushed out of the room. At that moment, I had my gaze fixed on a rather slight crack in the middle of the vault; I saw that crack open up suddenly, the enormous stones of the vault become dislodged. I thought that the entire mass was going to collapse on my head and I fled, terrified" (1.293). The crumbling of her uncle's dwelling is symbolic (and in Fourier's system, symptomatic), of the crumbling of the old social order; in particular, the crack in the vault is suggestive of the "cracks" or contradictions running through patriarchal ideology, contradictions that are suddenly exposed in times of social upheaval. Yet this process of sudden upheaval is as terrifying to Tristan, the socially rebellious and illegitimate-born woman, as it is to those around her. The neglected "bastard" of the family, Tristan comes to make herself heard by those who would prefer not to acknowledge her existence. However, it is the earthquake whose "voice" is terrifying. The personification of the shuddering earth, described as having a belly and voice, gives us the ominous sense that destruction of the flawed paternal edifice is not the work of Tristan, but of another, mysteriously powerful entity.

This entity is identified with Arequipa's volcano, whose link to earthquakes is established in the text: "Sometimes the volcano spews smoke; that happens particularly in the evening: often, in that smoke, I saw flames; when there has not been any smoke for a long time, one expects an earthquake" (1.293). The belief that great, destructive earthquakes were connected to volcanoes was a popular myth in Peru and elsewhere; moreover, the association of volcanic activity with small, local shocks is not unscientific. Nonetheless, Tristan's dramatic accounts of earthquakes, as well as the important status of volcanoes in her text, suggest that this association also fulfills an important rhetorical purpose. A direct relationship exists between the smoldering substances trapped in the verticle structure of the volcano, and the perturbations felt for hundreds of miles in the plane surrounding its base. The volcano, like woman in Fourier's social theory, is presented here as a "pivotal" figure around which the harmonious functioning of an entire system seems to revolve. Yet for Tristan, as for Fourier, neither women nor volcanoes can be considered the ultimate source of disruption. Indeed, the volcano, when personified in Tristan's text, has attributes as magnificent as they are terrifying: "This giant, who hides its menacing head in the heavens, is one of the most magnificent spectacles that the earth offers to man's gaze." The terrifying destructiveness of the earthquake contrasts with the sublime beauty of the volcano. Volcanic eruptions are the spectacular manifestation of a more widespread geological instability, the physical source of which is never identified.

The link between geological upheaval and a woman's revolt against patriarchy is reinforced when the earthquake provides the occasion for Flora and Carmen to discuss women's financial and social powerlessness. Carmen laments that financial dependence and the yoke of marriage have forced her to live in a country constantly rocked by earthquakes: "My cousin gritted her

teeth in a movement of revolt which proved to me that she was
ill-disposed to slavery" (1:295). Shocked at Flora's declaration
that women should refuse to be slaves, Carmen remains silent,
"blowing rings and fantastic patterns with the smoke from her
cigar" (1:296). The autobiographer then resumes without transition her account of the widespread damage resulting from the
earthquake, as if the intercalated discussion of women's oppression were naturally a part of that account.

Carmen, like the volcano, smokes and smolders, silently revolt-
ing against her oppression. So, too, do the nuns imprisoned in
a nearby convent Tristan often contemplates, as she watches the
sun disappear behind the three volcanoes: "Inside these large
buildings, instead of the tomb-like peace that their somber and
cold exterior had led one to imagine, one finds only feverish
activity that discipline confines but does not stifle; muffled,
veiled, it bubbles like the lava in the flanks of the volcano that
contains it" (2:137). Condemned to passivity, women rage inside,
brewing with energy and potential revolt. The word "flancs" in
this passage underscores the link between a woman's active sexuality and the expression of her own will, both of which are un-
evenly but vigorously held in check by patriarchal institutions.
Men's consciousness of women's will is held at bay, as is their
consciousness of the enormous volcano bordering the city of
Arequipa. In times of political upheaval, the startling truth of
women's will may become apparent, but it is the iron grip of
oppression that creates the conditions for revolt among women,
as well as other exploited groups.

Just as geological upheaval is linked to women's oppression,
so, too, is political violence. Flora reacts with outrage when Pio
de Tristan refuses to accord her the sum of money to which she
would have been entitled as the legitimate daughter of Mariano.
This event is closely interwoven in the text with an account of
the revolution that breaks out in Peru, leaving property owners
"stricken by terror."[17] Pio, having managed to protect "his" property from Flora, must eventually submit to the demands of the
warring political factions for money. He thereby loses property
all the same, a circumstance which Tristan is tempted to interpret as an act of divine retribution (2:50). The mystical connections of social unrest to Tristan's personal experience are further
underscored by the apocalpytic description of crowds in the
streets. The "muffled sound" arising from masses of people echoes the "muffled sound" or "voice" of the earthquake: "A long,
muffled sound, which escaped from those domes as from a tomb,

drew me out of my day-dreaming. That whole mass animated by the same feeling had only one voice!" (2:212–13). In a later passage, the crowd once more echoes the "muffled sound" heard during the earthquake, which, as we recall, had similarly been compared to the movement of waves: "A muffled and confused sound came out of those colossal masses, and the continual movement by which they were shaken resembled the roar of the waves of an angry sea."[18] The autobiographer thus deftly weaves the personal with the political, the private with the public, and the social with the geological.

Tristan's *Pérégrinations d'une paria* relocates the sources of terror in a manner that is pertinent to recent scholarship focusing on the relationships between castration anxiety, women's reproductive power, and fear of revolutionary violence. The cultural association of women with revolutionary violence and loss of property has been traced to men's castration fear, to what is perceived as the terrifying weakness—or power—of the female organs (Hertz). It is understandable that the volcano, as an enormous conical structure that discharges lava, may become associated with the terror-inspiring womb. But in Tristan's text, the womb-like volcano is at once a figure of terror and joy that promises the birth of a new social order. This response is notably different from that of Chateaubriand and Alexandre Dumas, both of whom emphasize climbing to the very highest point of a volcano in order to be face to face with its immense crater.[19] Perhaps the description, as well as the adventure itself, of climbing great heights in order to confront the abyss is both a reenactment of the terrifying castration scene and an act of phallic defiance that is typical of the male romantic's fascination with the volcano. For Tristan, however, there is no singular abyss, no unique source of terror. Rather, there are earthquakes in diverse places, suggesting that the repercussions of oppression are far more terrible than the sharing of power and property.

Vassar College

NOTES

1. My information on volcano tourism was obtained from Krafft 1993.

2. Tristan 1838. For more information on Flora Tristan, see Desanti 1972. See also Moses and Rabine 1993.

3. Tristan's parents had been married by a French émigré priest in 1802,

unbeknownst to the rest of the Tristan clan in Peru, and the marriage was never legally contracted.

4. "Social progress and changes of period take place because of women's progress toward liberty"—Fourier 1:132. Tristan writes: "The degree of civilization which various human societies have reached has always been proportional to the degree of independence that women have enjoyed in them" (1:xxv). For more on the theories of Fourier, see Beecher 1986.

5. See Adler 1979. See also Moses 1984.

6. Indeed, Moses and Rabine suggest that the *Saint-Simoniennes* created "the first consciously separatist women's movement in history" (1993, 7).

7. For more on the figures of spiritual autobiography, see Fleishman 1983.

8. Kari Weil suggests that Saint-Simonian men sought "a means to interpret the feminization of the Romantic man not as a 'malady,' but as evidence of a plenitudinous or androgynous power" (Weil 232).

9. *L'émancipation de la femme* was completed from Tristan's notes by Alphonse Constant and published by him in 1845, a year after her death.

10. Louis-Jean Baptiste de Turreil named his divinity "MERAMOURPERE," and its human counterpart "EVADAM." Simon Ganneau called himself Mapah, believing he "had known all the incarnations of man since the 'Evadam primitif'" (Bowman 320–21).

11. On *Saint-Simonienne*'s views concerning illegitimacy, see Moses and Rabine 58.

12. The association of woman with passivity and materiality facilitates the belief in man's exclusive prerogative to name and own his offspring. Sidonie Smith points out that in Genesis, "Adam recapitulates God's creation of the world through the word ... and establishes his patrilineal inheritance" (Smith 29).

13. She reminds an acquaintance that she is part Peruvian, stating: "I am from my father's country. . . . Look at my features and tell me to which nation I belong" (1:131). She quotes her paternal uncle as he affirms his belief that she is the daughter of his brother: "One sees too much of him in you to doubt it" (2:14).

14. The silencing of woman reflects a need to deny the gap between man's naming of "his" children and women's potential for infidelity. For this reason, argues Susan Hardy Aikin, the womb is "potentially the single most radical source of disruption in the paternal fiction of absolute control" (Aikin 1984).

15. Asked what will be the sign of the second coming, Jesus answers: "For nation shall rise against nation, and kingdom against kingdom: and there shall be famines, and pestilences, and earthquakes, in diverse places" (Matthew 24.7).

16. Had she been legally recognized as her father's daughter, Flora would have been entitled to 800,000 francs. She requested that her uncle give her only enough money to live on, a yearly pension of 20,000 piasters, or 5,000 francs. The yearly pension of 2,500 francs which he did send her was abruptly discontinued after the publication of *Pérégrinations*.

17. 2:206. According to Tristan's account, the causes of the revolution are as follows: Peru's official president was a Señor Gamarra, but his wife, interestingly, had usurped his role. When she began to lose control of the government, she named a new president. Various political factions rebelled, and named yet another president. Ultimately, Señora Gamarra died in exile. Despite the explanation given for this particular upheaval, Tristan attributes it above all to

the general failure of the Peruvian people to recognize the divine principle of interdependency.

18. 2:227. The homonymic association with a "*mère en courroux*" contributes to the symbolic richness of this passage.

19. "There I am on top of Vesuvius, writing while seated at the mouth of the volcano and ready to go down to the bottom of its crater" (Chateaubriand 1467). Recounting his visit to Etna, Dumas writes: "We were in front of the crater, that is, of an immense pit eight miles in circumference, 900 feet deep. . . . We were on one of the highest points" (Dumas 224).

4

Paintings of Terrorized *parlementaires* for the Bourbon Conseil d'état

JONATHAN P. RIBNER

DURING the Salon of 1827–28, visitors to the Louvre were permitted access to a suite of rooms occupied by one of government's most intimate and controversial organs, the Conseil d'état. On view was an extensive new ensemble of paintings. This official commission was shared by twenty-seven artists, including innovators such as Delacroix, Horace Vernet, and Paul Delaroche as well as bland Prix de Rome laureates. In my recent book, *Broken Tablets: The Cult of the Law in French Art from David to Delacroix*, I discuss the principal theme of the Conseil d'état paintings: the divine inspiration of law and the legislative preeminence of the French monarchy.[1] Here I will examine the manner in which this ambitious Bourbon decorative cycle addressed a troubling aspect of national history.

Looking up as they entered the principal room of the suite— that in which the Conseil d'état held its general assemblies— Salon visitors saw a ceiling painting by Méry-Joseph Blondel. Blondel's allegory of *France, in the midst of the Legislator Kings and French Jurisconsults, Receives the Constitutional Charter from Louis XVIII* glorifies the legislative stature of the late monarch while proclaiming the providential pedigree of the Bourbon Charter. Accompanied by Wisdom, Prudence, Justice, and Law, Louis XVIII, avuncular but august, is seated high above the Seine on "the throne of his Ancestors."[2] At his feet, a regal personification of France humbly receives the Charter. In the spirit of the preamble to that Charter, Blondel's allegory presents the regime's constitution as a product of traditional French monarchic largess.[3]

As Blondel's cloud-borne Louis XVIII grants the Charter to France, an assembly of monarchs and legists of the ancien régime

M.-J. Blondel, *France, in the midst of the Legislator Kings and French Juris-consults, Receives the Constitutional Charter from Louis XVIII*, 1827. Louvre, Paris (Photo © 1995 ARS, NY / SPADEM, Paris)

look on with approval. The enlightened Montesquieu (holding *L'esprit des lois*) relaxes in the unlikely company of a delighted Louis XIV. This reconciliation of the legacies of absolutism and the Enlightenment bears analogy to the political aspirations of vicomte Sosthène de La Rochefoucauld, superintendent of the Department of Fine Arts in the Ministry of the King's Household. This pious royalist, who saw in the Charter the sole means to sustain the monarchy that he cherished, shared responsibility for the decorative ensemble with the reputedly liberal comte de Forbin, general director of the Royal Museums. While the respective contributions of the two officials are undocumented, the program bears the stamp of La Rochefoucauld's conservative politics.

Advocates of the doctrine of providentially ordained kingship must have been pleased by the flattering correspondence between Blondel's allegory of Louis XVIII as lawgiver and the representations of divinely inspired legislators that could be viewed, ad nauseam, elsewhere in the Conseil d'état suite. Below Blondel's ceiling hung his portraits of Moses, Numa, Solon, and

Lycurgus. In the next room additional portraits of Moses and Numa hung near Delacroix's lost painting of the bejewelled Justinian, dictating his laws like an evangelist. For the ceiling of the fourth room, Jean-Baptiste Mauzaisse painted *Divine Wisdom Giving the Laws to the Kings and Legislators*. Here, Moses receives the law at the head of a crush of legislators that includes an Indian chief, George Washington, William Penn, Mohammed, and Confucius, as well as Numa, Solon, and Lycurgus. Envy and Calomny are banished by sword as Louis XVIII and other French monarchs preside from clouds in the upper left corner.

Deliberating amid this edifying decor was an institution deeply embroiled in the conflict between constitutional legality and royal prerogative that shaped the political history of the Restoration.[4] Derived from the corps of professional administrators who counseled ancien régime monarchs, and bearing the same title as one of the principal cogs in Bonaparte's political machine, the Conseil d'état bore an hereditary link to both monarchic absolutism and Napoleonic authoritarianism. Under the Restoration, the Conseil d'état functioned outside the scope of constitutional control, offering advice to the cabinet of royal ministers and arbitrating matters of administrative conflict. Particularly disliked by the liberal opposition, who objected to its extralegal character, the Conseil d'état had recently been moved to the royal palace of the Louvre in accord with its allegiance to the monarch, who symbolically presided over its members from an empty throne.

For its new royal setting, the Conseil d'état needed appropriate dress. The official habit of funereal Bourbon black, embroidered with black *fleurs-de-lys*, is worn with superb arrogance by comte Amédée-David de Pastoret, a star of ultra-royalist society known for his chivalric pretentions, in a portrait by Ingres (Salon of 1827–28; Art Institute of Chicago). Ingres's portrait of Pastoret was exhibited in the same Salon as the Conseil d'état paintings.[5]

Assembled beneath Blondel's allegory of France receiving the Charter, Pastoret and his colleagues could view four paintings of ancien régime *parlementaires* exhibiting courage and loyalty to the crown in the face of mob violence. With subjects drawn from the troubled history of late sixteenth- and mid-seventeenth-century France, the four paintings were all but one burnt in the Palais d'Orsay during the Commune. Fortunately, they were reproduced in that compendium of art by old and modern masters, Réveil's *Musée de peinture et de sculpture*. Unlike the chilly abstractions of Blondel's allegorical ceiling, the four paintings of

J.-B. Mauzaisse, *Divine Wisdom Giving the Laws to the Kings and Legislators,* **1827. Louvre, Paris (Photo © 1995 ARS, NY / SPADEM, Paris)**

A. Réveil after A.-J.-B. Thomas, *President Molé at the Barricades*, from Réveil and Duchesne aîné, *Musée de peinture et de sculpture*, IV, Paris, 1829. (Photo courtesy of the Thomas J. Watson Library, The Metropolitan Museum of Art; photograph by Jonathan P. Ribner)

parlementaires confronting political terror made an aggressively emotional appeal.

In one of the paintings, Antoine-Jean-Baptiste Thomas memorialized Mathieu Molé, first president of the *parlement* of Paris, who remained calm and resolutely loyal to the crown during an uprising of *frondeurs* on August 27, 1648. Regarding *President Molé at the Barricades*, the *livret* recounts how the chief magistrate heroically faced a homicidal mob.[6] The subject of Thomas's companion piece, *Les Seize au parlement* was inspired by the account in Voltaire's *Henriade* of the disturbances that followed

A. Réveil after A.-J.-B. Thomas, *Les Seize au parlement*, from Réveil and Duchesne aîné, *Musée de peinture et de sculpture*, IV, Paris, 1829. (Photo: courtesy of the Thomas J. Watson Library, The Metropolitan Museum of Art; photograph by Jonathan P. Ribner)

the murder of the duc de Guise in 1588.[7] The *livret* tells how Bussy le Clerc, one of the sixteen leading insurgents, "forced his way into the grand hall of the *parlement* and tried to force the first president [Achille de Harlay] to place in the record an order to no longer recognize the royal family" (*Explication* [1827] 1977, 20). This painting, previously exhibited by Thomas in the Salon of 1824 and retouched for its new location, apparently survived the Palais d'Orsay fire.[8] Bristling with halberds, Thomas's paintings contrast the virtuous calm of the *parlemen-*

taires with the disorder of vengeful assailants and panic-stricken compatriots. Thomas, who also exhibited in the Salon of 1827 a painting of Jesus following the flagellation and crowning with thorns, composed his paintings for the Conseil d'état in such a way as to recall representations of the taking of Christ. At the same time, Thomas revived a Louis Seize tradition that reconstructed historical confrontations between a heroic leader and would-be assailants. An example is a painting of *The Death of Admiral Coligny* (also inspired by *La Henriade*) exhibited by Joseph-Benoît Suvée in the Salon of 1787 (Dijon, Musée des Beaux-Arts; see Rosenblum and Janson, 28). More specifically, Thomas was inspired by François-André Vincent's *Président Molé Stopped by Insurgents during the Fronde* (Paris, Palais-Bourbon). Vincent's painting, exhibited in the Salon of 1779, was commissioned by the comte d'Angiviller as part of his program to direct the arts toward the commemoration of French heroes.[9] Vincent was Thomas's teacher, and the younger painter's dependence on artistic conventions dating from the reign of Louis XVI was in keeping with the Restoration's nostalgic ambition to reestablish continuity with the ancien régime.

Even more terrifying situations are presented by the other *parlementaire* paintings for the Conseil d'état. *The Death of Brisson* by Jean-Bruno Gassies and *The Death of Duranti* by Paul Delaroche reenact the final moments of two victims of the violence that followed the duc de Guise's murder. The *livret* describes how the *parlement's* acting first president, Barnabé Brisson, a "victim of his love for peace and for his king," was forced to kneel by a mob that "read him a sentence that condemned him to die for having corresponded with heretics . . . and without giving him time to defend himself, hung him"on the spot (*Explication* [1827] 1977, 19). The review of the Conseil d'état ensemble by the liberal critic Auguste Jal is peppered with anti-royalist and anti-clerical comment. But the critic was disarmed by this faithful magistrate bravely meeting his death at the hands of the populace. I quote from Jal: "In the background of his composition, M.Gassies has placed the rabble [*des hommes du peuple*] preparing the rope with which the president will be hung. . . . The expression of the president is well done; he confronts his enemies, but without swagger; he awaits martyrdom without protesting against the presumption of his executioners; fanaticism of duty sustains him without exaltation. Insults, cruelty, mockery, he will endure all; the sight of the noose does not frighten him, and his steadfastness will bring pallor to the

A. Réveil after J.-B. Gassies, *The Death of Brisson,* from Réveil and Duchesne aîné, *Musée dé peinture et de sculpture,* IV, Paris, 1829. (Photo courtesy of the Thomas J. Watson Library, The Metropolitan Museum of Art; photograph by Jonathan P. Ribner)

representative of the Hôtel de Ville who has come to deride his last moments" (Jal 421).

But the work that most deeply touched Jal was Delaroche's *Death of Duranti,* praised by the critic as "without contest the best work of the author, the most beautiful ornament of the rooms of the Conseil d'état, one of the most admirable paintings of the exhibition of 1827, and one of the most complete productions of the French school, since its regeneration."[10] The *livret* recounts how Duranti, first president of the *parlement* of Toulouse and opponent of the League, attempted unsuccessfully to calm the

A. Réveil after P. Delaroche, *The Death of Duranti,* from Réveil and Duchesne aîné, *Musée de peinture et de sculpture,* IV, Paris, 1829. (Photo courtesy of the Thomas J. Watson Library, The Metropolitan Museum of Art; photograph by Jonathan P. Ribner)

people following the murder of the duc de Guise: "Forced to seek refuge in a monastery with his wife and two children, Duranti is discovered by the populace who, in spite of the resistance of monks, priests, and his family, drag him from the monastery and kill him." A master *metteur en scène,* Delaroche rendered this subject with heartrending pathos. Here is Jal's description: "Duranti, seated at a table bearing a crucifix, offers the sacrifice of his life to God and to the king. Calm, he sees the fatal instant approach; . . . the wife of the president has thrown herself at the knees of her husband, whom she embraces for the last time; the

G. Lethière, *The Heroism of St. Louis at Damietta*, 1827. Musée National du Château de Versailles (Photo © R.M.N.)

elder of her children begs the murderers to spare a father. . . ." (Jal 425–26).

The intrepid righteousness of the four *parlementaires* had a medieval counterpart in the same room.[11] Guillaume Lethière's *The Heroism of St. Louis at Damietta* (Château de Versailles) treats a particularly heroic period in the career of this exemplary Christian ruler, his captivity in Egypt during the Crusades. Threatened at sword point by his captor, the saint maintains a calm resolve that contrasts with the consternation of his companions and echoes, across the centuries, the courage of Molé, Harlay, Brisson, and Duranti.[12] In its appeal to royalist sentiment, Lethière's painting follows the example set by François Ancelot's popular play, *Louis IX* (1819). Dedicated to Louis XVIII, Ancelot's drama of the virtuous king in captivity triumphantly concludes with the monarch's liberation.[13]

In the preceding room, Horace Vernet's *Philippe-Auguste before the Battle of Bouvines* offered yet another instructive medieval subject for the consideration of the Conseil d'état. Vernet reconstructed the day in 1214 when Philippe-Auguste was about to lead an army of commoners to victory under the auspices of the Church. According to a legend, reported as fact in the medieval chronicle of the Minstrel of Reims, the king offered his crown to any of his barons who might think they better deserved it. "This generous offer," noted Jal, "which I would not advise any current European prince to risk, is received by . . . oaths of faith and homage" (Jal 410). In the account of the Minstrel of Reims, the barons reply to their king: "We are ready to die for you" (Bossuat 64).

Such willingness to die for their monarch was also demonstrated by the *parlementaires,* whose defiance of popular opposition to the throne must have appealed to nostalgic conservatives uneasy with the representational system defined by the Charter. Unlike the legislators of the Chambre des députés, ancien régime *parlementaires* were magistrates who executed justice in the name of the king who, in theory, was the sole source of legislative authority. It was fitting for this ancien régime institution to be so honored before the Conseil d'état which, like the *parlement,* owed allegiance solely to the king.

In the same room as the *parlementaire* paintings hung a work that idealized the doctrine, embodied in the *parlements* and maintained by the Bourbon Charter, that "all justice emanates from the King." Georges Rouget's *Saint Louis Administering Justice under the Oak of Vincennes* reverently illustrates how Louis IX would either personally settle the disputes of his subjects or delegate this responsibility to his officers, as recounted by Jean de Joinville in *The Life of Saint Louis.* Like Lethière's painting of Saint Louis as prisoner, Rouget's painting had an ancien régime flavor. A series of paintings illustrating the life of Saint Louis had been commissioned in 1773–74 to decorate the Chapel of the Ecole militaire royale. That major undertaking had prepared the ground for the campaign to encourage the commemoration of France's *grands hommes* in works such as Vincent's *Président Molé.*[14]

H. Vernet, *Philippe-Auguste before the Battle of Bouvines*, 1827. Musée National du Château de Versailles (Photo © R.M.N.)

G. Rouget, *Saint Louis Administering Justice under the Oak of Vincennes,* **1826. Musée National du Château de Versailles (Photo © R.M.N.)**

The *parlementaire* paintings in the Conseil d'état suite drama-tized a warning voiced in the preamble to the Bourbon Charter: "when violence forces concessions from a weak government, public liberty is no less in danger than the throne." These words acquired an ironic resonance in the aftermath of July 1830, when the unwillingness of Charles X's ministers to respect public lib-erty provoked the civic violence that brought down the throne.

Established in the name of liberty, the July Monarchy was no less haunted by memories of revolutionary violence than the preceding regime. This is evident in one of the first decorative projects of the Orléans government, a competition of 1830 for monumental paintings intended to hang in the assembly hall of the Chambre des députés in the newly remodeled Palais-Bourbon.[15] The two subjects, culled from the history of the French Revolution, were intended to celebrate Liberty and Public Order, the governmental principles that the Orléans regime attempted to hold in balance, just as the Bourbon government had sought equilibrium between monarchic prerogative and the Charter. Louis-Philippe's prime minister, François Guizot drew up the program for the competition paintings in the belief that the two subjects exemplified the "opposition to despotism and opposition to insurrection [that] determine the limits of a deputy's responsibilities."[16] Intended to provide the Chambre des députés with stirring models of comportment, the competition paintings can be viewed as July Monarchy counterparts to the four *parlementaire* paintings for the Bourbon Conseil d'état.

In contrast to the *parlementaires'* unshakable fidelity to the crown, one of the 1830 competition paintings was to commemorate a famous act of resistance to arbitrary monarchic will. Contestants were asked to depict the defiant reply of Mirabeau when told by the chief of royal protocol, the marquis de Dreux-Brézé, to vacate the royal audience hall during the meeting of the Estates General. The pendant was to represent President François Boissy-d'Anglas during the uprising of May 20, 1795 when a mob invaded the Convention, decapitated a deputy, and brandished his severed head before the president. Like Mathieu Molé confronting agitated *frondeurs* on the barricades, Boissy-d'Anglas exhibited exemplary courage and saluted the bleeding remains of his fellow legislator.

In the version of *Boissy-d'Anglas* submitted to the competition by Alexandre-Evariste Fragonard, the president bows with bared head in deference to the victim of mob violence (1830; Musée du Louvre). Animated by accessory details—a dog lapping blood, for example—Fragonard's entry suggests the sensibility of a genre painter. In contrast, Delacroix submitted a sketch whose seething turbulence foreshadows the vision of irresistable crowd dynamism articulated at the fin-de-siècle by Gustave Le Bon (1831; Bordeaux, Musée des Beaux-Arts). In his version of *Boissy-d'Anglas*, Delacroix poignantly evokes a dark aspect of the revolutionary heritage that haunted the July Monarchy in its early years. As Michael Marrinan has suggested, so disturbing did the specter of disorder become in the wake of the uprisings of April 1834 that the paintings that won the competition were never placed in the Palais-Bourbon (Marrinan 105–108).

Whereas Guizot chose his subjects from the history of the Revolution, the Conseil d'état paintings condemned the revolutionary heritage through historical analogy. The absence of direct allusion to the Revolution in the Conseil d'état suite corresponded to an eagerness to forget stated in the preamble to the Bourbon Charter. That document, drafted on the ruins of the Revolution and Empire, addresses, as follows, the disruptions of French history since 1789: "By trying in this way to reestablish the chain of time, which disastrous errors had interrupted, we have erased from our memory, as we would like to be able to erase from history, all the wrongs that have afflicted our country during our absence." In the face of this royal will to forget, the *parlementaire* paintings for the Conseil d'état attest to the inability of the restored monarchy to efface the nation's memory of its Revolution. To the contrary, the paintings of Molé, Harlay, Brisson, and Duranti were products of what François Furet has called "the imagination of the Revolution"—that tyrannical impingement of the Revolution on future events and political sentiments (Furet 151–60). All but one destroyed by the Commune, these forgotten paintings were as inescapably tied to France's heritage of revolutionary violence as the regime for which they were painted.

Boston University

NOTES

1. (Ribner 1993), 54–60. The present article is based on a paper read at the nineteenth Annual Colloquium in Nineteenth-Century French Studies at the University of Kansas, Lawrence, Kansas, 28–31 October 1993. I am grateful to Barbara T. Cooper for suggesting the relevance of this material to the Colloquium topic, "Terror and Terrorism." I also extend thanks to David Wisner for sharing with me the manuscript for a forthcoming study of the Conseil d'état paintings.

2. Quoted from a description of the program sent by the comte de Forbin to the Minister of Justice, 6 October 1826. Archives Nationales BB17A, 49, dossier 1, item 12.

3. References to the 1814 Charter are from Godechot, 217–24.

4. See Olivier-Martin 1941 and Léonardi 1909.

5. See the catalogue entry by Jacques Foucart, in French Painting, 1774–1830, no. 111.

6. References to the *livret* are to Explication des ouvrages de peinture . . . le 4 novembre 1827 [1827] 1977, 15–23.

7. This painting is reproduced in the *Musée de peinture et de sculpture* with the erroneous caption, "Mathieu Molé insulted by the people." While Voltaire referred to a Molé as being among those harassed by les Seize, this was apparently Edouard Molé, a counsellor to the *parlement* who died in 1634.

8. The painting (Louvre inv. no. 8159) was deposited in the museum of Auxerre in 1876.

9. The paintings by Vincent and Suvée are reproduced, and discussed in the context of d'Angiviller's patronage, in Crow 192–97.   .

10. *Esquisses*, 425, quoted in the principal study of the artist, Ziff, 65. A copy of Delaroche's *The Death of Duranti* by Léon-Désiré Alexandre (1869) was commissioned by the state and is in the Palais de Justice, Bordeaux.

11. Two paintings in the same room by Jean-Victor Schnetz offered additional historical exemplars of courage and fidelity to the king. One represented Cardinal Mazarin on his deathbed presenting Colbert to Louis XIV (apparently destroyed in the museum of Reims during World War I). He says to the king, according to the *livret*, "Sire, I owe everything to your Majesty, but I believe I am repaying you by giving you M. Colbert." The other painting commemorated the last moments of Boethius, counsellor to Theodoric, who was imprisoned and executed by the ruler he served so well. Schnetz showed Boethius in prison, receiving the last farewells of his daughter and grandson before being led to execution. *Explication* [1827] 1977, 19–20.

12. The *livret* provides the following account: "Saint Louis, a prisoner at Damietta, turns down the odious proposition of the emir Octaï, who, after having assassinated the sultan Moadan, offers the holy King liberty and a throne if he agrees to make him a knight" (*Explication* [1827] 1977, 19).

13. Having won a spiritual victory over his Islamic adversaries, Louis is asked by the Syrian prince Nouradin to be their new legislator:

> The Muslim, struck by thy sublime virtue,
> Bows before thee, reveres thee, honors thee;
>
> . . . .
> This nation, these warriors, speak to thee through my voice,
> Good Louis, consent to grant them laws.
>
> (Ancelot 64)

In his dedication, Ancelot draws the kind of flattering historical parallel offered by the paintings for the Conseil d'état: "Under the rule of YOUR MAJESTY, it was simple for me to recount the virtues of the father of the Bourbons; and if my work has received some praise, I doubtless owe it to the pleasure the French have felt in rediscovering the image of the present in the memories of the past."

14. For the Ecole militaire cycle, see Cummings 33–34; and Goodman 382–86.

15. For the competition, and reproductions of the paintings in question, see Marrinan 79–98.

16. Quoted in Marrinan 95.

5

Le dandysme: Terrorism with Style

PAMELA A. GENOVA

In today's society, with its progressively more complicated cultural atmosphere, where questions of identity have given rise to an impassioned rage for new terms and a flourish of ideological "isms" such as postmodernism, multiculturalism, and new historicism, we are reminded that the variety of possible responses to the end of a century can be considerable. In late nineteenth-century France, too, faced with the ambivalent effects of a rapidly changing culture, artists and writers sought new ways of understanding and integrating the modern. In fin-de-siècle aesthetics, writers turned to the eccentric, the strange, and the unnatural to express their creative vision. Figures from Greek mythology, the Bible, and regional legend converge in an atmosphere of experimental writing and artistic play to overturn aesthetic tradition and to question social mores. This alternate aesthetic universe of satyrs, hermaphrodites, vampires, and androgynes utilized unsettling figures of lore and imagination to mirror the unique forms and subjects of the art itself.

From among the complex combinations of referential motifs carefully constructed by unconventional nineteenth-century artists and writers, one figure emerges who distinguishes himself through his outlandish mores, peculiar image, and unusual art: the dandy. As if to reflect its own inherent duality, nineteenth-century dandyism existed both as an actual social phenomenon and as a literary construct. In French society, critics, columnists, and aesthetically minded salon-goers argued over dandy status, capriciously granting the title of dandy to such figures as d'Orsay, Musset, Gautier, Montesquiou, and Oscar Wilde. During an afternoon stroll on a Parisian boulevard in the mid-1800s, one would surely meet up with a member of the dandy clan, recognizable by an impeccably tailored suit, a delicately carved walking stick, various accessories of lace and velvet, and a general air of detachment, of cool disinterest.

As a cultural phenomenon, French dandyism began in the 1820s as an import from England, modeled on the flamboyant figures of men such as Beau Brummell and Lord Byron. The stylish fashion of dandyism held unsuspected artistic potential, and a serious literary interest in the dandy soon began to flourish, sparked by Balzac's extremely popular "Traité de la vie élégante," and continued by the work of other celebrated poets and novelists, such as Gautier, Musset, and Stendhal.[1] A relationship of reciprocity was established between the great dandies of society who inspired literary models, and the figures of books themselves who in turn inspired the birth of new social dandies. Heir to the legacy of the elegant eighteenth-century *beau* and the English gentleman-poet, the French dandy of the nineteenth century infiltrated the social and aesthetic sensibility of his time as a symbol of difference. With cultural ancestry traced back to Alcibiades—who, incidentally, made his name as an esteemed dandy forerunner by cutting the tails off his prize dogs so they would stand out among the canine rabble[2]—the nineteenth-century dandy established a reputation of lucid originality, stoicism, challenge, and revolt. Throughout the 1800s, the individual who made his début as an elegant, useless fop gradually blossomed into an intellectual creature, ready to defy order through art, set willingly against the grain in social and aesthetic traditions. By the end of the century, the dandy came to embody a living legend by taking deliberate advantage of rumor and scandal, while his strict ideological credo lent to his persona a sense of continuity and systematic meaning.

Conscious of his marginalized social role, the fin-de-siècle dandy formulated a subtle, aesthetically-grounded style of cultural terrorism that attacked the foundations of art, morality, and convention by consistently questioning those very foundations, hoping to weaken them not through direct attacks, but through insinuation and innuendo. Faced with an increasingly more problematic cultural context, the dandy created a unique response to the splenetic ennui and chaos that accompanied the ambivalent promise of a new century.[3] Baudelaire's "Le dandy" emphasizes the political implications of dandyism and considers the dandy as a figure indicative of change, whose appearance in a society denotes a moment of cultural transition and instability: "Dandyism appears especially in transitional periods in which democracy is not yet all-powerful, in which the aristocracy is only partially weakened and debased" (Baudelaire 1958, 351). The dandy's striking silhouette on the boulevard spoke out as a vote against the ideological move of the end of the century towards the Americanization of Europe and the decadence of French aesthetic sensibility.[4] He stood up against the rising tide of egalitarian forces, against the movement to level off society at the lowest common denominator, and saw in the developing democratization of France a threat to a unique aristocracy, not that of riches and material possessions, but of a superiority of mind, of the individualistic nature of an aesthetic subject. As Roland Barthes writes, "Dandyism does not at all oppose the upper class and the lower class, but only and absolutely the individual and the vulgar."[5] In fact, the dandy's stance of independence and revolt synthesizes a wide range of distinctive human attitudes, culminating in a universal, even archetypal inner nature: "The dandy possesses the attributes found in relative degrees in the poet, the priest and the soldier: the man who sings, the man who blesses and the man who sacrifices others as well as himself" (Rhodes 390). Calling themselves "unemployed adventurers" and "knights of the ephemeral"[6] dandies challenged the practicality of the commonplace with the exigencies of art, negating the quotidian, scorning the social icons of family, marriage, labor, profit, and love.[7]

To understand the subtle dynamics of nineteenth-century dandy terrorism, it is helpful to examine the definitions of dandyism offered by the writers of the epoch who, fascinated by the paradoxical nature of the figure of the dandy, perceived in him a powerful vehicle for unique self-expression and important social critique. Two decisive theoretical voices, those of Barbey d'Aurevilly and of Baudelaire, clarified the ubiquitous yet elusive phenomenon of dandyism, positing the figure of the dandy as a sign of intellectual revolt and aesthetic terrorism. Barbey's 1843 text, *Du dandysme et de George Brummell*, and Baudelaire's 1868 essay, "Le dandy," represent the most in-depth, illuminating studies of the century, for Barbey and Baudelaire recognize the dandy as a creature of paradox. Barbey first emphasizes the reverential discipline of the rigorous dandy code, while Baudelaire describes dandies as the "priests and victims" of their own strange cult, "a kind of religion" (Baudelaire 1958, 351). As detailed as the language of flowers, the code systematized rules of conduct, dress, speech, and behavior. Yet Barbey insists on the role of the individual within the generalized system of dandyism to carry out the whim of his private desire, to embody the caprice of his singular imagination: "There are undoubtedly, in questions of Dandyism, some principles and traditions; but all of that is dominated by fantasy, and fantasy is permitted only for those it suits and who consecrate it, by exercising it" (Barbey 118). It is interesting to note that on this point Barbey and Baudelaire differ distinctly, since for Baudelaire the systematic rules of the outlaw dandy code must ultimately override individual character: "Dandyism, which is an institution outside the law, has rigorous laws to which all its adherents are subject, whatever may be, otherwise, the spirit and independence of their character" (Baudelaire 349). In Baudelaire's vision, the singularity and non-conformity of the dandy is integrated into an archetypal posture, appropriating as a comprehensive symbol the extraordinary nature of any given dandy.

Certain core guidelines emerge from Barbey's book, such as the authentic representation of the individual, the transgression without complete rupture of established values, and the eternal quest for impassibility. In Barbey's terms, "one of the consequences of Dandyism, one of its principal characteristics, [is] to always produce the unexpected, that which the mind accustomed to the constraints of rules cannot logically expect . . . Dandyism . . . defies rules and yet still respects them" (Barbey 101). At the heart of these guidelines lies the notion of distance. The dandy is inherently different; he is alienated from the other. This distance, which can be political, social, intellectual, or aesthetic, illustrates an important dialectic. Society predictably reacted strongly to the dandy's presence, rejecting him as an outcast, exiling him to a marginal position. Perceived as effete, eccentric, daring, and odd, the dandy was ridiculed for his paisley and pastel, scorned for his sexual ambiguity, and belittled for his devotion to his art. Not unlike the superfluous man of nineteenth-century Russia or Sartre's *homme de trop*, the dandy was threatened by a menace more subtle than outright repression—the danger of irrelevancy, of remaining a strange but harmless curio. Yet public outcry against the flamboyant mores and unpredictable aesthetics of dandyism did not stifle the dandy's energy or silence his voice. The dandy welcomed the distance; he emphasized his deviance and sought to accentuate the gulf that separated him from convention. Dandyism implies living the distance, maintaining it, playing off its multiple implications.[8] The prejudice held against Disraëli for his Jewish heritage or against Oscar Wilde for his homosexuality is quickly diffused when the dandy transforms these very characteristics into insignias, into unique weapons of reaction.

The subversive terrorism of the dandy also builds on the idea that he takes his power from qualities generally considered undesirable and unworthy. Uselessness, for instance, becomes a key element in the dandy character. Baudelaire describes the dandy as a "an idle Hercules,"[9] and emphasizes the heroic character of the dandy who, when faced with an overwhelmingly utilitarian social context, deliberately chooses to embody an attitude of idleness. Dandyism makes of frivolity a way of life, in an attitude of theatrical indifference to the most popular social and moral concerns of the time. To uselessness, the dandy adds a cold impassibility; he wears a fixed mask of stoicism. Described in fact as a "a pink stoic, a stoic of frivolity" (Ormesson 446), the dandy's camouflage includes an irritatingly elegant, inscrutable disguise of paisley and lace to upset and negate the tranquil banality of bourgeois culture. Baudelaire argues, "The dandy's beauty lies especially in the cold expression which comes from the unshakable resolution not to be moved; one might say the latent fire which allows itself to be noticed, which could, but does not want to, glow" ("Le dandy" 352), and Barbey quotes Machiavelli in his praise of cold dandy stoicism: "The world belongs to dispassionate minds" (Barbey 111). Finally, the dandy is the herald of the unnatural, of artifice, the spokesman of that which goes against nature. When Baudelaire writes in "Le peintre de la vie moderne" that "evil comes effortlessly, *naturally*, by fatality; good is always the product of an art" (Baudelaire 1958, 1183), he gives voice to the dandy faith in art over nature. Oscar Wilde, in his characteristically acerbic opposition of nature and art, of course became the emblematic figure for this stance, calling for a radical rethinking of the power of aesthetics in a social world. As Wilde reminds us: "To be natural is such a very difficult pose to keep up" (Wilde 487).

Although the dandy chooses to embody a sleek indifference, turning a cool eye to society, he is not totally independent from the other; for in order to be a dandy, one must be seen. The mirror of society is essential in the formulation of the dandy response; he needs a public, he needs mores and morality as a form of comparision, as a means to shock and displease, as a mirror in which he may admire his reflection. This notion illuminates another aspect of dandy strategy elaborated by Barbey, that is, the need to dare with tact, to bend the rules without breaking them, to maintain a delicate balance and keep from going too far. Baudelaire echoes Barbey in his definition of the "passionate doctrine" of dandyism as "above all the burning need to confer upon oneself an originality, contained within the extreme limits of propriety" (Baudelaire 350). The social eye is the dandy's sun; without it he wilts and fades. A terrorist act from the dandy point of view must therefore be discreet, subtle, even secret. The act will be one of "opposition and revolt,"[10] while it will first provoke uncertainty, hesitation, and anxiety in its object. Dandy insults can be obscure; the recipient of a slight may not even be aware of the offense. Thus the dandy's activism is ironic. He avoids outright conflict in order to more effectively infiltrate and subvert systems of meaning.

An ancient Chinese proverb imparts the following insight: "Nature forms us for ourselves, not for others; to be, not to seem." Dandy thought asserts itself in total opposition to this pragmatic perspective, and it becomes clear in fact that the peculiar form of terrorism practiced by the dandy takes as its ultimate foundation the distinction between the être and the paraître. Dandy activism takes aim at this timeless opposition, and turns it to the dandy's own advantage through the imprévu, through shock, surprise, and the attack on what might be called the rational, positivist culture of the nineteenth century. Baudelaire writes that the "cult of one's self" of dandyism can be succinctly defined through the manipulation of the dynamic between habitual expectations and actual perceptions: "It is the pleasure of astonishing and the proud satisfaction of never being astonished" (Baudelaire 350). The dandy is a master of the game between the être and the paraître, enjoying the pleasures of being different than he seems, leading his onlookers into a semantic labyrinth of mirrors and dead ends.[11] He aims to transform life into art, self into chef-d'oeuvre. In his 1889 study of fin-de-siècle society, Les contemporains, Jules Lemaître captures the magic of the dandy's power to transform reality: "From an ensemble of insignificant and useless practices he makes an art which carries his personal mark, which pleases and seduces like a witty work. He conveys to small features of costume, dress, and language a sense and a power which they do not have naturally. In short, he makes others believe in that which does not exist" (Lemaître 57–58). As the viewer struggles to keep his eye on the deceiving lace and velvet gloves, the dandy continually escapes capture, leaving his public in annoyance, awe, and even terror, faced with a phenomenon they cannot quite fathom. As Wilde writes in his preface to The Portrait of Dorian Gray: "All art is at once surface and symbol. Those who go beneath the surface do so at their peril. Those who *read* the symbol do so at their peril. It is the spectator, and not life, that art really mirrors" (Wilde 17). Society looks at the dandy and scorns that which *seems* to be different from it; what it actually condemns is that which *is* the same. By focusing on the duality of being and seeming, dandyism questions social structures and systems of signification, reflecting the falseness, the ambiguity, and the disturbing way of eluding definition inherent in social institutions. Dandyism reflects the very illusions of an era, in a gesture that affirms its own coherence. The dandy problematizes the apparently simple; he mythifies the mundane.[12]

Thus in midcentury Baudelaire and Barbey formulated the core principles of a theoretical system of dandyism. They described an ideal, whether in fiction or in the Paris streets, of the ultimate dandy, unsurpassable in his style, untouchable in his singular purity. As the century progressed, dandies became more visible, as writers, artists, and the general public showed a growing interest in the subversive dynamics of dandyism. By the end of the century, dandyism had become an integral part of French aesthetic sensibility, a voice of refusal and revolt, as more individuals attempted to put into practice what Baudelaire and Barbey had projected in theory. The pragmatic question of how to utilize dandyism, how to control its acrobatics of negation and its subversive sleights of hand, became a pressing concern for dandy hopefuls. They learned that first, and most visibly, the force of dandy terrorism comes forth through clothes. In fact, it is this aspect of dandyism that has become the most recognizable, and has led to a popular misconception, to the fixed image of the dandy as based solely on his clothes, as a man whose wardrobe is more complex and more interesting than his mind. In an 1883 essay, "The Dandiacal Body," Thomas Carlyle claims: "A dandy is a Clothes-wearing Man, a Man whose trade, office and existence consists in the wearing of Clothes. Every faculty of soul, spirit, purse and person is heroically consecrated to this one object . . . , so that as others dress to live, he lives to dress" (Carlyle 158). Balzac too added to the misconception when he compared the faddish dandy's intelligence to that of "a piece of bedroom furniture,"[13] and one may be tempted to accept the trendy stereotype when faced with some of the more ridiculous commentaries proclaimed by second-rate dandies. One such hanger-on, Maurice Donnay, was apparently proud to announce:

"It makes no difference to me that I appear stupid provided that I have English chic."[14]

The exterior trappings of the dandy, his fashion and frivolity, quickly took hold in the France of Louis-Philippe, overshadowing the aesthetic and intellectual implications of dandyism, and as the trend became popular, many faddish treatises appeared on the subject of elegance, such as those of Emile-Marc Hilaire, "The art of wearing one's tie" and "The art of never dining at home and of always dining at friends' houses" (Carassus 98). Yet there is more to dandyism than the clothes that seem to make the man, and Barbey insists that dandyism utilizes elegance in a truly unique and essential fashion, working from it as a point of departure. Reminding his readers that "dandyism is not the brutal art of wearing a tie. There are even dandies who have never worn one" (Barbey 130), Barbey explains: "The reality of Dandyism is human, social, and spiritual. . . . It is not an outfit which can walk around on its own. On the contrary! It is a certain way of wearing it that creates dandyism. One can be a dandy with a wrinkled outfit. Dandyism is a complete mode of being, and one is not a dandy solely by the materially visible side" (Barbey 98–99).

Terrorist dandy ideology adopted clothes as its most effective weapon in the project to reevaluate and reorganize social and aesthetic values, because of the ubiquitous, seemingly banal nature of wardrobe. Yet the multiple possibilities of colors, fabrics, and styles of fashion represented for the dandy a palette of artistic and political potential, as unlikely yet surprisingly useful tools in the project to embody the ambivalence of the modern.[15] For not only does a singular wardrobe hold the power to question the values of an external world, it also can become the key to reshaping the nature of the self. In a 1959 essay, "Language and Clothing," Barthes suggests that clothes represent a powerful force in the creation of image and identity: "At first sight, human clothing is a wonderful subject for research and reflection: it is a complete event whose study calls simultaneously for a history, an economy, an ethnology, a technology, and perhaps even . . . a linguistic model. But most of all, as the very object of *appearance*, it flatters this very modern curiosity that we have about social psychology, it invites us to go beyond the outdated limits of individual and society: what interests us in it is that it seems to participate in the greatest depth and in the greatest sociability" (Barthes 242). Dandies used clothes to create an artificial personality, social status, political attitude, or intellectual stance. When

Wilde writes that "one should either be a work of art or wear a work of art" (Wilde 1206), he brings to light this power of seduction and of meaning inherent in cloaks and masks. Of course, the French male wardrobe of the nineteenth century hardly stands as a hallmark of innovation and variety. Its overwhelming uniformity, with its range of hues, shades, and tones of black, aimed to underscore the notions of respectability, taste, and good manners that soon would be threatened by fin-de-siècle aesthetics.[16] Through elegance, the dandy stood out, made a statement, turned heads. The dandy made of himself the designer, the model, and the product of an aesthetic act whose message must be decoded.

It is the poetic nature of clothing, the power to create visual art and symbolic communication, that attracts the dandy to a seductive wardrobe. Barthes argues in fact that, applying Saussurian linguistic distinctions, the clothing styles proposed by society are like the *langue*, abstract, institutional, defined though function, while the individual's choice in dress, selected from among the various styles, represents his own *parole*, a personalized voice, an authored sign. In defamiliarizing the system of signs inherent in the communication of clothes, the visual image becomes a signature, a personal statement of rebellion meant to "speak" to those confronted by it.[17] The dandy weaves elegance into the stuff of the singular personal history he alone can write. A legend has it that Gautier or Nerval or Villiers de l'Isle-Adam (in any case, a dandy so stylized that his name has become obscured) ruffled many a feather, not only because of his unconventional costume, but because he did his boulevard-strolling with a companion: on a leash of powder-blue ribbon, the mythical dandy took his pet lobster out for air. Through an elegant or outlandish image, the dandy takes a crucial first step in his terrorist strategy: he captures the attention of his audience.

Dandy terrorism did not stop with the creation of a disturbing visual image; having captured a public, the dandy turned to the written text to keep it. Dandyism escaped triviality through art; by putting pen to paper and translating his paradoxical nature of flamboyant stoicism into discourse, the dandy writer upset aesthetic convention and called for a redefinition of art. Dandyism combined the artistic with the social, to politicize literature and adapt the realm of the written word into an arena for subtle confrontation and revolt.

In dandy writing, the text illustrates the characteristics of the dandy code itself, presenting a seemingly indifferent independence, a surface frivolity, and an aim of bending convention and

custom without an outright rupture.[18] The dandy wrote mock-
ingly of "serious" subjects, while he wrote solemnly of frivolous
ones, aptly illustrating the Baudelairian notion of the "gravity in
frivolity." Through such techniques as irony, paradox, hyperbole,
and pastiche, the dandy constructed a unique form of discursive
response to the *mal du siècle*. Dandy writing manipulates structure through experimentation with epigraphs, notes, margins,
and citations, leaving much to the reader, opening itself to wild
speculation, to rampant imagination. It presents itself as a puzzle, as a labyrinthine construction where innuendo, suggestion,
and the *non-dit* play a role as essential as the enunciated discourse itself.

Elements of dandyism permeate a variety of styles and genres
in nineteenth-century writing. Some writers, such as Huysmans,
chose the image of the dandy as a vehicle for the creation of an
imagined artistic world, personal, luxurious, and peculiar, his
own "Private Idaho" offered as an alternate reality, as a rival to
the banality of the everyday world.[19] Other writers experiment
with dandy techniques to confront society more directly, to mock
or deconstruct contemporary reality by emphasizing the very
aspects of that reality that society struggles to keep secret. In
their literary texts, both Barbey and Baudelaire present a vision
of Paris that undermines the legendary, coherent image of the
city as a celebrated crossroads for poets and painters, the undis-
puted capital of nineteenth-century aesthetics. These dandy
writers perceived in the urban hub a mirror of the self, and
worked to illuminate in the shadows of the city of lights a hidden
sister soul, as veiled, painted, and mysterious as their own. The
iconoclastic power of the dandy critique of society rests in its
ambivalence. Baudelaire's Paris of *Les fleurs du mal* is animated
by the marginalized figures of the poet, the prostitute, and the
flâneur, whose voyeuristic perspectives observe a dark Paris, self-
conscious and unsettling, teeming with the contradictions of contemporary life. Barbey too, in *Les diaboliques*, uncovers a Paris
ripe with the fruits of crime and the phantoms of adultery, madness, and murder. By concentrating on the dark private plots
thickening in public squares, Barbey reveals a modern Sodom,
one more insipid and more dangerous than the biblical city of
sin, because of the cloaked nature of the bourgeois hypocrisy of
the era. Barbey's revolutionary energy against the banal can be
understood as a celebration of excess, as a focus on the perverse,
the unnatural, and the genuinely ambivalent nature of progress
and modernity.

Baudelaire and Barbey aim to expose the diabolism of scandal and sin in a city overwhelmed by the confusion of good and evil, yet in their texts the cultural landscape of Paris is not so exaggerated or disfigured as to become fantastic or unrecognizable. Their writing illustrates one of the most essential characteristics of dandyism, that is, to play with the established system, to bend and subtly subvert it without a melodramatic refusal or blatant disavowal. By incorporating a mode of writing and authorial stance animated by the theories of dandyism, Baudelaire and Barbey could infiltrate the social consciousness of the epoch, undermining its widespread bad faith and self-deception. By avoiding an outright condemnation of the evils of modernity, by raising vice to a more universal, more ambiguous level, where such supposedly negative elements as abandon, decrepitude, and alienation evoke a certain odd, unexpected attraction, writers like Baudelaire and Barbey shocked their public all the more effectively.

Baudelaire writes of the dandy that he is the "final magnificence of heroism in decadence" (Baudelaire 351), capable of transcending the ideal of his vision through the provocative act of writing. Barbey writes that the dandy is forever: "One will never again see a Dandy like Brummell; but there will always be men such as he. They attest to the magnificent variety of divine creation: they are as eternal as caprice. . . . Double and multiple natures, of an indeterminate intellectual sex, in whom grace is all the more graceful in strength, and in whom strength is to be found again in grace; [They are] androgynes of history, no longer of Fable" (Barbey 151–52). In the image cherished by Baudelaire, that of the *thyrse*, the dandy combines masculine and feminine, overt and secret, self and other. Moreover, in the dandy, Baudelaire perceives a dual symbol that foreshadows a new perspective on the human condition which would see the day in twentieth-century Modernist writing. Problematic subjectivity, fragmentation in the perception of reality, alienation of the individual lost in the mass, such key aspects of Modernism find an important precursor in the dandyism of the 1800s. As the herald of the new, the fin-de-siècle dandy indeed embodies a certain timelessness, recognizable in any age.

Yet is it entirely true that dandyism is as timeless as Baudelaire and Barbey would have us believe? Perhaps these authors were blinded by their own social context, and the seeming universality of the complex figure of the dandy is in the end too particular to the nineteenth century, and especially to the fin de siècle, to hold meaning in other cultural environments. For while nineteenth-century French dandyism can claim the success of not going unremarked, it certainly has not escaped criticism. Surprisingly, in the twentieth century, when aesthetic revolt against convention has been especially popular, dandyism appears to have provoked more harsh words than praise. Among the various critical approaches of the twentieth century, certain voices stand out, for they illustrate a common critique, and considered together present a systematic motif of opposition. Jean Starobinski, in his *Portrait de l'artiste en saltimbanque*, suggests that the textualized figure of the dandy loses force and becomes a mere mask, a shadowy caricature of the author behind him. This critique rests on the notion, elaborated by Kempf, that the dandy writer is continually faced with the temptation of projecting his own image into that of the dandy character, and that often, as Kempf would have it, "an essay on dandyism is a dandy essay" (Kempf 29). Starobinski works from a similar idea and argues that the writer of a dandy text is enslaved to his own idealized image of the dandy and that his text inevitably takes on the very qualities of dandyism it aims to present in a fictional framework. Like Narcissus trapped in his corporeal body, forever condemned to a chimeric desire, the dandy cannot overcome the perfection of his vision: "Here he is, frozen, invulnerable, masked, a provisional inhabitant of his appearance, and almost reduced—by his own will—to the state of a ghost" (Starobinski 66). Leroy too has described the nature of dandyism as a threat to the very texts it animates, due to the "accent on the reflexive and autocritical character of a text on dandyism" (Leroy 262). A dandy text takes itself as model and object of study, and apparently cannot overcome the very qualities it strives to depict.

Along with the criticism of self-reflexive caricature, the dandy is also haunted by the threat of remaining purely illusory; trapped by the mirror, the dandy's *être* succumbs to his *paraître*. Albert Camus contends, in *L'homme révolté*, that dandyism cannot overcome its own potentiality, and that ultimately it fails to comprehend the very paradoxes and ambiguities that animate it, and cannot integrate its double nature into a meaningful philosophical stance. Presenting dandyism as "a degraded form of asceticism" (72), Camus holds that it is the dandy's dependence on others that debilitates his desired revolt, and that finally, a dandy cannot be, he can only seem to be, as a mirage in the ever-present mirror of society: "Dissipated as a person deprived of rules, he will be coherent as a character. But a character presupposes a public; the dandy can only pose by opposing. He can assure himself of his existence only by finding it in the face of others. Others are the mirror. A mirror quickly obscured, it is true, for man's attention span is limited. It must be constantly reawakened, spurred by provocation.... He performs his life, because he is unable to live it" (Camus 73). Reminiscent of a decadent Sisyphus, the dandy is condemned to carry out forever his project of nihilistic provocation, keeping close eye on the eyes of others, hoping they do not look away. Always apparently on the verge of revolt, the dandy remains incapable of taking the final step. It is this eternal pose, suggests Camus, that reduces the dandy's freedom to a sterile stance of empty gestures and masks.

Jean-Paul Sartre also critiques the idealism of dandyism of the nineteenth century, particularly as it is presented by Baudelaire. Sartre attacks Baudelairian dandyism on grounds not unlike the argument of Camus, that the seeming terrorism of dandyism merely ennobles the ephemeral, projects an empty sign, and in fact can do nothing, except sabotage art itself: "The still too utilitarian exercise of the artistic profession becomes the absolute ceremony of dress, the cult of beauty which produces stable and lasting works is changed into a love of elegance, because elegance is ephemeral, sterile, and perishable; the creative act of the painter or the poet, emptied of its substance, takes the form of an act which is wholly gratuitous, in the Gidian sense, and even absurd, the aesthetic invention transforms itself into mystification; the passion to create becomes fixed in insensitivity" (Sartre 1947, 167–68). The existential critique thus condemns the dandy claim to action as the ultimate embodiment of absurdity, as the refusal of social or philosophical commitment, as a decorative attitude emptied of practical and intellectual value. "Pure spirituality," claims Sartre, is all that remains of what may have originally held the promise of an active position of revolt. Dandyism can only mimic revolt, since it carries within it the seeds of its own dissipation: "Dandyism is a 'club of suicide victims,' and the life of each of its members is only the exercise of a continuous suicide" (Sartre 1972, 196).

Finally, Maurice Blanchot adds to the critique of dandy activism in his essay, "L'échec de Baudelaire," suggesting that dandyism can be reduced to a "a little game of revolt" and "the weakest of alibis," again emphasizing the overriding force of the *paraître* for what he considers as an institution incapable of transforming the game into the real: "Baudelaire's bad faith, so well analyzed by Sartre, is also his superior morality as a poet,

that morality which leads him to the transvestism, to the superficial effects of dandyism. In this new subterfuge, he is undoubtedly still looking for a way out of poetic impossibility, but at the
same time, he uses it to denounce that other overly-satisfying
subterfuge, the word. Dandyism scarcely figures into his story,
and no one better than he has judged the limited significance
of this *cult* in which he found himself with too many of his
contemporaries to have really appreciated it, he who, in matters
of social caste, would have liked only the one in which he would
have been alone" (Blanchot 142–43). Linked inherently to the
problematic impossibility of poetry itself to resolve the dialectics
of the human condition, dandyism for Blanchot can lead only
to one choice, that of the void, of the ultimate negation of choice.
It embodies impotence, sterility, and skepticism. Depicted as a
force opposing the writer in Baudelaire, the dandy hinders artistic production and works against the possibilities of aesthetic
and spiritual freedom.

These various perspectives share the critique of dandy terrorism on the grounds that it attempts to replace the real with the
illusory, that it weakens the integrity of art and the unity of
individual consciousness through its infinite system of mirrors
and misleading masks. The multiple irony of dandyism apparently threatens most profoundly the fundamental core of the
modern subject, necessary to a cohesive ideological attitude. The
dandy's cynical, skeptical view appears to negate the possibility
of a systematic answer to the philosophical questions of our
modern condition.

Yet are these critics right? Is the twentieth-century perspective
incapable of appreciating and even adopting the terrorist force
of nineteenth-century dandyism? And how do we answer the
question: "What is the dandy?" Knight of individualism, provoc-
ateur, hero of the modern? Or façade, sham, parasitic perversion?
Even Baudelaire likens dandyism to "a setting sun; like a fading
star, it is superb, without heat and full of melancholy" (Baudelaire 351). Has the sun of dandyism set forever? Could it be that
in the end the dandy symbolizes the impotence of an era, the
failure to formulate a coherently active response to culture? Or
could the seeming emptiness, the apparent contradictions and
the surface sterility of the fin-de-siècle dandy still signify something, behind the mask? Leroy suggests that the ambiguity of
dandyism itself, through both its mythic resonances and its contemporary relevance, "puts into doubt the categories of the serious and the comic, celebrates ambivalence" (Leroy 268). This

Bahktinian conception of the dandy rests on his power to question the complex relationship between reality and representation. Leroy continues, "this parading man, through his staging, would pose the problem of the conditions of his representation, of all representation" (Leroy 264), and posits that the inherent ambiguity of the dandy manifests itself systematically through an exquisite use of irony, the rhetorical figure described by Barbey as, "a genius which dispenses with all others. It casts on a man the air of a sphinx which disconcerts like mystery and troubles like danger" (Barbey 123). Refering to the many mythic dandy masks, such as those of Sisyphus, Janus, and Pygmalion, Leroy concludes, "Adopting one after the other those famous masks, substituting them endlessly, the dandy gives birth to the myth of irony, an irony which takes the myth itself as object" (Leroy 268). Is it not heroic in itself that the dandy simply is, that he personifies the impossible goal of unity in his own dual nature, and that he reflects that same impossibility in society, in convention, in art? Could it be that we have taken seriously that which overrides the serious? Have we forgotten how to play the game, the dandy rules lost to us over many decades of science, rigor, and system?

It may be that in our century, that of the undeniable rise and dominance of literary criticism in academic and intellectual circles, we have lost sight of an important dynamic of dandyism, lost touch with its *humor*. André Breton reminds us that the *humour noir* of a dandy writer such as Baudelaire represents the very force and energy of his poetry, the reflection of his inner conflict as well as the representation of that conflict in his writing: "Humor in Baudelaire is an integral part of his conception of *dandyism*. We know that, for him, 'the word dandy implies a quintessence of character and a subtle understanding of the entire moral mechanism of this world.' No one more than he has taken care to define humor in opposition to the trivial gaiety or the sardonic sarcasm in which 'French wit' likes to recognize itself" (Breton 133). If the dandy may represent the problem of representation itself, particularly relevant to the aesthetic exploration of the first decades of the twentieth century, if he reflects the incongruities of a particular moment in history, how can we then understand dandyism today? Does it no longer hold meaning in the postmodern cultural context, too limited to a specific social and artistic situation?

Susan Sontag suggested in 1964 that in fact the modern era still is animated by the dynamics of dandyism, ever-present in

the multifaceted sensibilities of contemporary life, yet most striking in the unconventional and peculiar phenomenon of camp. In
her essay, "Notes on Camp," Sontag highlights the fundamental
principles of this esoteric artistic and social stance and argues
that the dandy lives on in the campy love of the unnatural, of
artifice and exaggeration; in the contrast between richly elaborate form and esoteric, unlikely content; and in the consistently
aesthetic world-view of camp. She concludes: "Detachment is
the prerogative of an elite; and as the dandy is the nineteenth
century's surrogate for the aristocrat in matters of culture, so
Camp is the modern dandyism. Camp is the answer to the problem: how to be a dandy in the age of mass culture" (Sontag 288).
In the tradition of dandyism, camp aims to dethrone the serious,
to upset the conventional, to throw a note of discord into a seemingly harmonious social system. Through humor and through an
emphasis on hyperbole, "bad taste," and kitch, camp integrates
the basic dandy tactic of playing off the dialectic of the *être*
and the *paraître*. Sontag suggests that camp sees everything in
quotation marks; similar to the dandy perspective, nothing is to
be taken at face value, nothing taken for granted, nothing accepted in the way it first presents itself. To transform experience,
to stylize and defamiliarize the world in order to bring about
inquiry and doubt, new definition and understanding, therein
lies the importance of camp, hidden under the trappings of the
strange and the silly. It illustrates the notorious maxim of Wilde,
"Art is the only serious thing in the world. And the artist is the
only person who is never serious" (Sontag 1203).

Finally, when Wilde writes that "life is much too important a
thing ever to talk seriously about" (Wilde 665), perhaps he
touches on the very core of the question. Have we indeed taken
dandyism at face value? Have we, by evaluating this unique artistic phenomenon by worn-out criteria and dangerously serious
standards, prevented ourselves from understanding and appreciating the enigma that dandyism offers? Have we, quite simply,
missed the point? If dandyism can be understood as a versatile
and remarkable means to formulate a response to an overwhelming cultural predicament, perhaps in the end it is exactly what
we have been looking for, a uniquely individual yet coherently
systematized artistic form of expression and revolt. I would suggest that we are not completely beyond hope. The realm of literary criticism, often accused of taking itself much too seriously,
has had in fact its moments of dandy joy. If we look to Roland
Barthes's play with language, cultural signs, and aesthetic sys-

tems, exemplified in books such as *Fragments d'un discours amoureux* and *Roland Barthes par Roland Barthes*, perhaps there we can hear the dandy laughter, carnavalesque and bawdy, yet still smooth and ironic, of the true pleasure of the text, of the *jouissance* of the dandy game. The contagious dandy humor has undoubtedly spread to other aesthetic realms, as well. Andy Warhol's soup cans, William Burroughs's junkies, Philippe Sollers's misogyny, Peter Greenaway's patterns of repetition, John Cage's portrayal of chance: perhaps in the end our "postmodernity" has not completely failed to learn techniques of dandy terrorism, taking aim at the very issues and concerns that haunt human sensibility the most deeply, and has come to comprehend them more accurately and with more style, through the uneasy, yet undeniably pleasurable dandy smile, provoked through our art.

University of Oklahoma

NOTES

1. For an excellent overview of the historical and aesthetic development of dandyism, see Carassus 1971.
2. The figure of Alcibiades has inspired a great deal of interesting speculation. Plutarch points out some of his dandyesque faults, in his *Lives of the Noble Grecians:* "but with all this sagacity and eloquence, he intermingled luxury and wantonness, in his eating and drinking and dissolute living; wore long purple robes like a woman . . . ; [and] caused the planks of his galley to be cut away, so that he might lie the softer" (199). In his essay "Le dandy," Baudelaire also lauds Alcibiades, along with Caesar and Catullus, as a "brilliant prototype" of dandyism (1958, 349).
3. Favardin and Boüexière make use of the early example of Musset to illustrate a conception of dandyism as a unique response to the increasingly problematic moral and aesthetic atmosphere of the nineteenth-century: "In *La confession d'un enfant du siècle,* after having proclaimed the skepticism and despair of a generation, he advances dandyism as a cynical solution, suicidal but full of panache, to the doubt which gnaws at him and also as the means of contributing to the struggle against the mediocrity of a bourgeois society" (Favardin and Boüexière 76).
4. As Coblence succinctly argues: "Disconcerting, dandyism combines two attitudes. As an affirmation of the superiority of an aristocracy, it leads to the denunciation of universal rights, of the rationality of wisdom, of progress, of equality. But for all that, in this perspective, it does not claim to call into question political equality, considered as acquired . . . Dandyism concedes that political equality does not stem from a hypothetical natural equality, that instituted political equality cannot destroy the fundamental hierarchy, the profound inequality that predominates among minds, and which manifests iself, according to Baudelaire, in the dandy's eternal superiority" (Coblence 1981, 289).
5. Barthes 1971, 312. See also Baudelaire, for whom material elegance and

riches, "are, for the perfect dandy, only a symbol of the aristocratic superiority of his mind" (1958, 350).

6. Carassus 36, 94.

7. Baudelaire himself, in "Mon coeur mis à nu," uses terms much less metaphoric to describe the dandy's relationship to woman, for example, in an allegorical passage opposing nature and artifice: "Woman is the opposite of the Dandy. Thus she must inspire loathing. Woman is hungry, and she wants to eat; thirsty, and she wants to drink. She is in heat, and she wants to be screwed. . . . Woman is natural, that is to say, abominable. She is therefore always vulgar, that is, the opposite of the Dandy" (Baudelaire 643).

8. As Coblence formulates the question: "Can one not call dandyism that way of living, of 'acting out' (while inverting it) a situation of exclusion?" (1981, 279).

9. Baudelaire 1958, 352. Baudelaire continues in "Mon coeur mis à nu": "At a time . . . when men allow themselves to be dulled by the sole idea of utility, I believe that there is no great harm in exaggerating a bit in the opposite direction" (344), contrasting the distinctive dandy character with the banality of society at large: "Other men are subject to taxes, made for menial work, that is, for what are called *professions*" (Baudelaire 1958, 649).

10. To use Baudelaire's terms: "all draw on the same character of opposition and revolt; all are representatives of what is best in human pride, of this need, too rare in our contemporaries, to combat and to destroy triviality" (Baudelaire 351).

11. In his description of Alcibiades, Maurice Barrès emphasizes the secret world of the dandy, hidden behind his flamboyant masks: "He organized an unknown life for himself. He tasted ferociously the joy of being different from the way he appeared. *Etre et paraître!* The great adventurers claim that they find in it an intensity of nervous pleasure which triples life's domains" (Barrès 103).

12. Carassus argues: "The world refuses all unity to the man torn apart; the dandy endeavors to establish that otherwise imposssible unity on the aesthetic plain by making an attitude for himself. A being of defiance and refusal, the dandy seeks his coherence in the creation of a character" (Carassus 11). See also Favardin and Boüexière, who point to the autonomous power of the dandy to construct his own mythology by subverting the myths of popular culture: "dandyism was the manifestation of the individual power. He transforms reality into myth by sowing confusion in the basic values of a society" (Favardin and Boüexière 76–77).

13. "In making himself a dandy, a man becomes a piece of bedroom furniture, an extremely ingenious mannequin who can pose on a horse or a sofa, who skillfully bites or sucks the end of his cane, but a thinking man . . . never!" (Balzac 1938, 177). Yet Balzac also writes that "The man who sees only fashion in fashion is a fool. *The elegant life* excludes neither thought nor reason, it sanctions them" (ibid.).

14. Carassus 25. Carassus makes clear the prejudice against dandyism in his discussion of the definition most commonly given to the word "dandy": "For most people, the dandy had no interest other than his supreme elegance. The Robert dictionary says nothing more: 'A man who takes pride in an extreme elegance in his dress and his manners.' Moreover, the argument has been made that demotes the elegant man to the level of the merely extravagant individual. Witness Littré: 'A man affected in his dress and exaggerating fashion to the point of the ridiculous'" (Carassus 6).

15. As Coblence points out, the very deliberate dandy plan to reinterpret the cultral modes of fashion and aesthetics represents an essential facet of dandy tactics: "To reestablish the links between fashion and aesthetics, to show the beauty in the capricious and the transitory, to revalorize clothing, innovation: such is the dandy's task" (Coblence 111).

16. In his 1834 *La confession d'un enfant du siècle*, Alfred de Musset describes the oppressive power of the *habit noir* that permeated male fashion as a sign of desperation and apathy: "Let there be no mistake: this black clothing worn by men in our time is a terrible symbol; to arrive at this point, armor had to fall piece by piece and embroidery flower by flower. It is human reason which has overturned all illusions; but it carries mourning in itself, so that one will console it" (Musset 72). See also Barthes: "the great movement of uniformization and democratization of the male outfit, encouraged by the Revolution, formally nourished by an appeal to the austerity of Quaker dress, was bringing about an entire revision of clothing values" (Barthes 1959, 245).

17. See Stanton: "In the dandy's system, every ornament, every object, was tapped for its potential significance and special contribution to the overdetermination of the intended message" (Stanton 161), while Kempf suggests that clothing can be best understood as an "object of scrutiny and research, a means of distinction, an argument of elusive or indescribable exploits, constantly corrupted by the mission given to it" (Kempf 177).

18. See Stanton: "With language, as with the other elements of dandyism, innovation and eccentricity, paradox and hyperbole numbered among the techniques that created a contrast to an established norm. As a speaking subject, the dandy sought to strike, wherever possible and profitable, an opposing, paradoxical stance that would singularize him" (171).

19. See Michel Lemaire, who perceives in the extravagant apartment of Des Esseintes the desire to realize an isolated, personal world of beauty, where the art and the dandy reciprocally mirror each other's style: "Above all, [the dandy] places himself in a reciprocal relationship with the works of art with which he furnishes his retreat. He becomes the creative center of it. In the same way that the hollow middle of a wheel concentrates and realizes the work of the spokes, . . . he brings into being, with his gaze, the beauty which surrounds him, a beauty which, inversely, inspires him to raise himself to its level" (Lemaire 187).

Part 2
Play

6

Terre ferme, terreur des femmes: Le cou(p) de grâce chez Maupassant et Mallarmé

RICHARD E. GOODKIN

Au premier abord, trouver un parallèle quelconque entre Maupassant et Mallarmé semblerait une tâche ingrate. On parle de chacun de ces deux génies en conjonction avec d'autres figures contemporaines ou antérieures, mais pratiquement jamais ensemble. Dans le cas de Mallarmé, le précurseur de choix serait sans doute Baudelaire, et pour Maupassant ce serait Flaubert, qui partage ses origines normandes et qui a donné au jeune écrivain un soutien précieux au début de sa carrière littéraire. Il y a, bien sûr, une convergence de genre qui lie ces deux derniers: bien que Flaubert soit plutôt connu pour ses romans de proportions épiques, *Madame Bovary* et *L'éducation sentimentale*, que pour ses récits plus courts, à la fin de sa vie, au moment précis où Maupassant se lançait, il s'est aventuré dans le domaine du conte: en 1877, Flaubert réserve à son jeune protégé la primeur des *Trois contes*.[1]

Justement, n'est-ce pas une différence de genre qui a fixé Maupassant et Mallarmé dans deux domaines critiques séparés par une cloison tout à fait étanche? Bien qu'ils aient tous les deux la réputation d'avoir porté un certain genre littéraire à son apogée pendant la même période, au premier coup d'oeil ces deux genres semblent être séparés par une distance infranchissable. Qu'est-ce qu'il y a en commun entre le conte ou le récit court perfectionné par Maupassant, et la poésie lyrique—et notamment le sonnet—renouvelée par Mallarmé? Où trouver un point d'intersection entre ces deux grands courants de la deuxième moitié du 19è siècle, le réalisme et le symbolisme?

Il est vrai que bien des choses séparent ces deux courants: le symbolisme caractérisé par le goût du détail, de la miniature, du vague, le réalisme par les édifices littéraires de grande taille tels

95

que l'oeuvre d'un Zola et même d'un certain Flaubert.[2] Pourtant il y a des ponts évidents entre ces deux continents artistiques: justement, une oeuvre comme les *Trois contes* de Flaubert semble viser une telle liaison, avec l'opposition entre "Un coeur simple" et "Saint-Julien l'hospitalier," qui peuvent être lus, respectivement, comme des exemples de réalisme et de symbolisme en prose. D'ailleurs même si l'oeuvre de Maupassant est généralement classifiée avec le réalisme, l'édifice littéraire qui la constitue est principalement composé de pierres bien petites, d'une accumulation de petits "détails" en prose: c'est moins à ses romans qu'à ses contes qu'il doit sa réputation. Oui, il est très prolixe, mais par petits bouts. Sa production littéraire fait penser à la phrase célèbre de Proust parlant du père de Swann: "souvent, mais peu à la fois" (Proust 1:15).

D'ailleurs plusieurs critiques ont essayé de tenir compte de l'ouverture de l'oeuvre de Maupassant à l'univers symboliste. Greimas, par exemple, dans son étude sémiotique du conte "Deux amis" de Maupassant, en arrive même à considérer Maupassant comme un écrivain symboliste:

> Alors que, par exemple, toute la littérature classique s'oppose en bloc à la littérature romantique, la distinction entre poésie et prose n'en étant qu'une sous-articulation interne, le XIXe siècle procède, dans sa deuxième moitié, à l'inversion hiérarchique de ces rapports, en faisant diverger les deux courants sous des étiquettes de "symbolisme" et de "réalisme," en apparence incompatibles. . . . Cependant, on ne peut manquer de se demander naïvement comment il est possible que des hommes appartenant à la même génération . . . soient si différents dans leurs productions. . . . Nos analyses . . . en arrivent à la conclusion que Maupassant est presque tout autant un écrivain "symboliste" que ses contemporains; d'autre part, le conte, en tant que genre, peut être considéré comme l'équivalent, en prose, . . . d'un poème.
>
> (Greimas 11–12)

En effet, plusieurs facteurs justifient l'exploration d'un rapport possible entre Maupassant et Mallarmé. Les deux hommes se connaissaient. Ils se sont rencontrés dès 1875, à un moment où Mallarmé est déjà très connu alors que Maupassant fait ses débuts, et Maupassant a fréquenté les fameux jeudis de Mallarmé au 87, rue de Rome pendant un certain temps (Maupassant 1974, lxix). Je passe sur des raisons potentielles apparemment plus frivoles: par exemple, comment ne pas spéculer que le cratylisme connu de Mallarmé—son désir de fonder un rapport motivé plu-

tôt que conventionnel entre les noms et les choses[3]—a dû sa-
vourer la coïncidence apparente du nom de Maupassant? La
prolixité du jeune prosateur semble être anticipée par l'image de
mots qui passent à une vitesse qui devait être en même temps
source d'admiration et source de mépris pour le roi des
symbolistes.

D'ailleurs la prolixité réaliste et la concentration linguistique
favorisée par les symbolistes, qui ont souvent été utilisées pour
fonder la distinction entre ces deux mouvements, n'ont pas été
assez souvent mises en question. Elles peuvent nous faire
oublier, par exemple, le rôle considérable que joue le silence
chez Maupassant. Francis Marcoin parle du statut du silence
chez Maupassant, dans une discussion qui fait penser à Mallarmé, avec sa quasi-divinisation du silence: "[Chez Maupas-
sant], le silence des personnages recouvre le mutisme de l'auteur,
cette aspiration à en dire moins, . . . cette aspiration à un silence
moins animal que post-humain, un silence ayant franchi les limites de la parole. . . . [Maupassant] porte la question de ce silence au coeur même de l'acte de lecture. Maupassant le simple
ainsi devient énigmatique, le texte apparemment clos de la nouvelle reste ouvert, et le silence de l'auteur apparaît comme la
condition même d'une possibilité de lire" (Marcoin 68–69).

Il me semble que la distinction générique qui a séparé jusqu'à
présent ces deux génies littéraires peut également servir de base
à une lecture intertextuelle de deux oeuvres appartenant à des
genres différents mais qui ont par ailleurs des points de contact
significatifs; tel est mon propos dans cet article. Il s'agit donc
d'un des premiers récits publiés par Maupassant, "Sur l'eau,"
paru d'abord sous le titre "En canot," en mars 1876, et d'un des
premiers poèmes de Mallarmé, "Brise marine," publié dans le
Parnasse contemporain du 12 mai 1866. (Je ferai également référence au "Sonneur" de Mallarmé, republié dans le même numéro.) Mon but n'est pas d'assimiler ces deux textes l'un à l'autre,
ni de niveler leurs différences considérables, mais plutôt d'examiner comment leurs points de contact cristallisent quelque
chose de fondamental dans l'oeuvre de ces écrivains.

Je voudrais que le statut précis de cette juxtaposition de textes
reste flexible: je ne prétends pas, par exemple, que ces poèmes
de Mallarmé aient forcément influencé Maupassant directement,
bien que ce soit possible: après tout, Maupassant fait la connaissance de Mallarmé et commence à fréquenter ses jeudis au moment même où il est vraisemblablement en train de composer
"Sur l'eau." La valeur de cette juxtaposition de textes réside dans

l'idée que l'on peut les comprendre mieux—ou au moins autrement—en les lisant ensemble qu'en les lisant isolément. Non
seulement il y a une liaison thématique importante entre ces
deux oeuvres, comme nous verrons, mais chacune, composée
dans les premières années d'une carrière littéraire, peut être lue
rétrospectivement comme une sorte de point de départ de tout
un itinéraire artistique.

Quels sont les points communs entre ces deux textes, aussi
bien thématiques que structuraux? Les deux oeuvres traitent
d'une tentative de départ qui n'a pas lieu, et ce qui fait obstacle
au départ dans les deux cas est une figure féminine. "Brise marine," qui commence par l'un des vers les plus célèbres de Mallarmé, "La chair est triste, hélas! et j'ai lu tous les livres,"[4] décrit
le désir d'évasion d'un narrateur qui proclame qu'il partira, mais
dont le départ n'est jamais raconté au présent: "Je partirai!
Steamer balançant ta mâture, / Lève l'ancre pour une exotique
nature!" Parmi les "ancres" que le poète doit découvrir la force
de soulever avant d'entreprendre son voyage se trouve une image
non seulement de femme, mais de mère:

> Rien, ni les vieux jardins reflétés par les yeux
> Ne retiendra ce coeur qui dans la mer se trempe
> O nuits! ni la clarté déserte de ma lampe
> Sur le vide papier que la blancheur défend
> Et ni la jeune femme allaitant son enfant.

L'opposition "mer"/"mère" est déjà suggérée si ce n'est expli-
citée par ces vers. Cette figure maternelle représente le monde
familier et conventionnel de la domesticité, de la terre ferme, et
de la matière, par contraste à l'attrait d'une quête spirituelle en
mer; et les amateurs d'analyse biographique de souligner précipi-
tamment la ressemblance entre cette jeune femme et Madame
Mallarmé nourrissant la petite Geneviève à l'époque de la composition de ce poème. Cette figure féminine "retient" le poète;
elle l'ancre dans le port du monde domestique. N'oublions pas
l'étymologie du mot "matière": *materia*, considéré par Aristote
comme élément maternel par contraste à l'esprit, élément pa-
ternel.[5] Cette "ancre" du poète n'est pas la jeune mère elle-même
mais tout ce qu'elle représente pour lui: l'existence dans le temps,
la triste et inévitable mise en chair de toute aspiration au spirituel, et la naissance comme emblème du poids lourd de la condition humaine.

C'est justement cette image de la femme comme ancre du poète qui nous fournit un premier point de contact, d'ailleurs assez inouï, avec "Sur l'eau." Dans le poème de Mallarmé, une ancre métaphorique associée avec une femme retient le poète. Dans le conte de Maupassant, il s'agit d'une ancre littérale et d'une femme qui s'y trouve littéralement attachée: à la fin du conte le narrateur tire de la Seine son ancre, à laquelle est attachée une femme, ou plus précisément un cadavre de femme. Résumons brièvement ce récit.[6]

Un vieux canotier qui habite près de la Seine raconte à un de ses voisins une aventure qui lui est arrivée. En rentrant un soir en bateau, il décide de s'arrêter un instant pour "reprendre haleine" et fumer une pipe. Il jette donc son ancre dans la rivière, écoute les cris des bêtes tout autour, allume sa pipe. Soudain il a mal au coeur et cesse de fumer. Il essaie de chanter un peu, mais trouve le son de sa voix désagréable. Saisi d'une inquiétude mal définie, il veut repartir mais n'arrive pas à remonter l'ancre. Il fait beau, il a du rhum: il décide de passer la nuit à la belle étoile dans son bateau.

Subitement, et au beau milieu de son récit, sonne contre son bateau "un petit coup" (57) dont il n'arrive pas à bien préciser la source. Il tire désespérément sur la chaîne, mais l'ancre ne bouge pas. Et à partir du moment où il entend ce petit coup mystérieux commence un cauchemar éveillé. Il découvre sans aucun avertissement ni transition que la rivière est couverte d'un brouillard tellement épais qu'en se mettant debout il n'arrive plus à voir ses pieds. Il pousse des cris d'épouvante jusqu'à ce que son gosier soit "absolument paralysé" (58), boit du rhum, s'assoupit. Au petit matin, deux autres marins passent et l'aident à remonter l'ancre. Et voici les dernières phrases du récit: "Alors, peu à peu, l'ancre céda. Elle montait, mais doucement, doucement, et chargée d'un poids considérable. Enfin nous aperçûmes une masse noire, et nous la tirâmes à mon bord: c'était le cadavre d'une vieille femme qui avait une grosse pierre au cou" (59).

Si on arrive momentanément à faire abstraction de leurs différences, par ailleurs considérables, de tonalité, de technique, et de procédés stylistiques—pour tout dire, de leur différence de genre—ces deux oeuvres peuvent se résumer en termes analogues. Un homme veut partir en bateau; une femme-ancre le retient. Dans le poème de Mallarmé, on se doute que le poète ne partira jamais, ne pourra pas "lever l'ancre"; il n'entend qu'en lui-même, qu'en son coeur, le "chant des matelots" qui termine le poème. Par contre, à la fin du récit de Maupassant, l'homme lève l'ancre et peut repartir. Il s'agit donc de deux situations

analogues avec deux résolutions opposées, opposition qui souligne justement la valeur opposée de ces deux figures féminines.

La figure féminine de "Sur l'eau" représente non pas un monde
domestiqué et familier, mais plutôt le monde de l'insaisissable,
de l'indicible, de l'inexprimable qui donne à l'oeuvre de Maupassant son pouvoir. Alors que la jeune mère semble avoir disparu
à la fin de "Brise marine," le conte de Maupassant clôt sur la
première entrée en scène de la vieille. Le récit peut être lu
comme une sorte de plus-que-parfait macabre: à la fin on découvre que dès le début la vieille était déjà morte, vraisemblable-
ment par le suicide.[7] Figure de la rivière, c'est une sorte d'anti-
sirène, ou de "sirène à l'envers" (pour citer un autre poème de
Mallarmé, "Salut"), c'est-à-dire une sirène vieille, qui ne chante
pas, et qui habite la rivière plutôt que la mer.

Dans "Brise marine," comme nous l'avons vu, la mère s'oppose
très fortement à la mer; ici les deux homophones sont assimilés
métaphoriquement l'un à l'autre, et les deux s'opposent à la figure
complexe de la vieille femme, qui est métaphore de la rivière
comme la rivière est métaphore d'elle: "la rivière. . . . c'est la
chose mystérieuse, profonde, inconnue, le pays des mirages . . .
où l'on voit, la nuit, des choses qui ne sont pas, où on entend
des bruits que l'on ne connaît point, où l'on tremble sans savoir
pourquoi, comme en traversant un cimetière: et c'est en effet le
plus sinistre des cimetières, celui où l'on n'a point de tombeau. . . . la rivière est illimitée. . . . la mer . . . crie, elle hurle,
elle est loyale, la grande mer; tandis que la rivière est silencieuse
et perfide. Elle ne gronde pas, elle coule toujours sans bruit, et
ce mouvement éternel de l'eau qui coule est plus effrayant pour
moi que les hautes vagues de l'Océan" (54–55). Au centre de
cette description terrifiante de la rivière se trouve une déstabili-
sation de la temporalité réglée: le "mouvement éternel de l'eau
qui coule" inspire chez le canotier une terreur inexplicable. Dans
le poème de Mallarmé la mère fait obstacle au voyage en mer
justement parce que cette femme qui nourrit son enfant est métaphore de la temporalité domestiquée, d'un rapport réglé entre
les générations, l'une des conventions de base de la civilisation.
Le poète croit devoir délaisser cette figure maternelle à cause de
son désir de dépasser la temporalité normative en tant que signe
de l'état déchu de l'existence humaine aussi bien que du langage
conventionnel. Par son désir de départ, le poète résiste à la nécessité, qui du reste se trouve au centre de l'entreprise réaliste, de
s'exprimer dans un cadre où liaisons logiques et articulations
chronologiques conspirent au développement de la pensée à tra-

vers l'espace bien ordonné de l'écriture et le temps séquentiel de la lecture.

Mais dans le passage de "Sur l'eau" qui décrit la rivière, la mer ne s'oppose pas à une mère, elle ressemble plutôt à une mère; la vraie opposition est entre la mer et la rivière. La mer, comme une mère, gronde, hurle, et crie; elle peut être dure et méchante mais elle est loyale, liée à un modèle de conduite passé; c'est une force non pas totalement prévisible mais tout au moins compréhensible. On peut lutter et se mesurer contre elle, et cette lutte est justement génératrice de la civilisation. Par contre la rivière, domaine de la vieille, est "illimitée," non domesticable. Depuis Héraclite elle représente la temporalité instable, le flux, l'insaisissable. Non seulement le canotier est balloté par le courant, mais la scène est constamment en train de changer: en l'espace de quelques heures, il fait beau, il fait très chaud, il fait du brouillard, il refait beau, le ciel se couvre de nuages, il fait un temps "glacial," et il pleut. Ici comme chez Proust, par exemple, il y a une opposition entre les deux sens du mot "temps": temporalité et climat. Le temps météorologique représente le temps imprévisible, non contrôlé.[8] Chez Maupassant la rivière et la vieille sont associées avec une perte de contrôle de la temporalité.

Cette perte de contrôle est cristallisée par la comparaison entre la rivière et un cimetière sans tombeau, comparaison qui préfigure bien sûr la fin du conte. Il faut supposer que le but de la vieille en se jetant à la rivière est non seulement de se suicider, mais aussi d'échapper à l'enterrement: si son projet avait réussi, la rivière serait restée son cimetière aquatique. L'enterrement, composante essentielle de la civilisation humaine, signale la tentative par excellence de domestiquer la mortalité et la temporalité qui la sous-tend.

La rivière représente non seulement une temporalité déréglée, mais aussi une mise en question de la causalité. C'est le domaine non seulement des émotions fortes comme la terreur, mais aussi celui de l'incompréhension, où l'on ne sait même pas pourquoi on a peur: "on tremble sans savoir pourquoi." Toute cette aventure est pénétrée d'une perte progressive de causalité. Au début le canotier explique pourquoi il veut s'arrêter. Il fait beau, il veut fumer, il lance son ancre dans la rivière: en effet, il est toujours "ancré" dans le monde des explications.

Mais dès que le canotier jette son ancre, il commence à se perdre, et la perte progressive de toute causalité claire est signalée par la répétition du mot "cependant," utilisé la première fois dans son sens logique et la deuxième fois dans son sens chronologique. Le canotier, qui aime fumer, ne comprend pas pourquoi sa pipe lui fait mal au coeur, et il utilise le mot "cependant" dans son sens logique pour signaler sa confusion: "je résolus de fumer un peu pour me distraire. Cependant, quoique je fusse un culotteur de pipes renommé, je ne pus pas" (56). Ici le canotier continue à chercher des causes, même s'il n'en trouve pas. Mais après que sonne le petit coup mystérieux qui déclenche son cauchemar, la perte de tout raisonnement causal est signalée par la répétition du mot "cependant" dans son sens chronologique: "Je saisis ma chaîne et me raidis dans un effort désespéré. L'ancre tint bon. Je me rassis épuisé. Cependant, la rivière s'était peu à peu couverte d'un brouillard blanc très épais . . ." (57). "Cependant" ici n'a aucune valeur logique; le mot veut dire simplement "pendant ce temps." Et justement c'est ici que la suite des événements commence à devenir tout à fait illogique. Le canotier explique au début de son récit qu'il s'est arrêté parce qu'il faisait "un temps magnifique" (55). Mais ici, peu de temps après, il nous dit sans explication qu'un brouillard épais s'est levé, pas subitement, mais "peu à peu": on ne sait quand ni comment. Et dès maintenant, les énigmes se multiplient, et l'insuffisance croissante de la raison mène à la terreur: "Cet effroi bête et inexplicable grandissait toujours et devenait de la terreur" (58).

Un parallèle curieux avec ce double usage du mot "Cependant" se trouve dans un autre poème de Mallarmé publié dans le même numéro du *Parnasse contemporain* que "Brise marine," "Le sonneur," sonnet qui lui aussi a bien des résonances avec "Sur l'eau." Ce poème décrit une triple action simultanée, une scène à trois "étages" régie par le premier mot du poème, "Cependant," indicateur de son synchronisme. Au deuxième étage, en haut d'un clocher, une cloche est sonnée grâce à une corde attachée à une pierre. Le bas de cette corde est tenu par le poète, qui se trouve au premier étage. Sa séparation d'avec la cloche elle-même est significative, car il dit qu'il a "beau tirer le câble à sonner l'Idéal," il a perdu la foi; il ne peut pas atteindre les hauteurs spirituelles où la cloche est située. La naïveté et la ferveur qu'il a perdues sont représentées dans le poème par un troisième niveau, le rez-de-chaussée pour ainsi dire, où un enfant passe devant l'église et, comprenant que les prières du matin sont annoncées par la cloche, récite ou chante très naturellement ses prières.

Ce qui risque de décourager le poète, c'est justement la "tristesse de la chair," le poids de la mortalité, ici représentée par la pierre qui ancre la cloche. La fin du sonnet, où le poète imagine qu'il se pendra un jour du désespoir de ne pas "sonner l'Idéal," boucle littéralement—et mortellement—la boucle chronologique ouverte par le premier mot du poème, "Cependant": "Mais, un jour, fatigué d'avoir en vain tiré, / O Satan, j'ôterai la pierre et me pendrai." "Cependant," utilisé dans ce poème dans son sens chronologique, est emblématique de ce même aspect de la temporalité humaine qui faisait déjà problème dans "Brise marine": la nécessité fâcheuse de vivre les moments de la vie l'un après l'autre, étalés dans le temps et donc séparés de toute totalisation potentielle, la difficulté d'une vision synoptique dans un monde sans foi. Et justement, à la fin du sonnet, le mot "cependant," signe d'un désir de faire confondre ou correspondre le physique et le spirituel, de faire s'effondrer l'axe temporel, échoue: le mot est transformé en "me pendrai." "Cependant," homophone du participe présent impersonnel de "se pendre" ("se pendant"), est conjugué, ancré dans le temps. Le poète, lui-même transformé en "ancre" de la cloche, s'avoue vaincu par la temporalité et la mortalité; il se pendra avec la corde séculaire, le fil même du temps.

Si on retourne maintenant à "Sur l'eau," on voit en même temps un parallèle avec l'image de la pendaison qui fait le "coup de grâce" du "Sonneur" et les fonctions diamétralement opposées qu'elle joue dans les deux oeuvres. La vieille femme de "Sur l'eau" ne se pend pas: elle est obligée d'attacher une pierre autour du cou justement parce que la force de la gravité est bien moindre dans l'eau que sur terre. En quittant la terre et en entrant dans l'eau, on a l'impression de retourner aux sources de la vie, au moment de la conception, à l'instant où l'esprit prend forme et matière. La vieille femme n'est pas étranglée par la corde, plutôt elle se noie; la preuve, dans une image grotesque et en même temps absurde typique de Maupassant, c'est qu'elle continue à pouvoir "parler." C'est elle qui émet le "petit coup" qui met la terreur masculine en marche.

L'une des plus grandes ironies du conte, c'est que le canotier prétend aimer l'eau mais s'avère être une figure terrestre qui reste bien attachée à la terre des hommes. Le résultat de son action de jeter l'ancre, c'est d'imposer un enterrement à cette vieille femme qui est repêchée à la fin du conte et sera sans doute identifiée et enterrée. Encore une fois cette figure féminine s'oppose très fortement à celle de "Brise marine": chez Maupassant elle ne représente ni la matière ni le monde domestiqué. Elle est plutôt de nature flottante: elle est obligée d'attacher une pierre à son cou car sans cela elle flotterait, comme la rivière elle-même. Ce conte est le modèle même du mélange maupassantien du morbide et du risible, car on peut imaginer que si la vieille s'est jetée dans la Seine juste avant l'arrivée du canotier, celui-ci, en jetant l'ancre, devient son bourreau. Il tire le coup de grâce en achevant une femme mourante—peut-être même que les mouvements du bateau et le petit coup mystérieux sont causés par la dernière lutte de celle-ci avec l'ancre. En laissant tomber une ancre sur une femme en train de se noyer, il la tue à la façon des terriens et non pas à la façon de la rivière. Pour emprunter un jeu de mots à Mallarmé, le canotier, créature de la terre, fait taire une créature aquatique. L'effet de jeter l'ancre, c'est de transformer la noyade de cette étrange naïade en perte de connaissance ultime.

Ici nous touchons à un autre point d'intersection entre Maupassant et Mallarmé: le statut même de la parole et du silence, et les implications de ce statut pour la question de la clôture essentielle à ces deux écrivains. La poétique de Mallarmé est dominée par un désir de clôture: le projet du Livre absolu serait l'expression ultime et par là même le dépassement de la vie. Dans "Brise marine," le poète veut quitter le monde domestiqué de la "chair triste," de la *mater* et de la *materia*, mais il ne rejette pas les livres, ni même la chair: il trouve simplement que les livres qu'il a lus n'arrivent pas à dépasser la tristesse de la chair. N'oublions pas que pour Mallarmé, le tombeau est une métaphore du poème: les "Tombeaux" d'Edgar Poe, de Baudelaire, etc., sont censés faire revivre les défunts en tant qu'essences.[9] Les tombeaux de Mallarmé sont des clôtures, des domestications de la mort par un des plus grands outils de la civilisation: la parole.

Donc le silence si cher à Mallarmé va de pair avec l'idéal de la clôture: par la perfection esthétique il vise une rédemption de la mortalité, une sorte de grâce ou de "salut," l'une des images-clef de sa poésie. Dans "Brise marine," le mot "ancre," avec son homophone "encre," illustre cette idée. "Lever l'ancre," c'est soulever ou sublimer par le voyage poétique le poids de la matière représenté par la jeune mère; mais cette sublimation, ce mouvement vers un niveau plus élevé, ne veut pas ajouter un autre poids mort à celui qui est son point de départ, d'où l'idéal litotique de Mallarmé et la minceur de son corpus. Un poème idéal rejoint ou recrée le silence: "lever l'ancre" est le point de départ, mais "lever l'encre" est la destination visée: la page blanche.

Si on retourne maintenant à Maupassant, on voit que le statut de la clôture est tout à fait autre. L'ancre représente un encadrement, une stabilité, un ancrage dans le monde des institutions et des structures sociales dont le canotier a besoin. La femme morte représente tout ce qui échappe à ce monde. Les récits de Maupassant créent constamment des ouvertures sur ce monde "autre," mais il reste dans une grande mesure indicible. La valeur déstabilisante de la fin de "Sur l'eau" est tout à fait emblématique des récits de Maupassant, car au niveau du "réel" elle semble fournir une explication d'un mystère antérieur, mais on ne découvre pas la réaction du narrateur, ni celle de son interlocuteur; et, surtout, on ne sait pas du tout comment réagir soi-même. Dans un sens il n'y a pas de clôture narrative. L'ordre chronologique rétabli à la fin du conte ne rend pas compte de l'impression finale de désordonnement narratif. A la fin, face à une image d'altérité pure, le canotier se tait, et ce silence est signe non pas d'une clôture mais d'une interdiction—il ne faut pas aller plus loin.

Effectivement, on peut lire ce conte comme un apprentissage au silence. Il y a ici une sorte de chiasme de la parole et du silence: le narrateur est réduit peu à peu au silence, et le monde de la rivière s'exprime de plus en plus. Au début le narrateur chante, mais n'aime pas sa voix; ensuite il pousse des cris d'épouvante, mais sa voix s'éteint. Et il finit par accepter le besoin de se taire: "je me soulevai avec des précautions infinies, comme si ma vie eût dépendu du moindre bruit que j'aurais fait" (58). Par contre, le monde de la rivière au début se tait: il y a un "silence extraordinaire," les bêtes se taisent. Mais plus tard elles parlent, et c'est en écoutant le coassement furieux des grenouilles et la note "monotone" des crapauds que le narrateur surmonte sa terreur: "Chose étrange, je n'avais plus peur."

Evidemment, la voix la plus importante du récit, c'est celle de la vieille, figure qui est infiniment plus puissante que la figure féminine de "Brise marine." La voix à laquelle le récit de Maupassant reste ouvert, la voix à laquelle il semble faire constamment allusion mais qui reste potentielle, sur le point de parler, c'est celle de la femme morte. Ce qui déclenche la vraie terreur du canotier, c'est le "petit coup" qui sonne contre son bateau au milieu de son récit. La vraie source de ce "petit coup," n'est-ce pas la vieille qui, ballotée par le courant, ou peut-être luttant contre la mort, "tire" sur l'ancre et fait basculer le petit bateau?

Ce "petit coup" ne fait-il pas écho à la dernière phrase du récit, son "coup de grâce," la description de la vieille femme morte "qui avait une grosse pierre au cou"? Le mot "cou" sans "p" décrit le site dont émane la parole—le canotier lui-même dit qu'il a "paralysé" son gosier en essayant de crier sa terreur. Mais alors que la terreur croissante du canotier n'arrive jamais à produire que des cris inarticulés de bête, on a l'impression à la fin du conte, par une dernière image grotesque et absurde, que le cadavre de la vieille femme pourrait continuer à parler, comme la tête de Saint Jean-Baptiste dans "Hérodiade" de Mallarmé qui au moment de la décapitation récite un cantique, chant d'action de grâces qui est en même temps le poème lui-même. Même quand sa tête est en train de se séparer de son corps, Saint Jean fait un dernier signe de tête littéralement grâcieux: il "penche un salut," le salut ou la grâce de la mortalité provenant chez Mallarmé de la perfection et de la complétude, de la clôture du poème qui essaie de racheter la séparation radicale entre la tête (esprit) et le corps (matière).

De même on a l'impression que la vieille pourrait continuer à parler: après tout, elle n'a pas été décapitée comme Saint-Jean, ni ne s'est pendue comme "Le sonneur," qui se termine lui aussi par l'image d'une pierre autour d'un cou, mais plutôt elle s'est noyée. Sa voix est restée potentiellement intacte. Oui, elle a une grosse pierre au cou, mais en cela diffère-t-elle de Mathilde Loisel de "La parure," qui emprunte un collier décrit comme une "rivière de diamants" (Maupassant 1974, 1201) qui lui est plus ou moins fatal, à elle aussi, quand elle le place "autour de la gorge"? La grosse pierre autour du cou de la vieille, bijou de la mort, a une ambiguïté essentielle à la compréhension de la terreur du canotier devant cette femme littéralement "inouïe": elle est en même temps signe de valeur potentielle, comme une pierre précieuse, et noeud coulant qui empêche la vieille d'exprimer cette valeur terrifiante, qui refuse l'accès à un monde extra-terrestre, autre. Même si le canotier achève pour ainsi dire une femme mourante, lui tire le coup de grâce, Maupassant lui-même ne peut pas l'"'achever" d'un point de vue littéraire. A la fin de ce voyage sur la rivière, il a trop besoin de la terre des hommes, et trop de terreur devant cette créature non-terrienne, pour lui accorder une complétude, une clôture, un cou et des cordes vocales plutôt qu'un coup d'ancre et une corde autour du cou.

Donc, pour revenir à notre point de départ, j'espère avoir suggéré par cette conjonction de textes non pas que les deux textes se ressemblent, mais plutôt qu'ils se parlent, qu'ils se complémentent dans leur différence, qu'ils ont quelque chose à se dire. Le projet symboliste de Mallarmé prend comme point de départ un ancrage dans le réel incarné par la figure d'une jeune femme pleine de vie mais d'une vie excessive, de trop—le projet symboliste consiste justement à soulever cette ancre. Par contre le projet réaliste de Maupassant est ancré dans le réel, mais l'ancre ne fonctionne pas toujours comme prévue. Ce projet réaliste effleure constamment un univers au-delà du réel, mais la réaction implicite de l'auteur face à cet au-delà reste ambivalente: désir de dépassement du réel, et terreur devant ce désir.

En fin de compte (et de conte), il n'y a pas de vrai échange entre le monde "réel" du canotier et le monde autre de la vieille. Quand il la voit surgir de l'eau, il ne lui dit même pas "salut," signe chez Mallarmé d'un contact fugace avec l'idéal. Chez Maupassant il n'y a pas de salut. Le coup de grâce de la ressemblance entre Maupassant et Mallarmé, ce qui finit par l'achever ou tout au moins par la faire taire, c'est que le "coup de grâce" de "Sur l'eau" n'est pas, finalement, source de grâce.

University of Wisconsin

NOTES

1. Voir Guy de Maupassant 1974, lxx. Il est difficile de ne pas admirer la symétrie de ces deux carrières qui se touchent brièvement mais de façon significative: le conte est une sorte d'aboutissement pour Flaubert—les *Trois contes* seront la dernière de ses oeuvres parue de son vivant—et un point de départ pour Maupassant.

2. Une définition précise et détaillée des distinctions entre ces deux mouvements serait ici hors de propos, je me limite donc à en esquisser les grandes lignes.

3. Genette suggère que Mallarmé, héritier de Socrate, est un "cratyliste déçu" (Genette 36).

4. Les poèmes de Mallarmé sont cités dans Mallarmé 1945: "Brise marine" (38), "Le sonneur" (36), et "Cantique de Saint Jean" (49).

5. Voir Aristote, *La génération des animaux*. Pour une excellente discussion des avatars de cette théorie, voir Roger, surtout 49–94.

6. Maupassant 1974, 54–59.

7. Etant donnée l'absence totale de clarification à la fin du conte, le suicide de cette femme n'est pas la seule explication possible; elle a pu être tuée. La dernière phrase du conte est typique de Maupassant justement en ce qu'elle donne un détail grotesque dont on se serait passé volontiers—la position précise de la corde autour du cou de la vieille femme plutôt qu'autour de ses pieds, par exemple—mais s'obstine à faire taire les circonstances de sa mort.

Pourtant cette position de la corde suggère, me semble-t-il, plutôt un suicide qu'un meurtre.

8. Le père du jeune Marcel, qui fait tout par chimère et reste absolument imprévisible (Proust 1:27; 1:36), n'a qu'une passion dans la vie, la météo, alors que sa mère et sa grand-mère n'ont aucun sens du temps qu'il fait—celle-ci se promène résolument sous la pluie (1:11)—mais représentent une temporalité réglée et domestiquée.

9. Voir, par exemple, Davies.

7

"La vérité est inutile": Visionaries of the Terror in Nodier and Nerval

MARY JANE COWLES

IN his rewriting of his evaluation of Pichegru's role in the Revolution included in the *Souvenirs de la Révolution et de l'Empire*, Charles Nodier seeks to correct earlier condemnations of the revolutionary general, including his own. At its conclusion, Nodier says of his apologia:

> I did not write it for the republicans.
> I did not write it for the legitimists. . . .
> I did not write it for Pichegru's children.
> I did not write it for his parents.
> I did not write it for his noble and unoffendable memory.
> I did not write it for history.
> I wrote it for the truth.
>
> (1872, 87)

At first, the reader may well be taken in by such rhetorical flourishes. Here truth is affirmed as a value beyond partisan positions, a kind of transcendence nonetheless attainable by the author. If I write in the name of truth, the author implies, then what I write is true. The kind of truth that transcends history and that Nodier proclaims here in the "Préface" of the third edition is surprising indeed in these *Souvenirs* which begin under the sign of the most subjective of verities: ". . . I will certainly not try to prove that perceptions half-erased by time have attained, in going from my head and heart to the paper to which I commit them, that absolute precision of mathematical truths which is desirable every day in more essential and more positive matters. What I vouch for is that they are mine, that they came to me this way, as my organs took them in" (Nodier 1872, 6).

We must read this "vérité" in whose name Nodier writes not

as the truth of History, but as that truth of a subjective vision which draws its authenticity from lived experience, or from perception, or, as would more often be the case for Nodier, from some secret correspondence between fantasy and metaphysics. Certainly, this is the truth that most "littérateurs" would claim as their own, along with the belief that the work of art gives meaning to experience by shaping it.

Yet in one of his "Contes," "Jean-François les Bas-Bleus" of 1832, Nodier presents a different formulation of the same problem: in the words of the narrator's father, the very words with which the tale ends: "Truth is useless" ("La vérité est inutile"). This dictum undercuts both of the other stances with respect to truth. What difference does it make whether truth is transcendent or subjective when it is literally useless? These words reflect not only on the nature of Nodier's fictional enterprise, but also on the events of the French Revolution which influence, albeit indirectly, the object of the narration. But, as is so often the case with Nodier's irony, the concluding maxim must be read against as well as with the narrative to reveal its meaning.

The story centers around the young narrator's encounters with one of the local oddities in Besançon: Jean-François Touvet, "an idiot, a monomaniac, a madman" (Nodier 1961, 364). Aside from these encounters, the narrative is fairly uneventful, and is devoted to relating details of Jean-François's "madness," the narrator's reactions to it, and the narrator's conversations with his father. The narrator presents the tale as memory and structures it around a few dates—first the year, 1793, and then specific days: 16 October and the 29th of Prairial—and these dates function as anchors in this evocation of Jean-François's "madness." They serve as if to guarantee the veracity of facts, especially since the history they authenticate is a personal one. In evoking his second significant encounter with Jean-François, the narrator recalls the date with precision because it was the "first day of the school year," "and therefore October 16, 1793" (371). Of course, the use of the first-person narration and the recall of specific historical dates are time-honored techniques for creating the illusion of truth, or history, in fiction.

More importantly, the use of dates contrasts with the timelessness in which the protagonist Jean-François dwells: "One of the most remarkable peculiarities of the madness of this nice young man is that it was only perceptible in unimportant conversations in which the mind focuses on familiar things. If one approached him to talk about the rain, the nice weather, the show, the newspaper, what was being said around the city, the country's affairs, he would listen attentively and answer politely; but the words which came to his lips rushed forth so tumultuously that they would become confused before the end of the first sentence, in some kind of inexplicable gibberish from which he was unable to disentangle his thought" (365). Whatever is timely becomes nonsense to Jean-François, but whatever aspires to the immutable reveals his clairvoyance. When discussion turns to a philosophical or scientific matter. "Then the rays of this diseased intelligence, so divergent and so scattered, would come together suddenly in a beam, . . . and would give so much brilliance to his speech that one is entitled to doubt that Jean-François had ever been wiser, clearer, and more persuasive in the entire use of his reason" (366). Thus, the fundamental duality of our character—his differing notions of scientific laws and principles, and of life's ephemera—implies a rejection of objective history, a rejection which the narrator sympathetically shares. But where does the truth lie now? With historical fact which Jean-François fails to understand, or with questions of philosophy or science about which he has never been wiser nor saner?

The portrait of Jean-François is further complicated when historical fact appears to verify the vision, when mundane reality is not at odds with the truth spoken by the madman. On his return from school on 16 October 1793, the narrator finds Jean-François gazing overhead, surrounded by a crowd in the middle of an intersection. The narrator then asks him what he sees in the subtle matter of space. Jean-François replies: "Follow those traces of blood with your eyes and you will see Marie-Antoinette, Queen of France, going to heaven" (372). The narrator's initial reaction is one of surprise at Jean-François's awareness of the name of France's queen: ". . . I went away . . . marveling only that Jean-François les Bas-Bleus had stumbled so accurately on the name of the last of our queens, that pragmatic particularity belonging to the category of true facts of which he had lost all knowledge" (372). In other words, the truth of Jean-François's vision has precisely to do with the moment of intersection of the transient and the eternal, the appearance of the supernatural in the world of the real. The truth for Jean-François, and for the narrator, is the very definition of the genre of the fantastic.

It is no coincidence that the narrator alone holds the key to Jean-François's alienation (as he himself reports: "I know the wand which pulls him out of his spells" [367])—no coincidence because the narrator himself functions as the madman's double. The narrator of "Jean-François" is, according to Lucienne Frappier-Mazur, a "narrator-intermediary" ("narrateur-relais") who, through the character of the madman "objectivizes a part of himself in which he believes without taking full responsibility for it. He exalts his dreams as the truth, all the while stationing them in the Other, the incarnation of his unconscious desires" (Frappier-Mazur 35). We cannot fail to note here the importance of the narrator's belief in this Other that allows him to distance himself and entertain, at the same time, both scepticism and credulity. The narrator hypothesizes that the split in Jean-François between the madman and the genius comes from his having two souls, and his father, too, refers to Jean-François's differing responses as a "double language." If the narrator's father repeatedly warns his son against Jean-François's illusions (370, 374), it is because he fears his son might be susceptible to them. Indeed, the narrator resembles Jean-François by being himself double. He usually speaks to Jean-François only "in the name of the aorist or the logarithm, of the hypotenuse or of the trope, and of some similar difficulties of my double study" (367). Like his protagonist, our narrator is caught between two principles: not so much between the present and the eternal like Jean-François, but between mathematics and rhetoric: in other words, between reason, "the absolute precision of mathematical truths," and literature, all the more removed from the conventional claims of truth through the reference to the figurative language of tropes. Such an opposition symbolizes, too, both the narrator's scepticism, allied with notions of mathematical precision, and his youthful credulity, encouraged by the seductions of rhetoric. This duality is articulated on another level as the position between the "reason" of the father and the "illusion" of Jean-François.

Once Jean-François's vision of the death of Marie-Antoinette has been indeed confirmed, the narrator's father, rationalist par excellence (cf. 370), is careful to attribute such clairvoyance to coincidence, to pure chance: "He spared nothing to convince me that chance was fertile in such encounters. . . ." (374). But eventually, even the narrator's father is forced to admit that Jean-François's insight proves true. When he can no longer assert that Jean-François's knowledge is pure coincidence, when he confronts the day and time of Jean-François's death with that of his beloved patrons, aristocratic victims of the Terror, the voice of reason counsels illusion. He tells the narrator:

"If you ever tell this story when you are a grown man, do not offer it as the truth, because it would expose you to ridicule."

"Are there reasons which can exempt a man from proclaiming openly that which he recognizes as the truth?" I answered respectfully.

"There is one which is worth all of them," said my father, shaking his head. "The truth is useless."

(375–76)

Hence the response of the rationalist is to erase the visionary in turn, in fact, to erase the "truth" of the narrative itself—and the way to do that is to proclaim it as fiction. And that is just what the dutiful son does—or is it?

In speaking of his two classmates who accompanied him part-way home from school, the narrator mentions them first as guar-antors of the truth of his account, then suggests that it would be inappropriate to name them in a "story in which, undoubtedly, one demands only the verisimilitude required for tales of the fantastic, and which in the final analysis I myself do not present as anything else" (371). And in the first few paragraphs of the story which serve as a kind of preface, the story is explicitly identified as "fantastic," but "a fantastic tale in which I promise you I will not put anything of my own" (364)—in which nothing of the author's own invention will be added. Perhaps what is most telling is that the narrator's father, in the passage just quoted above, says that the truth must be concealed, which im-plies, again, that the story of Jean-François is indeed true, and that the narrator is complying with the father's wishes by leading the reader to believe differently. But by including his father's words as part of the narrative, that very strategy is put in doubt. Clearly, the narrator's object here is not the pursuit of truth, but a process of mystification of which the narrator himself appears the first victim. Two brief passages from the introductory para-graphs, if they bring us no closer to the truth, at least strengthen the ties between the narrator and Jean-François:

The first essential condition for writing a good fantastic tale would be to believe firmly in it, and no one believes in that which he in-vents. (362)
I will never in my life write a fantastic tale, you can believe me, if I do not have as sincere a faith in it as in the most ordinary notions of my memory, as in the most daily facts of my existence.

(362–63)

Thus Nodier's final gesture, reflected in the dictum, "truth is useless," repeats, in a way, this initial gesture of both faith and doubt. Since he *believes* in this story—or so he says—it cannot be a fantastic tale. Or rather, if it is a fantastic tale, it is because the fantastic is as true as if it were a memory or a fact of life. Questions of faith or doubt, not reason, underwrite the fantastic. If reason dictates the erasure of the fantastic, improbable truth, the visionary requires the erasure of objective truth—but such an erasure cannot fail, in turn, to call itself into question.

But what of the Terror itself? Does this deliberate confusion of illusion and truth reflect the times which frame the story? First, Nodier's opposition of vision and reason implicitly questions the glorification of Reason from which many of the revolutionary principles emerged. Second, it is not irrelevant that Jean-François's passion for the daughter of his benefactress, thwarted by their difference in social status, seems to be the initial cause of his madness. Hence Jean-François's condition depends to some degree on a social hierarchy that the Revolution sought to undo. Although Nodier portrays Jean-François as a sympathetic monarchist, the social inequities that lead to his madness reveal Nodier's profound ambivalence towards the Revolution.[1] Third, the two specific events which reveal Jean-François's madness and insight are events of the Terror: Marie-Antoinette's execution and that of the aristocratic family to whom Jean-François was devoted. Those events constitute the moments of intersection of the temporal and the eternal, and their factual nature serves to prove the truth of his visions.

Nonetheless, the Terror itself, alluded to only through those two incidents, has no impact on the narrative except as it informs the visionary experience. Curiously, though these events give the tale its meaning and structure, the Terror and the Revolution are strangely absent from "Jean-François les Bas-Bleus." No actual violence occurs during the course of the narration, and references to the deaths of Marie-Antoinette and of the family of Jean-François's benefactress are made as discreetly and as abstractly as possible. The guillotine is never explicitly mentioned, nor do severed heads haunt the scene. Were it not for the allusion to Marie-Antoinette and for the few dates we have already seen scattered throughout the text, we might hardly perceive the somber shadow of the Revolution at all. Thus the text seems to effect a kind of erasure of the Revolution: revolutionary violence and social inequities appear only in filigree though the leveling gaze of the child narrator. Some sympathy is expressed for the queen's death ("that catastrophe") and for the noble family to whom Jean-François was devoted ("those innocent creatures"), but the narrator and his family remain resolutely non-partisan, distanced. In this way, the truth of the Terror seems useless indeed: the truth of the innocence of its victims cannot change their fate, and the narrator is virtually indifferent to its political reality.

If the events of the Terror overshadow the visionary experience while the narrator is in Strasbourg—". . . I easily forgot Jean-François in the midst of the everyday emotions which tormented society" (375)—that displacement is only momentary. The narrator's prompt return to Besançon reestablishes Jean-François as the center of the narrative and the primacy of the truth of vision over that of historical events. Even the critique of the cult of reason remains implicit. The inability of reason to account for Jean-François's prophecy serves more to affirm the functioning of the supernatural than to assess the historical consequences of the ascendancy of Reason. Indeed, the deaths alluded to in the story have far less effect on the narrator than the visions themselves: "Jean-François's conversation had left an impression which frightened me from time to time" (371). The terror of visions replaces even political terror.

The final erasure of the Revolution in "Jean-François les Bas-Bleus" may be glimpsed by comparing this tale with biographies of Nodier. Biographers generally recognize both Nodier and Nodier's own father in the traits of the narrator and his father (for example, Zaragoza 39–40). But unlike the narrator and his family, the Nodiers were fervent Jacobins, even the thirteen-year-old Charles. And following the end of the Reign of Terror, Charles became as avid an anti-Jacobin as he had been a Jacobin before. Isn't the truth "inutile" in a more profound way for this chameleon of political life, who, although he may claim to have always championed liberty "in the true acceptance of such a misunderstood word" (1872, 4), tends only to support the forces in power—first Jacobin, then anti-Jacobin—in his early life, and only to oppose them, whatever they may be, in adulthood? Nodier adroitly minimizes his narrator's involvement in the Revolution while he makes the mystical monarchist Jean-François a speaker of truth.

Like Nodier's narrator who finds in Jean-François's visions a source of horror more powerful than that of the Terror, Nerval's evocation of Jacques Cazotte's final days elides the political terror in favor of the sacred horror of the visionary. Although Cazotte's execution preceded the Reign of Terror per se, Cazotte lived through—barely—some of the bloodiest days of the Revolution, including the September massacres, before becoming the victim of the Revolution later that month in 1792. Yet Nerval's treatment of the Revolution in Cazotte's biography, while more immediate in its effect than that of "Jean-François les Bas-Bleus," serves solely to highlight the subject's visionary experience.

Nerval's study on Cazotte, first published as the preface to an edition of Cazotte's fantastic novel *Le diable amoureux* in 1845, appeared in a collection of biographical sketches entitled *Les illuminés ou les précurseurs du socialisme*, published in 1852. Many, though not all, of these sketches illustrate the lives of mystics or "excentriques," as Nerval calls them, during the Revolutionary period—Restif de la Bretonne, Quintus Aucler, Cagliostro.[2] Of all those portrayed, however, Cazotte is both the most truly visionary and the only one to face the guillotine. He is also, in this volume subtitled *Les précurseurs du socialisme*, the only royalist (Schaeffer 12, 35). It seems particularly appropriate to examine the effects of the Terror in this essay since the figure of Cazotte mediates a filiation between Nerval and Nodier, who himself had written an evocation of "Monsieur Cazotte" first published in 1836.

The centerpiece of Nerval's portrait contains a lengthy citation of La Harpe's memoirs recounting the prophecy made by Cazotte in 1788. In response to the guests' enthusiasm for "the revolution that Voltaire had made" (Nerval 1984, 1093) and for the reign of reason, Cazotte expresses first his scepticism, then his prediction: "You, M. de Condorcet, will expire stretched out on the stone floor of a prison cell. . . . M. De Chamfort . . . you will cut your veins with twenty-two razor strokes . . . You, M. de Nicolai, you will die on the scaffold. You, M. Bailly, on the scaffold. . . . You, Mme la duchesse, you will be led to the scaffold, you and many other ladies with you, in the executioner's cart, with your hands behind your back" (1094–96). The critique of reason implicit in "Jean-François les Bas-Bleus" is explicitly voiced by Cazotte in this scene. Initially, that critique is put in doubt as Nerval, following the lead of others, including Nodier, expresses reservations about the authenticity of La Harpe's report. Yet he is quick to provide additional evidence of Cazotte's prophetic abilities: ". . . we are going to relate a singular passage which is found in the poem *Ollivier*, published precisely thirty years before 93, and in which one noted a preoccupation with severed heads which may well pass, but more vaguely, for a prophetic hallucination" (1097). The passage from *Ollivier* describes the protagonist's adventures in an enchanted palace where she and her companions fall through a kind of trap door and are dismembered by a great wheel covered with blades. Most of the passage consists of the dialogue of detached heads, bored with their inactivity and disposed to quarrel. Nerval's commentary on the passage brings us still closer to revolutionary violence than even the preceding prophecy: "Is it not peculiar to find in a mock-heroic poem from the author's youth this bloody reverie of severed heads, of limbs separated from bodies, a strange association of ideas which brings together courtiers, warriors, women, dandies, commenting on and joking about details of torture, as later, at the Conciergerie, those lords, those women, those poets, who are Cazotte's contemporaries, will do" (1099).

In Nerval's gloss of *Ollivier* we find yet another form of the truth of the visionary experience. If Cazotte himself is condemned to speak the "useless truth" in his role as Cassandra, a comparison made explicitly by Nerval in two passages of the text, at least *Ollivier* becomes the art which life later imitates. The literary work is granted a kind of prophetic legitimacy that seems contested in the representation of lived experience. It is not surprising either that the further we stray from the revolution itself, the more its bloody horror can be articulated. Although this "poem" is the stuff of fairy tale, it can pass as prophecy. The Terror, for Nerval, becomes, on the other hand, " . . . [the] fantasies of that bloody fairy tale, which he had not foreseen having one day to call the Revolution" (1099). The tale itself seems to contaminate the Revolution, which becomes a horrible fantasy.

Nerval's use of Cazotte's dream from the feast of Saint-John, 1791, serves much the same purpose. Nerval repeatedly states throughout *Les illuminés* that mystics like the "martinistes" were extremely influential in the revolutionary movement. Yet each of the figures he presents, especially Cazotte, is defined in opposition to the more orthodox aspects of the revolutionary movement. Cazotte himself is resolutely Christian and monarchist: his letter to his father-in-law suggesting armed resistance to the six thousand soldiers of the Republic sent to Martinique is more than enough to condemn him in the eyes of the Revolutionary government. But Nerval's juxtaposition of this undeniably political act and Cazotte's dream of 1791 again undercuts any political aims in the case of Cazotte.[3] Speaking of this letter, Nerval writes: "One understands after all that such a piece was judged to be quite unpardonable by the revolutionary government; but it is unfortunate that it was not compared to the following document dating from the same period, and which would have shown that one must not pay any more heed to the reveries than to the dreams of the unfortunate old man" (1109). The three-page text of the dream that immediately follows, with its subjugation of recalcitrant spirits, lightning bolts, and decapitation of a white rooster, is a vision worthy of Nerval's own. Though his introduction to the dream, written as if to prepare the reader for the irrational effect of Cazotte's hallucination, portrays it in a derisive light, the conclusion Nerval draws is, typically, quite different: "Whatever judgment serious minds may bring to bear on this too-faithful portrait of certain dream hallucinations, . . . there is, in this series of bizarre visions, something terrible and mysterious. . . . His revelations, still marked by his monarchical opinions, tend to suggest connections to the vague predictions of the Apocalypse in everything happening at that time" (1112). While the remarks which preface the text portray Cazotte as a madman, the effect of the text itself suggests a certain truth, despite the narrator's disclaimers. What Nerval discounts here is Cazotte's monarchism; what he finds far more powerful is the vision itself.

Even as Cazotte stoically awaits his second arrest, the aspect that Nerval underscores is the vision which anticipates his arrest rather than his prison experience or even his death. Cazotte confides in his friend M. de Saint-Charles: "A moment before your arrival, I had a vision. I thought I saw a gendarme who was coming to get me on Pétion's orders: I had to follow him. . . . My time has come" (1116). At the conclusion of Cazotte's trial, the sentence pronounced by the president of the Tribunal Lavau, which Nerval quotes from Bastien's preface to Cazotte's work, exalts as much the mystical practices of Cazotte as it does the inexorable law of the nation. Finally, the confrontation with the guillotine is almost chastely veiled: " . . . Standing on the scaffold, he shouted in a very loud voice: 'I die as I have lived, faithful to God and to my King.' The execution took place on September 25, at seven o'clock in the evening, in the place du Carrousel" (1118).

Of course, one of the reasons Nerval privileges Cazotte's visionary quality is that his purpose in *Les illuminés* is to "portray certain *excentrics* of philosophy" (Nerval 885). His reflections on the "folies" of his subjects leads him to "develop especially the amusing and perhaps instructive side that the life and character of my *excentrics* could present.—Analyzing the multifaceted pattern of the human soul is moral physiology,—that is equal to the work of a naturalist, a paleographer, or an archeologist. . . . " (886). Nerval first plays with our expectations as he trivializes his undertaking, but by establishing an analogy between his literary portraits and "objective" sciences he brings this "folie" within the domain of the rational. At the same time, such a stance effectively removes Nerval's subjects from their history, situates them within the frame of a timeless moral philosophy rather than a particular political position and its disturbing consequences. Thus the royalist Cazotte can take his place with Restif: "All excentrics, the heroes see themselves, through the intermediary of the eccentric Nerval, offered the chance to participate in the poetic world of fundamental synthesis" (Schaeffer 14).

Here, then, we glimpse again that fusion of madness and lucidity, of the temporal and the eternal, that reveals a fundamental ambivalence on the part of the author. It is little wonder that Nerval's formulations echo so closely those of Nodier's definition of the fantastic: "But the poet who believes in his fable, the narrator who believes in his legend, the inventor who takes seriously the dream blossomed from his thought, that is what one scarcely expected to encounter in the middle of the eighteenth century. . . . " (1076). Nerval's prefatory remarks to Cazotte's biography are surely not as playful as Nodier's mystification. His description of the self-deluded poet puts Cazotte's creation into question more than it does his own. However, Nerval's repeated strategy of affirming, then retracting doubts as to the "truth" of visions of Jacques Cazotte, eventually does force him to play the same role of unwilling witness as did the narrator in "Jean-François les Bas-Bleus." If the conclusion of "Jacques Cazotte" lacks the clever aphorism of Nodier's tale, we can still discern traces of its ludic ambivalence in the words with which the preface to Les illuminés ends: "My poor uncle would often say: 'One must always turn one's tongue seven times in the mouth before speaking.' What should one do before writing?" (886).

Nerval's reasons for focusing on the visionary experience of Cazotte (and of the other "illuminés") do not seem to grow out of the author's personal experience with political life as much as is the case with Nodier. We may detect Nerval's egalitarian spirit in works such as his Prince des sots of 1831; he seemed to feel uneasy about having to ask favors from ministries under Louis-Philippe to fund his travel; he idolized Napoleon. While Nerval did not manifest the same degree of inconstancy as No-

dier, like Nodier, his political beliefs remained ill-defined. This
lack of definition suggests, in turn, the nature of his perception
of the Revolution. Referring to the events of the eighteenth century in his preface to Les illuminés, Nerval writes: "That period
has rubbed off on us more than one could have foreseen. Is that
good, is it bad—who knows?" If the values of the period left
him ambivalent, the confusion of madness and reason which
characterized both the violence of the revolution and its visions
were bound to fascinate Nerval. What better proof of a possible
correspondance between the visionary experience and the "outside" world than Cazotte's uncanny prophecies? What better way
to justify one's own visions while maintaining one's hold on
reason than by exploring them in another?

As much as Nerval affirms the influence of the "illuminés"
during the Revolution, he provides us with little hard evidence.
Indeed, just before describing the poet who believes in his own
creation, Nerval evokes, so as to establish a contrast, the more
typical writers of the eighteenth century: "The most serious writers, Montesquieu, Diderot, Voltaire, rocked and put to sleep, with
charming stories, that society which their principles were going
to destroy from top to bottom" (1075). He presents these authors,
then, as men of action who have radically changed the world.
Their fables and allegories must have had some "useful" truth
in order to have such a profound effect. The visionary, however,
he who believes in the truth of his own fiction, discovers indeed
that "la vérité est inutile": the visionary's truth is virtually useless to others, and the truth of outside realities is irrelevant to
him. Ultimately, though, as much as the visionary experience
willfully eludes the reality of the Revolution's horror, within its
frame it raises a fundamental question, the answer to which it
also eludes: which is the truth?

Kenyon College

NOTES

Part of the research for this paper was conducted in the summer of 1993
under the auspices of the Dartmouth/Dana Collaborative, which I would like
to thank for its support.
1. Réboul and Setbon explore Nodier's ambiguous and changing attitude
towards the Revolution, especially as revealed in his critical essays. Delon portrays the adult Nodier as more objective towards the revolutionaries than his
royalist sentiments would lead one to suppose.
2. Les illuminés has received relatively little critical attention. For a discus-

sion of the title of the collection, see Jean Richer, pp. 391–92 and Gérald Schaeffer, pp. 11–14.

3. Schaeffer sees Cazotte as a "révolté": "Communists (Restif et Aucler) or Royalist (Cazotte), all the heroes clash with the power of their epoch, of which they denounce both the social injustice and the spiritual errors" (Schaeffer 35).

8

Lamiel de Stendhal à feu et à sang

PAULINE WAHL WILLIS

*L*AMIEL ne cesse de fasciner. Le grand public se contente du pastiche beyliste de Jacques Laurent, *La fin de Lamiel;* les "happy few" se régalent des aventures de la jeune Normande malgré l'inachèvement du texte stendhalien; les érudits se disputent la lecture des manuscrits du roman tout en sachant finalement qu'"aucun éditeur de *Lamiel* ne peut être infaillible" (Meininger 325). Depuis la première édition de *Lamiel,* due à Casimir Stryienski en 1889, jusqu'à l'édition Folio, presqu'un siècle plus tard, préparée par Anne-Marie Meininger, il n'a cessé d'être question que de l'agencement des chapitres, plans, notes, brouillons et dessins qui forment ce qui reste aujourd'hui de ce roman. Bien que les lecteurs trouvent toujours un certain plaisir à tourner délicatement les pages du *Lamiel* en Pléiade, ou à froisser impunément le *Lamiel* en Folio, l'édition de travail du roman est devenue celle de Victor Del Litto parue au Cercle du Bibliophile en 1971: seule elle donne tout ce qui existe du roman dans l'ordre où l'écrivit Stendhal.[1]

Cette édition présente une première version du roman, commencée le 2 octobre 1839, précédée et suivie de plans, qui raconte en entier la diégèse: l'adoption de Lamiel par les Hautemare, son engagement comme lectrice chez la duchesse de Miossens, sa rencontre avec le fils de la duchesse, Fédor, et sa fugue avec celui-ci à Rouen, toutefois après la perte de sa virginité comme cliente payante d'un villageois, Jean Berville. Ensuite, à Paris, après avoir passé quelques moments avec le comte d'Aubigné (également appelé le comte de Nerwinde), Lamiel trouve "le véritable amour" (Stendhal 1971, 159) dans les bras de Valbaire, un forçat bientôt condamné aux galères perpétuelles, mais qui s'évade, "assassine au hasard (comme Lacenaire), est condamné [de nouveau et] se tue" (162–63). Lamiel périt aussi dans une tentative de venger son amant.

122

Del Litto fait suivre cette histoire d'une deuxième version à laquelle Stendhal travailla de janvier 1840 à mars 1841. Cette fois, *Lamiel* commence par deux chapitres dans lesquels un narrateur homodiégétique explique ses liens avec les habitants de Carville, bourg où démarre l'action. Après cette entrée en matière, la narration se fait hétérodiégétique et parle non plus uniquement de Lamiel, mais aussi du docteur Sansfin, lequel n'était mentionné qu'accessoirement dans la première version. Le deuxième *Lamiel*, qui s'arrête sur les lectures faites en cachette par la jeune héroïne, est suivi de maints brouillons qui orientent encore davantage la narration vers Sansfin.

Depuis l'édition par ordre chronologique de Victor Del Litto, la critique a pu fournir différentes explications à l'inachèvement du roman. Certains faits sont indiscutables, comme nous les rappelle Anne-Marie Meininger: Stendhal ne finit aucun roman à Civitavecchia, où il était constamment en proie à l'ennui et, même une fois de retour à Paris en 1841, l'écrivain se sentait trop malade pour travailler de façon suivie; enfin, sa mort interrompit la rédaction d'une scène sur laquelle il n'était revenu que dix jours auparavant (Meininger 1983, 9–11). En plus de ces faits, Meininger avance l'hypothèse que ce qui aurait empêché Stendhal d'achever son roman, c'est le choc qui dut se produire en lui quand il prit conscience que le modèle de Lamiel, Mélanie Guilbert, une actrice et la seule femme avec qui il ait jamais vécu, était sans doute une lesbienne (23–29). "En Lamiel," d'après Meininger, "*résidaient à la fois le principe de la création première et celui de sa destruction*" (23; Meininger souligne). Cette hypothèse s'ajoute à celle de Gilbert Chaitin, qui a vu dans la création et aussi dans l'inachèvement de *Lamiel* le résultat des fantasmes d'Henri Beyle (173–74). L'aspect pédagogique de *Lamiel*, qui est fortement marqué,[2] m'a permis de tirer une autre conclusion: la première version du roman semble examiner la liberté de l'étudiante qu'était Lamiel dans une relation de pygmalionisme, tandis que le contrôle qu'exerce le professeur dans une telle relation est étudié dans la deuxième version. Ainsi, la nature du pygmalionisme, tout en fournissant le sujet du roman, produit de nécessité, par le pouvoir écrasant du professeur dans une telle relation, son inachèvement (Wahl 117–18). Plus récemment, Naomi Schor, qui voit dans le premier *Lamiel* un des grands textes féminocentriques du dix-neuvième siècle, estime qu'il est, par là même, une écriture qui renferme les principes de sa propre destruction, autre forme d'inachèvement, mais qui était inéluctable à l'époque réaliste. Enfin, dans un article intitulé

"Gender and Class in *Lamiel*," Lynn R. Wilkinson montre comment Lamiel représente l'altérité, la rencontre inquiétante avec la foule. Son exclusion progressive de la diégèse, qui s'effectue en la remplaçant par des personnages masculins, figure le rejet définitif de la classe menaçante par les détenteurs du pouvoir.

Toutes ces tentatives qui se proposent d'expliquer l'inachèvement du roman, si différentes soient-elles, ont ceci en commun: elles situent dans le principe même qui déclenche l'histoire les germes de son effondrement. Quelle que soit la cause ou la signification de cet inachèvement, il demeure que le jaillissement du récit et son tarissement semblent naître d'une même source. Il ne serait donc pas indifférent d'identifier et d'analyser ce principe vital, mais en même temps mortel, de l'écriture. Dans *Lamiel*, ce principe me semble être la terreur, thème qui est véhiculé tout au long de l'histoire par les motifs du feu et du sang. Ces motifs font et défont le roman, parfois séparément, quelquefois ensemble. Dans *Feu la cendre*, Jacques Derrida signale poétiquement le rôle tout ensemble destructeur et durable du feu, et insiste sur la position privilégiée de la cendre, ce reste du feu: "J'ai maintenant l'impression que le meilleur paradigme de la trace, . . . ce n'est pas, comme certains l'ont cru, la piste de chasse, le frayage, le sillon dans le sable, le sillage dans la mer, l'amour du pas pour son empreinte, mais la cendre . . ." (43). Vers la fin du même livre, Derrida note la parenté homophonique entre la trace du feu et le sang, en y ajoutant d'autres termes qui s'avèrent étrangement importants dans *Lamiel:* "sans, sens, sang, cent DRE" (75). Voyons maintenant de plus près le texte de *Lamiel* et essayons de dégager le travail à la fois constructeur et ravageur du feu et du sang.

D'un bout à l'autre de *Lamiel*, la force motrice de l'action est la terreur, présentée comme une des armes maniée par la classe dirigeante dans la lutte acharnée qu'elle mène contre le peuple. Le premier *Lamiel* s'ouvre à Carville sur la description d'une mission évangélique protégée par les nobles des alentours et où le prédicateur se grise "d'éloquence sur le diable toujours présent partout pour séduire les fidèles, . . . se transformant tantôt en jeune homme libéral arrivant de Paris, tantôt en vieux grognard de l'empire parlant gloire et Napoléon" (14–15). Les plans de la fin de cette première version mettent en évidence, par la présentation du forçat Valbaire, la contrepartie de la terreur politique des dirigeants. Le criminel explique: "Je fais la guerre à la société qui me fait la guerre. Je lis Corneille et Molière. J'ai trop d'éducation pour travailler de mes mains et gagner 3 francs par dix heures de travail" (159). Dans ces deux positions antagonistes encore qu'également terroristes, le feu joue le rôle principal. Dans la prédication du début, derrière l'autel de l'église, on allume des pétards pour figurer l'enfer, tandis qu'à la fin, Lamiel incendie le Palais de Justice.

Mais les pétards du début font plus qu'effrayer les fidèles. Leur explosion est à l'origine de l'adoption de Lamiel et ils donnent ainsi naissance au roman de celle-ci, qui est souvent appelée "fille du diable" (13, 392n24). Le rôle dans la fiction de ce pouvoir géniteur du feu est constamment souligné. Ainsi, Stendhal signale l'efficacité du stratagème des pétards détonnés pendant "l'affreuse description" (19) du prédicateur, qui "parlait comme un roman de Mme Radcliffe" (19), référence intertextuelle qui fait à l'instant même de *Lamiel* un roman noir où, lors de l'explosion, "une lumière rouge et infernale illumina tous les visages pâles de terreur" (20). Pour renchérir sur le rôle du feu dans la création fictive, Stendhal fait en sorte que le couple Hautemare, où le mari allume les pétards et connaît le stratagème, soit néanmoins les gens qui sont les plus affectés par l'explosion.

Comme on le sait, la vie de Lamiel et le roman devaient également finir par le feu: "Elle incendie le Palais de Justice pour venger Valbaire; on trouve des ossements à demi-calcinés dans les débris de l'incendie,—ce sont ceux de Lamiel" (163). Assurément, c'est bien là la fin des événements, d'autant plus que cette phrase ne figure même pas dans le texte du roman proprement dit mais dans un plan rédigé le 1er décembre 1839. Pourtant, il faut remarquer ici que tout n'est pas complètement fini: Lamiel est bien morte mais sa trace reste. Elle demeure pour être repérée ("on trouve") et identifiée ("ce sont ceux de Lamiel") par d'autres. L'incendie est donc une fin, mais une fin qui s'ouvrirait sur une identification et par là, sur une reprise de la biographie de Lamiel.

En effet, le feu reprend de plus belle dans la deuxième version de *Lamiel*, comme s'il renaissait de ses cendres. La scène des pétards est refaite mais, cette fois, le lien entre feu et fiction est encore plus évident. Voulant à tout prix maintenir l'illusion infernale créée par l'explosion, le clergé de Carville s'inquiète beaucoup de la découverte des pétards, dont on essaie désespérément de gommer toutes les traces. Et le sermon, ce conte diabolique, est repris dans le cimetière à côté de l'église par le curé local qui, malgré des "yeux enflammés," n'est pas habité par le "feu d[e l'] inspiration" (182). Lorsqu'il s'embrouille tout à fait, son sermon, qui n'est déjà que la trace du premier, s'éteint comme le fera le roman. Mais il reste encore dans le deuxième *Lamiel* d'autres cendres d'où s'élèvent des fictions. Chez la duchesse de Miossens les convives passent la soirée à tracer dans la cendre de l'âtre des initiales de femmes qui leur ont fait faire des sottises humiliantes. Le docteur Sansfin, après avoir fièrement écrit quatre initiales, "était si attentif à ses idées que rien n'était capable de le réveiller. . . . [I]l inventait les détails d'un roman par lui préparé à l'avance" (174, voir aussi 332–33). C'est encore un exemple du feu qui laisse ses traces, qui suscite par ses ravages des fictions.

Entre le début et la fin de *Lamiel,* le feu brûle à plusieurs reprises (par exemple, 69, 147, 150, 231, 288). De tous ces cas, il en est un particulièrement digne d'attention parce qu'il constitue en quelque sorte une mise en abyme du texte romanesque. Lors de la mission, pour faire la cour au curé Flamand,—notons le nom moitié ironique, moitié incendiaire—le docteur Sansfin feint de brûler ses oeuvres complètes de Voltaire. "Mais au moment de l'exécution," lit-on, "Sansfin brûla dix volumes bien reliés et sauva tout son Voltaire, à l'exception du premier volume, qu'il remplaça à Paris moyennnant vingt francs" (42). Il serait aisé de penser que, comme les oeuvres de Voltaire, le roman de Stendhal s'incinère dans les flammes des bien-pensants. En réalité, il est sain et sauf. Comme le Voltaire, le premier volume est remplacé et il n'y a que le simulacre de sa destruction par le feu.

Les actions de Lamiel lui sont dictées par le désir qu'elle a de connaître l'amour. C'est au cours de sa recherche de la grande passion que le sang coule dans le roman. Dans la première version de l'histoire, lorsque Lamiel est dépucelée "sans transport, sans amour" (67) par Jean Berville, Stendhal note simplement entre parenthèses: "(Elle essuya le sang et songea un peu à la douleur)" (68). L'absence de tendresse est d'autant plus frappante que l'auteur renvoie le fait de nettoyer le sang à un espace quasiment effacé, à une parenthèse. Mais le sang continue à couler car une nouvelle version de cet incident clôt la deuxième rédaction du roman. Là, Sansfin, dans un accès de jalousie, poignarde le jeune homme, devenu un certain Fabien. Celui-ci ne survit à l'attaque que par "un léger mouvement de côté" (382) et à cause du "luxe d'empoi [sic]" utilisé dans "le repassage admirable" (383) de sa chemise. Le "signe de [la] violence," la "chemise sanglante," (383) s'étale, telle un drap de nouveaux mariés, à la fin du récit, dont le dernier mot est d'ailleurs "écorchure" (385).

Le sang est également présent dans le paratexte de *Lamiel*. Stendhal, malade comme on sait, mentionne, dans des notes qui suivent la deuxième version du roman, les saignées qu'il a dû subir. Le 16 mars [1841], il écrit le "Caractère de Mme de Myossens" "after sangsues" (365) et le lendemain, dans un plan daté "Saignée du 17 mars [1841]," il remarque: "Quoique je sois l'homme du monde le plus incapable d'imiter quand je le voudrais, j'écris ici pour me comprendre moi-même, en peu de mots les idées qui me sont venues la tête libre après la saignée" (370–71). La saignée, dont le propre est de rendre visible le sang mais aussi de l'absorber, facilite le rappel et l'expression écrite des idées habituellement fugaces de l'auteur. Ainsi, des traces de sang, comme des traces de feu, disparaissent et apparaissent, font et défont la diégèse.

Nous venons de voir brièvement comment les scènes de feu et de sang se relayent dans *Lamiel*. Le feu de la mission déclenche l'action du roman, dont la première version se termine par l'incendie du palais de justice. Ses débris semblent s'enflammer de nouveau dans la reprise de la scène des pétards et dans celle des invités autour du foyer. Le sang, en revanche, disparaît aussitôt qu'il coule dans le premier texte pour réapparaître ensuite, tache ineffaçable, à la fin du second *Lamiel*. Il pourrait donc s'établir facilement dans les deux versions du roman un schéma où alternent feu et sang. Cette alternance souligne un rapport de cause à effet entre ces deux motifs: l'écoulement du sang est l'effet du feu, comme on le sait bien. L'alternance met en relief la similarité de but existant entre ces images, lesquelles servent toutes à susciter et à étaler des fictions. En effet, la parenté entre ces deux motifs de *Lamiel* est d'autant plus forte qu'elle indique l'importance de personnages qui font du feu pour tuer, c'est-à-dire de chasseurs. Le feu et le sang, la cause et l'effet, sont des métonymies du chasseur, autre image fondamentale du roman. Ces chasseurs sont au nombre de deux et ils chassent ou, comme le feu et le sang, ils composent et décomposent l'héroïne et la fiction.

Dans la deuxième version du roman, le narrateur explique sa présence chez la duchesse en disant que "la chasse [est] superbe dans ce domaine et fort bien gardée" (172). Ce notaire, dont "un beau coup de fusil consol[e] de tout" (172), est également présenté comme quelqu'un qui a une affinité avec la fiction. Sa "belle voix" (178) lui vaut une offre d'emploi dans la troupe des

missionnaires; et il considère ainsi brièvement "le plaisir vif
[d']improviser en chaire" (178). Après quelques années d'une vie
autrement mouvementée, il revient chasser à Carville, où il est
saisi par la fantaisie d'écrire les aventures de Lamiel "afin de
devenir homme de lettres" (193). Curieusement, immédiatement
après, il disparaît en clamant "Ainsi, ô lecteur bénévole, adieu;
vous n'entendrez plus parler de moi" (193). Effectivement, on
n'entend plus rien dire du narrateur; il disparaît, comme le feu
et le sang. Comme eux, pourtant, il laisse des traces. On les
repère dans d'autres interpellations directes ou indirectes au lecteur (220–21, 233, 265), ce qui indique, toujours d'une façon
métonymique, son existence. Ainsi, ce chasseur de gibier et d'histoires attire l'attention sur la composition et la décomposition
de la fiction.

Le deuxième chasseur, le docteur Sansfin, ne s'intéresse nulle-
ment au gibier: il est, lui, chasseur d'êtres humains. Ce médecin
bossu ne sort jamais sans fusil pour pouvoir terroriser les imper-
tinents qui se permettraient des remarques déplaisantes sur sa
disgrâce physique. Lorsqu'il commence à traquer Lamiel, pourtant, son mobile n'est plus l'autodéfense; il cherche plutôt à exer-
cer son emprise sur l'esprit de la jeune fille. Dans une des scènes
capitales du roman, Sansfin s'assure la complicité de Lamiel en
la faisant participer à ce qui ressemble à une messe noire
(Berthier 53): "Je veux, [explique] Sansfin [à Lamiel] en riant,
que vous consentiez à un meurtre horrible: tous les huit jours,
je vous apporterais dans la poche *de ma veste de chasse* de Staub
(le tailleur à la mode) un oiseau vivant. Je lui couperai la tête.
Vous verserez le sang sur une petite éponge que vous placerez
dans votre bouche" (245–46; c'est moi qui souligne). Cette céré-
monie digne d'un prêtre satanique, ce stratagème qui fait pâlir
le feu des pétards et rejaillir le sang occulté, permet au docteur
d'entretenir tout seul Lamiel, qui, en la présence des tiers, feint
la maladie en crachant le sang. La force du chasseur diabolique
est d'autant plus remarquable ici qu'on ne peut s'empêcher de
comparer les liens par lesquels il entrave Lamiel avec la liberté
que lui laisse le garde-chasse Lairel, dont le nom se rapproche
curieusement de celui de l'héroïne. Ce garde-chasse complice
procure à l'héroïne un faux passeport lui donnant la possibilité
de s'éloigner de ses parents adoptifs. Quelle différence avec le
docteur Sansfin, qui réussit à immobiliser Lamiel pour pouvoir
lui parler sans distractions! Les conversations du docteur et de
la jeune fille tournent autour de la manière de raisonner: Sansfin
veut que Lamiel écrive dans son livre d'Heures sa "règle du

lierre" (247), moyen de se débarasser des idées reçues, et donc aussi un moyen de faire concurrence aux dogmes de l'église inscrits dans le même livre. La terreur qu'inspirent ces procédés chez la jeune fille la rend incapable de choisir définitivement entre la morale de Sansfin et celle, plus douce mais certes moins logique, de l'abbé Clément. A cause de cette hésitation, la chasse à l'esprit de Lamiel entreprise par Sansfin reste en suspens. Une fois de plus, le chasseur figure l'invention et la dissolution, cette fois encore plus fortement liées à la terreur.

Le gibier que poursuit le narrateur et l'oiseau décapité par Sansfin connaissent aussi des avatars qui marquent le texte. Plusieurs notes marginales de Stendhal, lui-même chasseur enthousiaste, parlent de ses succès à la chasse (201, 202, 324, 363), remarques qui font que le paratexte ici encore souligne l'importance des oiseaux dans le texte, tout en mettant en relief la fictionnalité de ceux-ci. A côté de certaines notes, il y a aussi des dessins de têtes d'oiseaux (18, 48, 268, 317), qu'on dirait être ceux que Sansfin avait décapités, comme si le processus de destruction du texte était figurativement restaurée par le paratexte. La première tête d'oiseau, qui est relativement de bonne taille et paraît à la première page de la version initiale (17), est encore plus intéressante. Stendhal écrit dans son 'franglais' habituel: "Dicté to [le dessin de tête d'oiseau]." Il se peut bien que le dessin représente le nom du copiste, Laigle peut-être (Meininger 246). Quoi qu'il en soit, il reste que la dictée du roman se fait, du moins en apparence, à la victime innocente de la chasse terroriste, l'oiseau. Puisque l'oiseau est en définitive le destinataire du texte comme matérialité, il revit par cette relation de dicter ou de raconter l'histoire. Lui aussi, comme le chasseur et comme ses métonymies, le feu et le sang, sert à faire, à défaire et à refaire le roman. Dans tous ces va-et-vient au sein de la terreur, il n'est donc pas surprenant que ce texte, tel un phénix qui renaît de ses cendres, soit, comme un de ses personnages principaux, sans fin (Sansfin).

University of Calgary

NOTES

1. Del Litto, préface, in Stendhal 1971, xviii. Pour de plus amples explications sur ce que contient cette édition, voir l'article de Hemmings.

2. Voir Simons, qui appelle *Lamiel* "la véritable réponse à Rousseau, le traité de l'éducation naturelle selon Stendhal" (272) et Pizzorusso (135–38).

9

Balzac at the Crossroads: The Emplotment of Terror in *Une ténébreuse affaire*

OWEN HEATHCOTE

I

THE aim of this paper is to examine the themes of terror, violence and death in *Une ténébreuse affaire*. The aim is to ask whether the novel can be seen as violent or non-violent, and, if violent, whether the violence is redeemed through suffering, expiation, punishment, or narration itself. In asking these questions, the paper will, therefore, address the issue of the relationship between violence and representation: to what extent is it possible for the representation of violence to critique that violence, or are such representations necessarily in complicity with the violence described?[1]

Une ténébreuse affaire is a singularly appropriate text for this task. The events of the narrative take place in the aftermath of the French Revolution and Terror, which are thus close enough to be recalled in their full horror, yet they are also becoming remote enough to be superseded by the pace of change. As Balzac himself observes towards the beginning of the novel: "The general need for peace and tranquility that everyone experienced after violent commotions engendered a complete forgetting of the most serious previous events. History was quickly growing old, constantly aged by new and intense interests" (Balzac 1976–81, 8:509). From the outset, then, *Une ténébreuse affaire* alludes to the complex relationship between both violence and history and violence and narrative. At the end of the novel Henri de Marsay also reflects on this aspect of the novel's agenda. Thus while noting that "The thing happened more than thirty years ago; it is as old as the death of Henri IV," he also claims that the affair illuminates "a famous passage in modern annals" (8:688). *Une ténébreuse affaire* is, therefore, a highly self-conscious historical narrative, resurrecting violence in terms which efface that violence but whose very act of effacement is also violent. A first section of this paper will accordingly examine the relation between violence and historical and narrative time, confronting the paradox that the very aging and death of violence is also a renewal of the violence of death.

The impact of recent violence and the fear of its renewal are also a function of the narrative setting. The setting is the former estate of the related aristocratic Simeuse/Cinq-Cygne families, which has been clandestinely purchased for a derisory sum by a rising star of post-revolutionary regimes, Malin de Gondreville. The setting is, therefore, a constant reminder of the violence wrought on the aristocracy and the émigrés, in terms of dislocation, uprooting, and the removal of property. As Baptiste-Marrey writes of the novel: "the only reality, the true *revolution* of those years, on which we still live, is the change in ownership of Gondreville" (Baptiste-Marrey 303). Since the marquis and marquise de Simeuse were also recently executed in nearby Troyes, the setting is a reminder that the violence of Revolution and Terror was at least as severe in provincial France as in Paris, particularly as Michu, former bailiff of the Simeuse, together with his deceased father-in-law, were active in the local Jacobin clubs and tribunals. Violence also pervades the estate's internal spaces: Michu lives in what was once a *pavillon de chasse* and one of its forests, Nodesme, hides a former monk's cell which serves as a refuge for pursued aristocrats and as a prison for the abducted Malin. A second section of this paper will, therefore, examine the geographical setting of Une ténébreuse affaire to see to what extent it endorses and "naturalizes" the violence described.

One of the main characteristics of the French Revolution was, according to Lynn Hunt, the execution of the "bad" father—and the "bad" mother—and their replacement by the "band of brothers" (Hunt 1992, 53–88). It is interesting, therefore, that fathers tend to be absent, debilitated or killed in Une ténébreuse affaire, whether in history or in the present. In history, the absence of a father stimulated five Cinq-Cygne daughters to defend their castle in a "fait d'armes" which gave the family renown and enabled the name Cinq-Cygne to pass through the female line (8:534; see Taylor 8). In the present, the marquis de Cinq-Cygne has been executed, and the aging aristocratic fathers such as the marquis de Chargeboeuf and even M. d'Hauteserre are thought to be compromised by the new regime, at least according to the recent, more militant generation, the d'Hauteserre brothers, the Simeuse twins, and their Charlotte Corday-style cousin, Laurence de Cinq-Cygne. Une ténébreuse affaire can, therefore, be seen to offer an interesting variant on Hunt's "family romance of the revolution." Given the presence of more active replacement "fathers," from the police to the politicians and to Napoleon, the novel also perhaps prepares for a rehabilitation of the father which, for Hunt, characterizes the Napoleonic period (see Hunt 151–91). It can be seen that gender issues permeate the representation of violence which, by relating to the presentation of different generations, either with or without fathers, also relate to violence and history. Given the different relationship these generations have to emigration and property, with the older generation cultivating their reduced lands and the younger exiled from them, the representation of violence, history, gender, and geography are shown to be equally inseparable.

A final section to this paper will bring these various strands together in order to see whether the narrativization of violence in time, location, and gender enables that violence to be explained, owned, or redeemed. The narrative is recounted at a considerable distance, from the perspective of the Paris of 1833, when Henri de Marsay, the then Prime Minister, explains to an elite coterie why Laurence de Cinq-Cygne still feels so violently towards Malin de Gondreville that his mere presence at their gathering could jeopardize a marriage between her daughter, Berthe, and the son of their host, Georges de Maufrigneuse. The timing and placing of this explanation emphasizes both the remoteness and yet the durability of the violence described: the direct and indirect violence suffered by Laurence from Malin is so obscure and so distant that it has to be explained, even to her friends. At the same time, the violence is still so deeply felt by Laurence that the affront and the loss will never be erased. The act of narration thus epitomizes the ambivalence of Une ténébreuse affaire towards violence—narration both reawakens a sense of abuse or loss and yet also confirms the loss of that sense of loss. A final section of this paper will, therefore, examine the ambivalences of the narrativization of violence, or of what would now be called its mediatization: does that mediatization serve the violent or the violated? Or is it, in a sense, neutral? And is the privileging of the representation of violence in this paper itself a distortion and a misrepresentation of Une ténébreuse affaire?

II
TIME AND HISTORY

One of the most important sources of violence in Une ténébreuse affaire is undoubtedly the French Revolution and the

Terror. This is hardly surprising. As Claudie Bernard writes in her study of "le chouan romanesque": "Origin of our contemporary in the broad sense, the Revolution also founds our national consciousness" (Bernard 1989, 48). The Revolution, and in particular the guillotine, mark a division between what becomes the past and a new vision of present and future. As again Bernard writes: "Another privileged figure, metaphor and metonymy of the revolutionary rupture: the guillotine blade. Its bloody stroke also cleaves History and the social body while cutting the biological body: it precisely delimits the ancien and nouveau régimes, the country and its periphery, the good citizens and the bad" (Bernard 50). The revolutionary period thus acquires the status of a violent foundationalist moment which seals the past and inaugurates a new future. This future is embodied, as Hunt has shown, in new visions of time, space and gender. For Hunt, the "profound revolution in the notion of political time" was accompanied by a transformation of the family and by "a different model of the location of the sacred" (Hunt 198). The narrative of the Revolution combines with the revolutionary narrative in a fusion of history and story to generate violent, foundationalist myth.[2]

There is some evidence that Une ténébreuse affaire can be seen as one such myth. Not least among this evidence is the retrospective coherence given to the narrative by Henri de Marsay. If Balzac changed the position of this explanation from that of introduction to conclusion of Une ténébreuse affaire (8:1472–78), the change has the effect of making that coherence the culmination rather than the prolegomenon to the novel. However mysterious Une ténébreuse affaire, there is some final emphasis on light. Darkness is followed by revelation, the profane by a glimpse of at least secular salvation. The sacred may indeed be relocated: it may be relocated in the explanatory insights and almost superhuman power of one of Balzac's most prestigious narrators, Henri de Marsay, whose nearness to his own death gives his words the almost posthumous conviction of an apocalyptic "memoir from beyond the grave": "De Marsay, like lamps which are close to going out, was shining with a final brillance" (8:686). If the executed Simeuse parents leave Laurence a reliquary of locks of hair and final letters, de Marsay bequeathes to posterity and to history Une ténébreuse affaire. The power of the foundationalist narrative is established.

This coherence and this power also apply to the linking of the two plots—the royalist counterrevolutionary plot and the abduction plot against Malin de Gondreville. Here again Balzac moves

time, placing the Gondreville plot in 1806, some six years after
the Clément de Ris plot of 1800 on which it was based.[3] The
Gondreville plot can thereby be made to follow the royalist plot
of Cadoudal and be linked to it by a seeming overlap of characters, from Michu to Laurence and Fouché.[4] The royalist plot is
made into a kind of curtain-raiser to the abduction plot, justifying the violence of both. The violence is made to spread both
from the Jacobin Michu forwards to the counterrevolutionary
Michu and sideways between the "naturally" savage bailiff and
the "naturally" insurgent aristocrats. The violence of both Michu
and aristocrats is thereby represented as fanning outwards and
forwards from its revolutionary beginnings, inflaming all levels
of the population from commoners to courtiers and all political
persuasions from Jacobin to royalist. The choice of target of violence is, therefore, incidental. What matters is mayhem and murder; what motivates is plotting against a new establishment
which also increasingly looks like a replica of the old, with corruption, privilege, patronage, and power simply changing sides
but not in nature. If, as Janet Beizer has argued, Balzac's plots
are "narrative constructs which can never be purged of connotations of destruction" (Beizer 2), it is at least partly because the
first revolutionary plot is the master-plot of them all. If Laurence
takes as her role-model Charlotte Corday (8:535) it is partly because the revolutionary moment is a myth and a paradigm as
well as a movement to be reversed. Even for the militant aristocrat
the Revolution is a foundationalist fiction which Une ténébreuse
affaire charts with a gruesome grandeur, epitomized by the fear-
some Michu whose features forecast further terror and whose
neck invites—and receives—"the blade of Law" (8:503).

Such is the fascination with Michu and with his death-
prophesying features that his actual fate seems overdetermined
by presentiments, fear, and terror. He almost embodies what Bernard has called "the overinvestment of the Revolution" (Bernard
46). Michu is so explicitly linked to past and future violence that
he draws attention to the dangerous fascination and contagious
power of foundationalist violence. Does Une ténébreuse affaire
not only exploit but also question this fascination? Are the internal and retrospective coherences of the novel and the ensuing
coherence of its violence also questioned, problematized, and
fractured, as André Vanoncini suggests happens in this period
(Vanoncini 17, 27, 48)? Or does Balzac allow history to dissolve
into a continuum of violence which Henri de Marsay uncovers

in a demonstration of his own authority, for his and his audience's pleasure?

There is evidence in Une ténébreuse affaire that the myth of foundationalist violence is by no means monolithic. For the violence of the novel, although in some senses foundationalist, is by no means isolated, unique, or attributable to a single, sacrificial source. On the contrary, in the history of the families of the Simeuse/Cinq-Cygne, the Revolution may mark a "high-point" of violent reprisals and counterreprisals, but it is only one of several such milestones of the families' long career throughout history. It is clear that from the "vieux frondeur" marquis de Cinq-Cygne (8:504) through to the combative Cinq-Cygne sisters and through to Laurence's brother, "dead before Mayence" (8:508), violence is the watchword of these families. Hence their mottoes, "To die singing" (8:534) and "Here I die!" (8:683) which are actually declaimed by the Simeuse twins as they perish in battle. Violence is, therefore, integral to the family tradition, for both sexes. Counterrevolutionary plots are but one of a series of violent acts either committed by them or against them. Ultimately it matters little whether they fight against or for a King, against or for an Emperor. The less prestigious, elderly relatives, the d'Hauteserre and the Chargeboeuf, are sidelined: for the younger generation as for their ancestors throughout history, violence is the norm. As Arlette Michel concludes after an analysis of Laurence: "The distinctive feature of nobility is to die" (Michel 70).

Although, then, the foundationalist violence of the French Revolution and Terror by no means monopolizes Une ténébreuse affaire, the demotion of a specific Revolution and a specific Terror does not result in a more general demotion of violence. On the contrary, the violence of the Revolution is demoted by being incorporated into a greater and wider pattern of violence extending back to the Fronde and forward to the Napoleonic wars. This incorporation means that, however exceptional, the Revolution is simply one of a series of violent events in a history where violence becomes both the exception and the norm. History is a series of violent exceptions and it is the task of the novel to expose this series, turning it into a chain where the exception becomes the rule. Whether this particular emplotment of history is true or not matters little. It may be the police who construct connections which do not exist, as with the counterrevolutionary and abduction plots. Or it may be Henri de Marsay making connections, attributing responsibility to Fouché. Or it may be Balzac himself, turning "family plots" into a "family romance of the revolution." For it does not matter finally whether the serial violence constructed in Une ténébreuse affaire is imagined or real. It does not need the "clandestine conductor," whether Fouché, Napoleon, de Marsay, or Balzac, to demonize the violence, for the violence is devastating whether it is explicable or inexplicable. For the mere juxtaposition of the explicable or inexplicable violences of history combines the violence of foundationalist fiction with the violence of the arbitrary series and thereby converts these two violences into the story that is Une ténébreuse affaire. Violence has become serial, whether the repetitions make sense or not, and Une ténébreuse affaire exploits that seriality to the full by making the violence seem comprehensible and yet arbitrary. It is this combination of a violence which is both plausible and aberrant, foundationalist and serial, which makes Une ténébreuse affaire such a disturbing text. This combination may account for Françoise Taylor's comment that "a great fear haunts the unconscious of the text."[5] For the "unconscious" of Une ténébreuse affaire is the all-pervasive presence and power of violence.

III
SETTING AND TOPOGRAPHY

The setting and the topography of a Balzac novel is almost invariably a subject worthy of study and Une ténébreuse affaire is no exception. As Arlette Michel writes in her study of Laurence de Cinq-Cygne: "A study of the spatio-temporal structures of the narrative would be fascinating" (Michel 53). One of the interesting features of the Gondreville estate is that it is a thoroughfare for journeys, whether these journeys are the comings and goings of local farmers such as Violette and Beauvisage, or the rather more sudden and mysterious visits of Malin to his new property, or the even more sinister arrival of the Paris police, Corentin and Peyrade, and their escort of gendarmes and soldiers. All these characters enter and exit as on the stage of a theatre, the "magnifique théâtre" of Gondreville (8:503), coming in "stage-left" and exiting "stage-right," and always, it seems, en route for another destination. The setting therefore represents a physical and emotional crossroads, between different routes represented by different generations, different political allegiances, different careers, and even different destinies, such as the destiny of life or of death.

The most frequent travellers are, of course, the younger generation of d'Hauteserre, Simeuse and Cinq-Cygne, who career across the French and European stages to further the royalist cause. This mobility both derives from, and feeds, a seemingly inexhaustible fund of restless energy, typified by Laurence who, as again Michel points out, is first and foremost "a horsewoman and we see her in her drawing room or her bedroom only between two 'expeditions'" (Michel 53). This mobility has, like the aforementioned violence, characterized the family over generations, from the "marquis frondeur" to his descendant, the sailor-marquis, and to the marquis who built the Gondreville estate "just to have a wonderful hunting ground" (8:504). The raison d'être of the estate has thus traditionally been not only as a stage for ceaseless movement but a movement associated with death. As Max Andréoli has pointed out, Une ténébreuse affaire is marked by "the ever-present motif of hunting" (Andréoli 108). The estate is designed as an arena for killing and for killing as sport, as pleasure, as entertainment. At Gondreville killing is, therefore, normalized and naturalized, leading seamlessly to "the man hunt" which is, for the police, "superior to the other hunt in the same proportion as the distance that exists between men and animals" (8:579). For the police—and for Michu—tracking down men is also a pleasure. At Gondreville, killing can be fun.

At the time of the main events of the narrative of Une ténébreuse affaire the use of the estate has become twofold. On the one hand it is being exploited by Malin as a basis for increasing his wealth and his influence throughout the region, for making himself into "the King of Aube" (8:613). It is also where he comes to have secret conferences with his advisors and hide the compromising documents, later burnt, publicizing the anticipated downfall of Napoleon. On the other hand, the estate is also the theatre for the real or supposed hunting parties of the Simeuse/d'Hauteserre/Cinq-Cygne after the release of the four aristocrats. Their use of the land is now illegal, but, as Michu argues: "it is difficult, in two months, to get out of the habit of things that one has been doing for two centuries" (8:616). Here again, violence and violations combine across both time and space; time and space converge to provide recurrent sites or theatres of violence.

The multiple uses of the estate are violent in other, perhaps less obvious, ways. If the "original" purpose of the estate, hunting, was already a distortion—or, possibly, the fulfilment—of nature, the usurpation of that land by Malin and its subsequent usurpation by the younger nobles constitute further violations, themselves compounded by the clandestinity of Malin and by the fact that the current hunting parties are cover-ups for counterrevolution. The land has witnessed an accumulation of usurpations, distortions, and perversions which contrast with the patient, constructive agricultural and social re-building by the older d'Hauteserre. But that is outside the Gondreville estate. For the "quasi-royal land" of Gondreville (8:504), "the most beautiful in the department of Aube" (8:503), is, despite its external impressiveness, a site of violence, abduction, and planned murder. It seems as if it could be the setting for a *Mansfield Park*, a kind of nineteenth-century version of Central Park, that "repository of nature in the heart of the city" and "antidote to urban over-civilization" (Seltzer 110). However, Gondreville is impregnated with the forbidding presence of Michu and his rifle-carbine. It is there where Corentin and Peyrade first appear (8:513) and where François Michu unhorses and wounds the pursuing brigadier (8:588). Gondreville, like Central Park, is a real if unexpected site of danger, violence, and "poorly-disguised terror" (8:502). Its soft earth betrays horses' hoofprints and its crossroads repeat "the ramifications of the plot" (8:541). Although physically as unlike the French Wild West of *Les Chouans,* so ably analyzed in the previously cited studies by Claudie Bernard and André Vanoncini, as it is unlike the dangerous urban Paris of the *Treize,* Gondreville is as violent as either. Its thoroughfares, forests, and crossroads are as terrifying as the ensnaring hedgerows and precipitous corniches of the Brittany of the Chouans and as the city of the "Dévorants" and the "buccaneers in yellow gloves."

Within the crossroads that is the whole of the Gondreville estate there are two particular, more obvious sets of crossroads, the "rond-point" dominated by Michu's impressive residence, former "hunting lodge," and the now disused intersection in the forest of Nodesme, the site of the monks' cell which houses first the four fleeing nobles and then the abducted Malin de Gondreville. The two intersections both concentrate and compound the violence already described, in two different but complementary ways. For while the "rond-point" inhabited by Michu seems, like the estate, to represent leisured and luxurious living, its very openness exposes its residents to the intrusive eyes of passing local farmers, spying servants, and professional spies and police. The horizontal openness of Michu's "rond-point" is as perilous as the vista indicated by Napoleon to Laurence on the eve of the battle of Jena (8:681). Both sites, whether "magnifique théâtre" or plateau, presage the massacre of innocents, whether one in the case of Michu, or thirty thousand in the case of Jena. Horizontal crossroads and vistas enable assailants to take aim and beseiged to foresee death.

These comments about horizontality relate to another constant in Balzac's works, to what Catherine Nesci, after Foucault (and Bachelard), has called "the 'metaphysics of depth'" (Nesci 39). As she also writes: "By constantly relating a surface to a depth, like Lavater, Balzac opens up a space of internal laws" (Nesci 57). For in Une ténébreuse affaire violence by exposure is matched by the violence of concealment and burial, notably in the underground cell at Nodesme, also at a crossroads of "[the] five principal roads of the forest, several of which were obliterated" (8:564). This effacement and disguise of roads and monastery parallels the other disguises of the novel, from the masks worn by Malin's abductors to the clandestinity of plots and counterplots masquerading as "hunts."[6] The cell itself is doubly if not triply deceptive since it is discovered where Michu "felt the ground ring hollow," is hidden under an "artificial rock" and is only seemingly near "a lost fountain" (8:565). The cell at Nodesme is, therefore, disguise folded on disguise—and at the centre of that disguise is a hollow. Although, then, Françoise Taylor sees Nodesme as the lost "origin," center, and sacred of Une ténébreuse affaire (Taylor 16), that origin, center and sacred seem, from time immemorial, always already lost. The center is a hollow and the tomb is empty. The use of the cell for both nobles and Malin, for both protection and imprisonment shows that the cell is a mere function,[7] an empty sign, and, with its darkness, inaccessiblity and resemblance to a tomb, a particular kind of emptiness—the emptiness which is death. With its surrounding water it is almost an island, and thus reminiscent of those other islands of burial in the Comédie humaine, from the island where Raphaël de Valentin's mother is buried to the island contemplated by Véronique Graslin, which conceals the money stolen by the guillotined Tascheron.[8] In Les Chouans le château de la Vivetière is also surrounded by "two deep ponds" and, appropriately, given the massacre to follow, strikes Marie de Verneuil with "the funereal physiognomy of this tableau" (8:1026, 1027).

It follows that Une ténébreuse affaire is a tale of two centers, both of which open outwards or inwards to violence and death. For although both centers are geographically different they also share certain features. The "rond-point" of Michu is not only open but at the center of "two horse shoes," an inner "magnificent half-moon" formed by elm-planted embankments and an outer crescent framed by "clumps of exotic trees" (8:505). His pavillon thus stands at the center of three concentric circles— "rond-point" and layered crescents—and is therefore not only visible but carefully enclosed.[9] The center that is Nodesme is not only enclosed, but, as Taylor has remarked, increasingly public as the narrative progresses, invaded first by Michu, then by nobles, Malin, and police (Taylor 16). The two centers do, therefore, complement one another, with Nodesme acting as a kind of ghostly presence of threat and death beneath or beyond the "rond-point," living, or dying, "spectrally," like the shadow in the daguerreotype or atmospheric ideas in *Le cousin Pons* (7:587). The violence that overshadows the light, open surface of the "rond-point" seems to be recharged in the dark recesses of Nodesme. For Nodesme is both temporal and geographical ancestor to the violent pathways and crossroads of *Une ténébreuse affaire*, endowing the narrative with a violence and a terror which seem infinitely extensible through space and time, and underlying even the sacred itself. For if, as Taylor argues, in Nodesme "the sacred still pulses beneath the profane" (Taylor 16), the profane also rests beneath and beyond the sacred. Or perhaps, in time and space, at a final crossroad, the violences of sacred and profane are merging in another *ténébreuse affaire*.[10]

IV
SEXUALITY AND GENDER

As Lynn Hunt has shown, the execution of the father and his replacement by the "band of brothers" was the hallmark of the French revolutionary scenario (Hunt 53–88). According to Janet Beizer, one of the main concerns of the Balzac narrative, as indeed of many nineteenth-century novels, is "the father's death knell." As she writes of the detective or courtroom plot, which would include *Une ténébreuse affaire:* "what is on trial in these fictions is patriarchy itself" (Beizer 182, 183). *Une ténébreuse affaire* thus offers an interesting variant on these family plots or family romances, which repeat, regret, and yet fail to redeem the debility, demise, or deposition of the father. For, as noted above, *Une ténébreuse affaire* presents a number of absent or weakened fathers. As Françoise Taylor points out, the Cinq-Cygne daughters' defense of their castle, which marks "the founding myth of the Cinq-Cygne branch," occurs "in the absence of their father" (Taylor 8). M. d'Hauteserre and the marquis de Chargeboeuf also have a relatively low profile. Although, unlike his brother and the Simeuse twins, Adrien d'Hauteserre manages to return, wounded, from the Napoleonic wars, he later dies "in the arms of Laurence, of his father, of his mother, and of his children who adored him" (8:684). It is, therefore, left to Laurence to perpetuate the family name, to bring up her children, Berthe and Paul, and to live on into the *Monarchie de Juillet*. And to be the main character for de Marsay and Balzac in *Une ténébreuse affaire*. In Taylor's words: "Widowhood is a vocation for the Cinq-Cygne women" (Taylor 14).

A closer consideration of the novel does, however, suggest that the debility of some of these fathers is more apparent than real. M. d'Hauteserre and the marquis de Chargeboeuf are both slowly and painstakingly reconstructing their families' fortunes in terms of property and personal and political security: "that painful and slow restoration of things delighted M. and Mme d'Hauteserre" (8:547). The disinterment of family heirlooms and the extension of their farms signal a political awareness and an entrepreneurial energy which Benassis, Mme de Mortsauf, and Véronique Graslin would appreciate. They also turn the negative associations of horizontal spaces into a positive expansion of territory and reverse the trend towards burial and death. The marquis de Chargeboeuf offers practical advice and, even when it is disregarded, he supports his relatives throughout their trial and escorts Laurence to that other, more potent father, Napoleon, at Jena. The novel is, moreover, studded with other, substitute fathers, from the police who, according to Beizer, "are so many avatars of the father" (Beizer 183), to political masters such as Talleyrand and Henri de Marsay, and the supremos that are Napoleon and Louis XVIII. As Hunt argues, Napoleon ushers in a rehabilitation of father and family (Hunt 151–91), and Louis XVIII's policy of "union and forgetting" strives at a national level to achieve what, on a smaller scale, is the aim of the d'Hauteserre and Chargeboeuf.[11] If Louis omits to tell Laurence of his dealings with Malin, it is because he, like the fathers of her family, is seeking to purge the national plot of its "connotations of destruction" (Beizer 2).

Unlike the older and wiser males of her family, Laurence has been accused of non-cooperation, of anachronism, and misplaced idealism. As Arlette Michel writes: "Laurence rejects history" (Michel 64). For Max Andréoli, "Laurence survived like the debris of a very ancient time" (Andréoli 123). However, at least she does survive to promote her children's future, notably the marriage of her daughter, Berthe, to Georges de Maufrigneuse. In *L'envers de l'histoire contemporaine* she is, moreover,

"one of the leading aristocratic lights" (8:254), and in *Le député
d'Arcis* a force to be reckoned with at personal and political
levels. She will never permit her son to marry a Beauvisage and
she is likely to live long enough to prevent it, given "the health
of that woman still strong and almost beautiful at age sixty"
(8:757). With her energy, charisma, and likely longevity, Laurence
can afford to ignore history. She will outlive it. Not only through
herself, but through her daughter and later generations of Cinq-
Cygne women who will transmit, like their illustrious forbears,
their name and their vigor to posterity. If her older male relatives
can reverse the negative impact of horizontal spaces, she can
resist the threat posed by vertical space, by depth and burial,
represented by the deathly Nodesme. For Laurence has a power
which goes as deep as Nodesme, since "that sensitivity lay, in
her, like a treasure hidden at an infinite depth beneath a block
of granite" (8:588). Unlike Marthe Michu, who refuses to identify
with the statue of Liberty (8:507, 533), Laurence is not afraid of
either moral or historical petrification. That is her strength and
her survival. Whereas the males of the narrative counter violence
by proliferation, by splitting and doubling in a kind of lateral,
synchronic generation, Laurence will counter that violence by a
kind of diachronic vigor, by outliving successive generations
either in herself or in Berthe. The success of the males resembles
"la ramification du complot" and the open spaces of the "rond-
point." The success of Laurence extends inwards towards her
own, deeper resources. By thus both imitating and yet countering
the violences to which they are exposed, the survival of the characters at both kinds of crossroad is assured. Laurence survives
the threat of burial at Nodesme or Notre-Dame,[12] and even Michu
of the "rond-point" survives as a portrait in Laurence's salon and
through his son, François, whom Laurence promotes in *Le député d'Arcis*. Thus both fathers and mothers succeed, in their
different but complementary ways, to thwart the violence emplotted into time, space, and sexuality. They combine to ensure
that new generations survive to confront other sets of crossroads
such as *Le député d'Arcis* and the wider, further world of the
Comédie humaine.

V
VIOLENCE, EXPIATION, AND RETRIBUTION

It is apparent from the above that time and space combine to
make violence as immemorial as it is ubiquitous. It is also evi-

dent that mothers and fathers combine over time and space to engender a violence which is both widespread and durable: their very resistance to violence bears witness to its power and theirs. Each of the main characters is a temporary or permanent focus of violence, a crossroads through which violence passes. The longer a character survives, therefore, the more he or she bears witness to that violence. Laurence de Cinq-Cygne, in particular, like her female ancestors, becomes such a focus, but so, too, in their different ways are Michu, Napoleon and even Malin de Gondreville. Each of these characters bears witness to the emplotment of violence in terms of the times they live through, the spaces they inhabit, and in terms of their propensity to engender violence throughout their personal histories and territories. If a resolution to violence is to be sought it is not, therefore, in time, space or gender. It now remains to be seen whether such a solution can be found in the narrative itself, in the way violence is there represented and "mediatized."

As Joyce O. Lowrie remarks, the *Comédie humaine* is an immense and accommodating world which can tolerate a wide variety of apparently conflicting themes and perspectives (Lowrie 41). *Une ténébreuse affaire* is, despite similarities with other Balzac works, an unusual novel in the way it concludes its representation of violence. Unlike works such as *Pierrette* and *La fille aux yeux d'or* it does not end with a disclaimer or a quip. Unlike *La cousine Bette* or *Albert Savarus* it does not end with a form of retribution being visited on at least some of the offenders. And unlike novels, particularly in the *Scènes de la vie de campagne*, such as *Le médecin de campagne*, *Le curé de village*, and even *Le lys dans la vallée*, it does not culminate in a confession. *Une ténébreuse affaire* does not end with the final revelation that the main character committed a crime, be it deception, complicity with murder, or infidelity, which is exorcized by self-inflicted mortification, service to others, and silent suffering. Nor is it a novel where a sense of guilt and a corresponding need for expiation are transferred from one party to another as in *Les Marana* or *Un épisode sous la Terreur*, where the executioner assumes and purges collective responsiblity for the killing of the King.[13]

In *Une ténébreuse affaire*, however, no character or characters assume the violence and thus there is no evidence of guilt, responsibility, punishment, or expiation. Indeed, the only character who is punished is Michu, and if he is innocent, then, as Napoleon points out, so are three hundred thousand others who will die on the field of battle (8:681). As for the violence of the counterrevolution, that was too widespread and too abortive to be appropriately punished and, in any case, *raison d'état* dictates otherwise. The young nobles were little given to redemptive suffering and even Laurence, despite her association with Mme de la Chanterie in *L'envers de l'histoire contemporaine*, feels too indignant and too innocent herself to feel she has anything to expiate. Her motto is "To die singing!" not "To wounded hearts, shadow and silence."[14] Unusually for Balzac, there are no clergy at hand to offer insight or support: the priests have become politicians like Talleyrand, and the Church seems to restrict itself to prayer.[15] Unusually for Balzac, therefore, the violence is left untouched and intact. The violent deaths of family, allies, friends and soldiers are too public, too generalized, too arbitrary and too unjust to be redeemed by a Benassis, a Véronique Graslin— or even an executioner. Furthermore, as noted above, sacred and profane are no longer distinguishable. The notions of both redemption and punishment have therefore lost their meaning.

An alternative ending to violence in Balzac is silence. Both the marquise de Rochefide at the end of *Sarrasine* and Camille Maupin at the end of *Honorine* are left mute and reflective after the narratives they have just heard. Hence, after reading Félix de Vandenesse's confession, Natalie de Manerville enjoins him to silence: "When one has such crimes on one's conscience, the least one can do is not tell them."[16] Confession and silence are then closer than might have first appeared, with the confession seen as a momentary lapse, preceded by the silence of suffering and followed by the silence of death. Although the word "silence" is indeed the last of *Une ténébreuse affaire*, it is the diplomatic silence of Louis XVIII, not the self-imposed silence of suffering, of "Fuge, late, tace" (*Le médecin de campagne* 9:574). It is in this different silence that the different violence of *Une ténébreuse affaire* lies. For Louis's silence shows that he knows the violence of the past to be unredeemed and unredeemable. Neither de Marsay's explanations nor Louis's silence can expiate a violence which is so deeply felt by an individual, Laurence, and by a nation after Revolution, Terror, and Napoleonic wars. The narrative is, therefore, caught in a double bind which carries with it yet further violence: any attempt by de Marsay or Louis to talk an audience through the violence of *Une ténébreuse affaire* will show that violence is ubiquitous yet arbitrary, eternal yet unjust. It will show that violence is fatally emplotted into history, space, and sexuality. It will, however, also be a first step towards the mediatization of that violence and, therefore, to its relativization and banalization. Thus, on the one hand the novel shows that no form of retribution is adequate, no trial will reassert mastery, and no confession will acknowledge sufficent guilt. And yet on the other hand, it shows that no silence is sufficently eloquent to convey the pain, the suffering, and the injustices it withholds. Hence Une ténébreuse affaire indeed shows Balzac at the crossroads, at the crossroads between the exposure and the non-exposure of violence, between the possiblity and the impossiblity of its adequate representation. For Une ténébreuse affaire is caught between complicity with violence if it is explained and complicity with violence if it is not. Explanations coopt and silence ignores. Une ténébreuse affaire is, therefore, itself at the crossroads, between the misrepresentation and the non-representation of violence, between the violence which it does, and yet cannot, speak. And even the compromise between speaking and not speaking preserves violence, in the mystery of Une ténébreuse affaire.

University of Bradford

NOTES

1. This paper develops work in progress on violence and representation, on both Balzac and other writers such as Marguerite Duras, Monique Wittig, Yukio Mishima, and Eric Jourdan. See also Heathcote 1992, 1993.

2. On the complex interrelations between history and story in the first half of the nineteenth century, see Bernard 7–44, and, for "a comparison of historical discourse and literary discourse," Vanoncini 29. For nineteenth-century historians' uncertainty of their own discourse, see Orr. Although reference can hardly be made to foundationalist violence without invoking the work of René Girard, this paper will not look for his "triangular structures" of mimetic sacrificial violence in Une ténébreuse affaire.

3. See Suzanne-J. Bérard's introduction to the novel, Pléiade 8:463. The similarities and differences between the Clément de Ris and Gondreville abductions, and the question of Fouché's involvement, have been recurrent issues in Une ténébreuse affaire criticism. In the most detailed analysis of the novel to date, Wells Chamberlin comments: "Balzac is a novelist, and he uses history instead of following it; he is not an historian, although he had certain pretensions to that title" (Chamberlin 508). For a more recent mise-au-point on the two affairs and on the involvement of Fouché, see Bérard 8:453–81.

4. For the importance of Fouché for Balzac, see Tulard's article, which concludes: "For the myth of Fouché to be born, one must wait for Une ténébreuse affaire" (Tulard 12).

5. Taylor 16. For Mireille Labouret, however, "The sublime terror of Les Chouans is tempered in Une ténébreuse affaire by a bitter integration into the social order" (Labouret 327).

6. For analyses of *Une ténébreuse affaire* as a site of games and gaming, with Malin as "joker," see Taylor, and Schuerewegen 1990.

7. The cell is, therefore, not unlike the Malin-"joker" described by Taylor as "the man of the sign" (Taylor 7) and by Schuerewegen as "an element with no fixed value" (Schuerewegen 1990, 378).

8. See *La peau de chagrin* 10:201 and *Le curé de village* 9:741.

9. It should be noted that the sites of the "rond-point" and Nodesme are not dissimilar to other locations in the *Comédie humaine*. For example, just as Montégnac offers "an immense horse-shoe" and "valleys placed like the tiers of an amphitheater" (9:775), the Couesnon valley in *Les Chouans* is an amphitheatre and Fougères comprises "a vast half-moon" and "a vast horse-shoe" (8:912, 1071). From the valleys of *Le lys* to the fiords and amphitheatres of *Séraphîta* (11:733) and to the theater/"horse-shoe" that is Paquita's boudoir in *La fille aux yeux d'or* (5:1087), a combination or alternation of open and closed forms is a constant of Balzacian topography. See O'Connor. Internment, too, whether actual or figurative, is of course another Balzac leitmotiv, not least in *Le colonel Chabert*.

10. Or as Louis Lambert expresses it: "Perhaps the words materialism and spiritualism express two sides of one and the same fact" (11:616).

11. See Butler 1991, 128. According to Butler, Talleyrand also embodied Balzac's belief in the need for "social reconciliation" (1985, 135). For Andréoli, however, "Michu's death is the death of the Napoleonic dream of fusion" (Andréoli 123).

12. It is tempting to add to the characteristics of this sacred central mound and cell in Nodesme, formerly Notre-Dame, those of femininity and maternity. Nodesme would, therefore, illustrate what Nicole Mozet has called "the assimilation of Mother and Province, place of origin and nourishing earth" (Mozet 1982, 39), particularly as Gondreville is almost certainly transposed to Champagne from Touraine (Maurice 1965). The mound could also be suggestive of the omphalos, connoting femininity, birth, and death: see Bronfen. It is also interesting that Mme de la Chanterie, another maternal figure who promotes life while grieving her lost daughter, operates from near another Notre-Dame, from the dark seclusion of another island, from la rue Chanoinesse "in the shadow of the cathedral" (see 8:227).

13. See Schuerewegen 1985. The importance of the theme of the severed head in Balzac has also been shown by Chollet, and developed in relation to head/hair-care in two papers presented at a recent Nineteenth-Century French Studies Colloquium: Carpenter 1992, and Winchell 1992. For analyses of the expiatory role of the executioner, see Queffélec; Dunn; Burton, also presented at the 1992 NCFS Conference.

14. See the epigraph to *Le médecin de campagne* 9:385 and also 9:568, 573, 574.

15. 8:617. On Balzac's priests, see Adamson.

16. 9:1228. As Michèle Hannoosh suggestively pointed out in a discussion of this paper, a similar silencing of past violences occurs at the end of *Les Chouans*, where Marche-à-Terre is rehabilitated from a killer of more than one hundred men into "a very good man!" (8:1211).

10

Huysmans le terrible: À propos du terrifiant dans l'écriture du rêve et la critique d'art de J.-K. Huysmans

FRÉDÉRIC CANOVAS

DANS la livraison de février 1885 de *La Revue Indépendante*, figure un article de Huysmans intitulé "Le nouvel album d'Odilon Redon" consacré à *L'hommage à Goya*, série de six lithographies inspirée de l'oeuvre gravé du peintre espagnol et illustrant un court poème en prose lui-même composé par Redon.[1] L'année suivante, une édition augmentée du recueil des *Croquis parisiens* de Huysmans paraît chez l'éditeur Léon Vanier. L'un des poèmes en prose, figurant pour la première fois dans la collection, s'intitule "Cauchemar."[2] Il s'agit, comme son nom l'indique, d'un récit de rêve. Or il se trouve que le poème en question n'est autre que le compte rendu de *L'hommage à Goya* publié l'année précédente. Huysmans a subrepticement troqué le titre original au profit d'un énigmatique "Cauchemar." L'article de *La Revue Indépendante* et le poème en prose des *Croquis parisiens* se montrent identiques à quelques variations près, les rares coupures pratiquées par l'auteur concernent essentiellement des épithètes.[3] Que faut-il déduire de ce tour de passe-passe littéraire?

La question du statut du texte surgit immédiatement. Statut mouvant et pour le moins équivoque d'un texte qui se dérobe à toute tentative de classification de genre, variant, selon son titre, la volonté de son auteur et les circonstances de sa publication, de la critique d'art au poème en prose. Statut récalcitrant qui ne fait que confirmer la troublante ambiguïté du texte lui-même dont la valeur des champs lexicaux, les effets de la syntaxe, l'utilisation de la comparaison ne se distinguent en rien des procédés d'écriture communs au récit de rêve et au commentaire pictural.

Dans un essai intitulé "L'écrivain et le désir de voir," récemment publié dans la revue *Littérature*, Max Milner fait du fantastique "un genre littéraire qui se prête mieux que les autres à une exploration psychanalytique du regard." D'après le critique, "les images s'[y] organisent selon des constellations où le travail de l'inconscient se donne à lire, mais la manière même dont elles sont appelées, dont elles s'imposent à l'esprit du lecteur, mime ce travail, qui est, toutes choses égales, analogue à celui du rêve" (Milner 9). Quatre ans plus tôt, dans les mêmes pages, Bernard Vouilloux déclarait qu'il fallait chercher l'"analogon de la peinture moderne . . . dans les espaces imaginaires déployés par le rêve et le fantasme" (Vouilloux 65). Certes notre propos n'est pas ici de nous livrer à l'étude des mécanismes psychiques qui ont présidé à l'élaboration du texte huysmansien, ces deux remarques nous permettent cependant, à défaut d'associer le texte à un genre particulier, de situer la zone de son activité: c'est à dire précisément à la jonction du fantastique, du rêve et de la peinture moderne. Ce qui nous intéresse ici n'est pas tant de définir le statut générique du texte de Huysmans que de nous interroger sur les raisons qui ont poussé l'auteur à établir une comparaison implicite entre l'écriture du rêve, d'une part, et celle du compte rendu artistique, de l'autre. Mon objectif, dans cet essai, sera de démontrer qu'il existe, au moins sur le plan formel, une écriture commune au deux.[4]

Qu'il soit commentaire de critique d'art ou bien récit de rêve fantastique, le texte de Huysmans n'en demeure pas moins dans les deux cas un discours de l'ordre métalinguistique. Barthes nous rappelle dans la "Rhétorique de l'image" que toute "description constitue déjà un métalangage" (Barthes 1964, 41). En évoquant l'album de lithographies d'Odilon Redon ou le souvenir d'images oniriques, Huysmans se livre à un traitement textuel d'une série d'images qui, dans un cas comme dans l'autre, constituent elles-mêmes un système comportant ses propres réseaux de significations. Le fait que l'image du rêve soit encore généralement appréhendée, à cette époque, de la même façon que celle, plus tangible, d'autres supports visuels explique en partie la raison pour laquelle le commentaire artistique a pu suggérer une méthode d'investigation de l'écriture onirique et fournir un modèle de traitement textuel en vue de la verbalisation des images du rêve.[5]

Le premier regard posé sur une image constitue déjà les prémices d'une lecture dans la mesure où il fournit le point de départ spatial et temporel autour et à partir duquel le reste de

la lecture va pouvoir s'organiser. Le regard du spectateur/des-
cripteur (Hamon 40) duplique en cela le travail du peintre ou
du rêveur, c'est à dire le travail de l'inconscient. Si nous partons
donc du fait que toute description de tableau, que tout récit de
rêve, est déjà une interprétation, il nous reste à démontrer dans
quelles mesures ces deux types de discours sont à la recherche
d'un ordre de signification qui leur est propre. C'est un poème
en prose de Redon qui a servi de support textuel à l'élaboration
des six lithographies de *L'hommage à Goya*.[6] A chaque segment
du poème correspond une illustration de telle sorte que l'ordre
de succession des planches est subjugé à celui du texte. Dans
le poème que voici, j'ai fait suivre par une lettre de l'alphabet
chaque segment se rapportant à l'une des six planches:

> Dans mon rêve, je vis au Ciel un VISAGE DE MYSTERE (a)/la FLEUR
> du MARECAGE, une tête humaine et triste (b)/Un FOU dans un
> morne paysage. (c)/Il y eut aussi des ETRES EMBRYONNAIRES (d)/
> Un étrange JONGLEUR.(e)/Au réveil j'aperçus la DEESSE de l'INTEL-
> LIGIBLE au profil sévère et dur.(f)

L'originalité du travail textuel de Huysmans, dans l'article de *La
Revue Indépendante*, consiste à perturber l'ordre dans lequel le
texte, qu'il soit pictural ou poétique, se donne à lire habituellement pour aboutir à la disposition suivante: [a] + [b] +
[d] + [e] + [c] + [f] à l'intérieur de laquelle le troisième segment se
voit relégué en cinquième position. Loin de s'en tenir à ce cas
d'inversion de la proposition, somme toute assez subtil pour ne
point choquer de prime abord le lecteur-spectateur, le descripteur en profite pour insérer dans le fil de la description l'évocation d'une autre lithographie de Redon dont la similitude avec
la seconde illustration de *L'hommage à Goya* fait ressurgir le
souvenir: "le spectacle parcouru défila encore, rappelant un ancien et analogue spectacle presque oublié depuis des ans. Ce fut
à la place de la fleur des marais, une autre fleur humaine naguère
vue dans une exposition" (Huysmans 8:162). Il s'agit, en fait, d'un
fusain que Huysmans décrit dans les pages de *L'art moderne*
consacrées à la seconde exposition de Redon organisée en 1882
par le journal *Le Gaulois* (Huysmans 6:299). Nous désignerons
cette planche par la lettre x. En altérant, au sein de son propre
texte, l'organisation spatiale de l'album sans tenir compte de la
numérotation des planches par Redon, en insérant un épisode
supplémentaire dans la séquence d'apparition des lithographies,
Huysmans bouleverse par contrecoup la logique du poème en

prose qui a inspiré à l'artiste les six illustrations de *L'hommage à Goya* et propose une grille de lecture différente, soit le schéma: [a] + [b] + [d] + [e] + [x] + [c] + [f].

Ainsi est-ce en fonction de son désir que le descripteur procède à une telle réorganisation textuelle de l'espace pictural ou du contenu manifeste du rêve, manipulant l'objet de son discours au gré du sens qu'il désire lui donner, sens qui, comme on l'imagine facilement, n'est pas forcément celui de l'auteur du tableau ni, dans le cas du rêve, celui de l'inconscient. Il nous semble légitime que Huysmans, fasciné par le rêve et encouragé par le poème en prose de Redon, ait abordé les dessins au fusain comme des témoignages de cauchemars et que, par la suite, sa lecture de l'album ait été intégralement subordonnée à son désir d'y voir effectivement un récit de rêve.[7] Car, de manière significative, ce n'est pas tant la succession des gravures fixée par Redon qui règle la structure de l'article, que les émotions se dégageant à leur vue et les effets qu'elles produisent sur le descripteur. Le terrifiant se pose comme le dénominateur commun le plus évident de l'écriture huysmansienne: le "paysage atroce" des *Croquis parisiens* (Huysmans 8:158) rappelle "le paysage minéral atroce" du cauchemar de des Esseintes (7:147), les "yeux effroyables" des créatures de Redon (8:161), ceux "terribles" de la figure de la Grande Vérole (7:144), "l'affreux sourire" de l'effroyable fleur (8:163) fait écho à "l'affreux regard" de la femme-fleur d'*A rebours* (AR, 144), enfin à "l'épouvantable vision" du roman de 1884 (7:145) succède l'"effrayante image" des *Croquis parisiens*.[8]

C'est donc bien la notion de terreur qui, comme l'indique la prolifération du lexique appartenant au champ sémantique de la peur, incite Huysmans à modifier l'ordre des planches, à les réorganiser, voire même à recourir à des éléments hors-texte de façon à produire une tension croissante et, par l'intermédiaire notamment de la répétition du motif de "l'effroyable fleur," à faire redoubler la terreur d'intensité avec chaque épisode. Désormais le désir de voir du descripteur, de lire dans cette suite d'images les visions d'un cauchemar, impose à son discours l'utilisation d'un vocabulaire hyperbolique et d'un rythme où dominent les figures binaires et ternaires: "à cette moderne vision des anciens âges, succéda un paysage atroce" (Huysmans 8:158), "Au pâle avoué . . . s'était substitué une vision non moins horrible" (8:160), quitte également à ménager ici et là de rares instants d'apaisement: "Il y eut dans ce cauchemar une courte trêve" (8:161), "Enfin une accalmie eut lieu" (8:162). Le sentiment de terreur n'en relance pas moins l'action avec plus de vigueur pour finalement atteindre le sommet du terrifiant et rompre le cauchemar dans un cri de terreur.

D'ailleurs tout contribue dans le texte à accroître le degré de terreur maximal. Les locutions prépositives de lieu qui orientent habituellement le regard du spectateur-lecteur dans la description du tableau ont disparu au profit des adverbes de temps, rappelant en cela l'attrait qu'a toujours éprouvé Huysmans pour les locutions adverbiales ainsi qu'en témoignent les titres de ces romans. Dans sa lecture, le critique d'art néglige totalement de décrire la répartition spatiale dans chacune des six planches: il n'est pas question une seule fois d'évoquer la droite, la gauche ou le centre, pas plus que le haut ou le bas des dessins. Le descripteur insiste au contraire sur la valeur épisodique qui lie les planches les unes aux autres mais surtout sur la puissance dramatique qui se dégage au sein même de chaque lithographie en ayant recours notamment à un nombre impressionnant d'adverbes et d'expressions de temps (*tout d'abord, soudain, puis, enfin, cette fois, alors, tout à coup, et voilà que, enfin, soudain, en même temps, enfin, encore, naguère, alors, subitement*). L'effet est immédiat: les figures semblent se mouvoir sous les yeux du lecteur, d'autant plus que les verbes indiquant une suite d'actions subites prolifèrent dans le texte de façon à produire un jeu de va-et-vient constant, de plus en plus rapide, entre les phases d'agitation et de répit qui déterminent l'activité onirique (notons au passage que le choix du passé simple est caractéristique de la volonté déterminée d'animer à tout prix la description): dans l'ordre d'apparition, on rencontre les verbes *surgir, disparaître, jaillir, sortir, crever, s'éteindre, bondir, sortir, disparaître, s'effacer, émerger, éclater, tomber, bondir, surgir, dresser, sortir, jaillir, éclore* pour finalement aboutir, dans un ultime accès de terreur, au réveil en sursaut: "Subitement le cauchemar se rompit" (8:163). N'est-ce pas ainsi que des Esseintes dans *A rebours* et Jacques Marles dans *En rade* parviennent à échapper l'un et l'autre aux visions nocturnes qui les assaillent?[9] Un effet de rêve s'est produit qui n'est autre qu'un effet de réel destiné à rendre le récit de rêve crédible aux lecteurs: "le réveil effaré s'opéra, alors que l'inflexible figure de la Certitude apparut" conclut le critique d'art (8:163). C'est le même pacte onirique qui vient clore le poème en prose de Redon: "Au réveil j'aperçus la DEESSE de l'INTELLIGIBLE au profil sévère et dur," certifiant, dans ce cas comme dans celui de l'article de Huysmans, que ce nous venons de lire relève effectivement du domaine du rêve.

J'ai défini ailleurs ce que j'entends par la notion de pacte onirique en établissant que seule une mention insérée dans le cours
du texte, dans la plupart des cas immédiatement avant ou après
la séquence onirique, peut permettre au lecteur de décider si un
texte ou une portion d'un texte est véritablement un récit de
rêve (Canovas). Ce pacte onirique a valeur de contrat passé entre
l'auteur et son lecteur d'une part et entre le narrateur et son
narrataire de l'autre. La clausule ou scène de réveil, telle que
nous venons de la voir, constitue avec l'incipit du récit de rêve
l'un des deux types principaux de pactes oniriques. Notons
d'emblée, dans l'article de *La Revue Indépendante*, le choix de
la formule introductrice: "*Ce fut* d'abord une énigmatique figure"
(Huysmans 8:157; c'est moi qui souligne). On reconnaît ici un
incipit familier: de manière symptomatique, la forme imperson-
nelle du verbe "être" domine à la fois les incipits des descriptions de toiles dans la critique d'art de Huysmans comme ceux
de ses récits de rêve: "*Ce fut.* . . . une autre fleur humaine"
(8:162), "ici *c'est* le cauchemar transporté dans l'art" (6:214), "ici
c'étaient des vibrions et des volvoces" (6:299), "*ce fut.* . . . un
autodafé de ciels immenses" (10:16–17) lit-on dans la critique
artistique de *L'art moderne* et de *Certains* (c'est moi qui souligne). Et le rêve de Jacques Marles au cinquième chapitre d'*En
rade* de débuter: "*C'était* au-delà de toutes limites, dans une fuite
indéfinie de l'oeil, un immense désert de plâtre" (9:99, c'est moi
qui souligne).

Dans *En lisant En écrivant*, Julien Gracq certifie que "[n]ul
artiste, bien entendu, ne peut rester tout à fait insensible, même
s'il passe outre, à ce vice de l'incipit qui marque tous les arts de
l'organisation de la durée: littérature, musique, à l'inverse des
oeuvres plastiques dont l'exécution, certes, s'insère elle aussi
dans le déroulement du temps, mais qui par leur achèvement,
effacent toute référence temporelle et se présentent, plus pure-
ment, comme un circuit fermé sur lui-même, sans commence-
ment ni fin" (Gracq 116). En circonscrivant son discours critique
à l'intérieur des limites fixées par des conventions propres au
récit de rêve littéraire, Huysmans pousse le vice de l'incipit au-
delà de toute analogie pratiquée jusqu'alors entre le rêve et l'oeuvre d'art. L'incipit du commentaire artistique fournit à ce type
de discours l'équivalent textuel du cadre d'une peinture ou du
pourtour d'un dessin. Elargir ce procédé technique à l'écriture
de la séquence onirique, c'est non seulement consentir à établir
implicitement une analogie entre l'élaboration du texte de critique artistique et celle du récit de rêve mais encore encourager

voire même perpétuer chez le lecteur une habitude de lecture qui consiste justement à lire les images du rêve comme s'il s'agissait de celles de l'oeuvre d'art visuelle. C'est sans doute parce que Huysmans était critique d'art qu'il écrit le rêve comme s'il évoquait un tableau, conscient que le traitement textuel des images oniriques comporte des difficultés similaires à celui des oeuvres picturales. Est-ce par l'acquisition des techniques permettant de rendre compte de la peinture moderne que l'écrivain pense parvenir à transposer le rêve verbalement? En remplaçant le titre de son article par celui de "Cauchemar", Huysmans semble suggérer qu'il est préférable de donner l'évocation d'une oeuvre d'art pour récit de rêve quitte à exagérer ses accents oniriques plutôt que de se lancer dans la reconstitution verbale des images du rêve.

Si, comme l'affirme Redon, la mission de l'artiste est de rendre l'invisible visible, celle du descripteur qui consisterait alors à rendre le visible dicible peut paraître problématique. Comme tout métalangage, la critique d'art et le récit de rêve ne parviennent pas à rendre compte de l'objet de leur discours dans son intégralité. Au-delà du travail de condensation et de déplacement du rêve, la mise en écriture des images oniriques implique nécessairement son propre travail de transformation ne serait-ce que parce que, malgré les moyens d'adaptation du langage, ses possibilités sont limitées et toute représentation textuelle du rêve partielle. Il y a dans le rêve, comme dans l'oeuvre picturale du reste, des éléments qui correspondent à des signes linguistiques et auxquels le descripteur parvient, tant bien que mal, à trouver des équivalents dans le langage verbal. Je reprendrai, pour désigner ces éléments, le terme barthésien de lexies, soit unités de signification. Le degré de réussite de la transposition d'un art dans un autre dépend directement de l'habileté du langage verbal à prendre en charge le plus grand nombre d'unités de lecture. Plus l'objet du discours est conçu en terme de langage, plus le traitement textuel des lexies aura de chance d'être efficace.

C'est désormais un lieu commun que d'affirmer que tout rêve est en grande partie élaboré à partir de matériaux linguistiques perçus à l'état de veille, qu'ils relèvent de l'oralité, tels que la parole prononcée et entendue, qu'ils soient d'ordre textuel comme l'écriture et la lecture, voire même visuel dans le cas de la production et de la vue d'images elles-mêmes conçues à partir du langage. Le récit de rêve d'*A rebours* en est une parfaite illustration puisqu'il mêle dans ses visions nocturnes, à la manière d'une mise en abyme, différents éléments du texte qui le précèdent à son point d'ancrage dans le récit, soit le souvenir de conversations, de lectures et de tableaux dont, entre autres, plusieurs lithographies de Redon tirées des trois albums précédant *L'hommage à Goya*.

Quant à dire des oeuvres de Redon qu'elles tiennent autant de la littérature que du domaine des arts, c'est reprendre ici encore un lieu commun de la critique. Rappelons simplement que Redon est passé maître dans l'art d'illustrer ses contemporains: Baudelaire, Destrées, Flaubert, Mallarmé, Poe, Verhaeren, et même Huysmans puisqu'il réalise un portrait de des Esseintes qui servira de frontispice à la réédition de 1888 d'*A rebours*.[10] Dès lors, il n'est pas surprenant qu'un artiste qui affirme dans son journal qu'"écrire et publier est le travail le plus noble, le plus délicat que puisse faire un homme" (Redon 1922, 38), pousse l'art de la transposition au point de ne pouvoir créer qu'à partir d'un support textuel. Il ne fait pas de doute que Redon n'a pu qu'emprunter les titres "Eclosion," "Germination" de ses premières lithographies au lexique que Baudelaire utilise pour définir l'art d'un autre grand poète visionnaire, Victor Hugo: "Germinations, éclosions, floraisons, éruptions successives, lentes ou soudaines, progressives ou complètes, d'astres, d'étoiles, de soleils, de constellations" (Baudelaire 1961, 710). Toute la production lithographique de Redon est contenue dans ces quelques mots tirées des *Réflexions sur quelques-uns de mes contemporains*. Curieusement, Redon a toujours repoussé les allégations des commentateurs trop pressés de le ranger sous l'étiquette des artistes-poètes. Dans une lettre du 21 juillet 1898 adressée à son biographe André Mellerio, Redon justifie sa préférence pour l'album *Dans le rêve* "parce qu'il est façonné sans aucun alliage de littérature. Le titre *Dans le rêve* n'étant en quelque sorte qu'une clé d'ouverture."[11]

A ceux qui l'accusent de peindre comme s'il écrivait, Redon rétorque sous forme de devinette: "Où est la limite de l'idée littéraire en peinture? On s'entend. Il y a idée littéraire toutes les fois qu'il n'y a pas invention plastique" (Mellerio 78). Est-ce à dire que tout ce qui, dans le système de signification de l'oeuvre picturale, parvient à transposer un discours verbal ou bien à être relayé par des mots dans le langage du descripteur, tombe forcément dans le domaine du littéraire?[12] Est-ce encore une façon de suggérer que le propre de l'art plastique moderne, sa caractéristique essentielle, réside justement dans son irréductibilité, dans le fait qu'une image résiste à toute tentative de description, qu'elle se dérobe aux pouvoirs du langage verbal? Où le visible deviendrait indicible. Comment interpréter autrement ce reproche adressé par Redon au descripteur: "la critique d'art n'est pas créatrice. On peut la tolérer chez des êtres pensifs, sensibles, . . . mais le commentaire pur n'a d'excuse que s'il refond les principes sans cesse, toujours nouvellement, à chaque frisson d'un art nouveau. Il doit proclamer les découvertes" (Redon 1922, 115). En s'exprimant ainsi, Redon pensait sans doute à l'auteur d'*A rebours*, ayant probablement en mémoire le souvenir des pages élogieuses qui lui y étaient consacrées et qui le révélèrent au grand public.

Alors que pour le descripteur, selon le mot de Christian Metz, "le tableau n'existe que par ce qu'on y lit" (Metz 9), Redon semble au contraire indiquer que le commentaire artistique ne peut exister qu'en dehors de la description pure: "Mes dessins inspirent et ne se définissent pas. Ils ne déterminent rien. Ils nous placent, ainsi que la musique, dans le monde ambigu de l'indéterminé" (Redon 1922). Le travail de Huysmans se résume alors à la narrativisation de l'image puisque c'est une des fonctions essentielles du romancier que de tenter inlassablement de raconter des histoires. Pour en revenir au rêve, la tâche du descripteur, dans la séquence onirique, ne consiste-t-elle pas à faire entrer coûte que coûte les éléments les plus hétéroclites à l'intérieur d'une mini-fiction—d'où l'aspect fourre-tout du rêve—de telle sorte que les anomalies révélées à la lecture provoquent un effet de rêve? Lorsque cette pratique textuelle est appliquée, comme dans le cas de la critique d'art de Huysmans, à la lecture d'une oeuvre picturale, elle laisse la porte ouverte à l'exagération parfois même à l'invention et mène donc tout droit à la fiction. Dans l'évocation des lithographies de Redon comme dans celles du rêve, c'est l'émotion qui domine, en l'occurence la terreur éprouvée à la vue de ces planches par un descripteur qui est aussi un romancier chevronné: la fonction critique prend ici le pas sur la fonction descriptive.

Le compte-rendu du nouvel album d'Odilon Redon brise le schéma traditionnel du commentaire artistique qui, de Diderot à Baudelaire, consistait en un premier temps à *faire voir* aux lecteurs les oeuvres exposées au Salon sans même qu'il soit question pour le critique d'art de soumettre un jugement quelconque.[13] C'est seulement une fois l'oeuvre scrupuleusement décrite que le critique pouvait alors faire connaître son appréciation esthétique. Notons que l'écriture du récit de rêve, avant et après Freud, procède selon un modèle identique où le compte-rendu objectif du rêve est censé précéder son interprétation. En laissant les fonctions descriptive et esthétique du commentaire artistique s'exprimer simultanément, Huysmans se libère à la fois de l'obligation de décrire et du devoir de juger. En effet, au terme de la lecture de l'article de *La Revue Indépendante*, le lecteur soucieux de s'informer ne sera pas plus avancé qu'il ne l'était au départ. Car s'il n'a pas vu les lithographies de Redon, il ne doit pas compter davantage sur l'avis du critique pour éclairer son propre jugement: la cinquième planche est à peine identifiable et la phrase "telles les visions évoquées . . . par Odilon Redon" au terme de l'article semble suggérer que *Cauchemar* n'est pas l'évocation de *L'hommage à Goya* que l'on serait en droit d'attendre même s'il supporte la comparaison avec celui-ci.

Le jeu des pronoms personnels brouille les pistes en mêlant la troisième personne de la description au "je" du critique, les planches de Redon au texte de Huysmans, l'univers métadiégétique à celui du narrateur. Comme dans le rêve, un effet de condensation s'est produit. C'est tout juste si le descripteur se risque à interrompre la suite de ses digressions pour glisser, à une ou deux reprises, un commentaire sur les deux premières estampes. L'interprétation se résume, dans le premier cas, à une litanie d'interrogations toutes aussi différentes et s'annulant l'une l'autre—"Est-ce le primitif pasteur d'homme . . . ?—Est-ce la figure de l'Immémoriale Mélancolie . . . ?—Est-ce enfin le Mythe, une fois de plus rajeuni, de la Vérité . . . ?" (8:157–58)—pour finalement conclure par deux fois à l'échec: "en vain je voulus scruter son regard perdu au loin; en vain je tentai de sonder s[on auguste] face" (8:158). La seconde tentative d'interprétation ne se montre pas plus concluante: "Je me demandais de quels maux excessifs cette face blafarde avait pu souffrir. . . . Mais je n'eus même point le temps de discerner la réponse qu'il [m']importait de faire à cette question que je me posais" (8:159–60). Emporté par le flot des images qui semble défiler sous ses yeux et qu'il n'a de cesse de transcrire, le narrateur s'excuse de ne pas être en mesure de fournir un quelconque élément de réponse. La remarque pour incidente qu'elle paraisse, ne relève pas moins du niveau de la métatextualité et contribue à perturber encore davantage l'ordre du discours critique. Autant dire immédiatement que l'article s'achèvera sans qu'il soit à nouveau question pour son auteur de trouver le temps ou la place d'apporter la moindre réponse. Si Huysmans se permet de fausser ainsi les règles du jeu, c'est sans doute qu'il n'a pas jugé nécessaire de décrire ce que les lecteurs pouvaient par ailleurs voir de leurs propres yeux. Une note au bas de la première page prend bien soin de fournir le nom et l'adresse du libraire auprès duquel les lecteurs pourront admirer de leurs propres yeux l'album de lithographies.

De tous les critiques qui se sont essayés à l'interprétation des fusains de Redon, Huysmans est peut-être le seul à être véritablement parvenu à dépasser le niveau de la pure description du visible pour atteindre cet au-delà qui est le propre du discours métalinguistique et répondre aux exigences en matière de critique d'art formulées par l'auteur de *L'hommage à Goya*. Un critique en conclut: "C'est au niveau du commentaire lyrique qu'il convient d['].entendre et de . . . juger [ces textes], en leur restituant leur nature spécifique: celle de la méditation sur l'oeuvre d'art par le moyen de l'écriture poétique, investie non du pouvoir de décrire ou d'expliciter, mais de suggérer à l'aide des rythmes et des métaphores un signifié porteur de sa connotation affective. L'oeuvre plastique est souvent pour Huysmans prétexte à un discours interprétatif, dont la vigueur tient à l'empreinte de la charge poétique" (Eigeldinger 215). Poésie, le mot est lancé. Il l'était déjà par Baudelaire, l'autre critique d'art de ce siècle, pour qui le seul commentaire pictural digne de ce nom ne pouvait être que poétique. "Ainsi le meilleur compte rendu d'un tableau pourra être un sonnet ou une élégie" propose-t-il dans son *Salon de 1846* (Baudelaire 1961, 877). Trente ans plus tard, Redon s'accordera au poète pour affirmer que seule "une parole sous forme d'art, un poème par exemple" peut parvenir à "laisser dans l'esprit une impression durable" d'un tableau (Redon 1922, 79).[14] Huysmans le comprit très tôt qui, progressivement, donna à ses articles de critique d'art la forme de poèmes en prose "de toutes les formes de la littérature . . . la forme préférée de des Esseintes" (7:301). Dès lors, récits de rêves et commentaires de tableaux ne représentent plus chez Huysmans qu'un aspect de son écriture poétique. Songeons à Jules Laforgue, poète qui "aurait mérité de figurer dans le florilège de des Esseintes" mais qui n'avait "encore rien imprimé à cette époque" (7:xx), correspondant à Berlin de *La Gazette des beaux arts:* "Je songe à une poésie qui serait de la psychologie dans une forme de rêve . . . je rêve de poésie qui ne dise rien, mais qui soit des bouts de rêverie, sans suite. Quand on veut dire quelque chose, il y a la prose" (Hautecoeur 213–14).

En projetant le commentaire pictural au niveau du poème en prose, Huysmans se révèle un écrivain déchiré entre la prose et la poésie, entre le désir et la volonté de s'exprimer sur l'art de ses contemporains, d'une part, la détermination et la tentation de se taire définitivement, de l'autre. L'article de *La Revue Indé-*

pendante marque une date dans l'histoire de la critique artistique de Huysmans. Celle du passage de la description de la
peinture objective à l'évocation de la figure abstraite dans l'oeuvre d'art moderne alors que la peinture tente justement de se
libérer de toutes les entraves qui l'ont maintenue jusqu'alors dans
le champ d'expression du langage verbal. La remise en question,
au même moment, du statut de la description dans et par le
roman justifie en partie les hésitations de Huysmans. Confrontée
à l'obstacle du langage et à la difficulté croissante à rendre
compte des oeuvres de ses contemporains, la critique d'art de
Huysmans devient un discours sur l'impossibilité de dire l'oeuvre picturale. Ainsi aurais-je tendance à interpréter l'insertion
tardive de l'article sur Redon dans le recueil des *Croquis parisiens* comme une tentative de dissimuler, par l'écriture elle-
même, l'échec de l'acte descriptif et, comme semble le suggérer
la figure de la première planche de *L'hommage à Goya*, "l'impuis-
sance avérée de la Joie, . . . l'inutilité absolue de toute chose."[15]

Cette surimposition d'un discours sur un autre, Jean de Palacio
nous rappelle encore qu'elle se trouve, de manière consubstan-
tielle, au coeur même de la dialectique décadente fin-de-siècle:
"curieux phénomène d'écriture narcissique, où l'écriture de l'autre devient le miroir de sa propre écriture qui se trouve par con-
séquent présente deux fois: à l'état d'écriture romanesque et
d'écriture critique. Cette analyse de soi (on n'ose parler d'autoa-
nalyse) est dans la logique de l'écriture fin-de-siècle, écriture
d'appropriation s'il en fut" (De Palacio 1994a, 168). Et le même
critique ajoute, dans un essai postérieur consacré à *A rebours*:
"Par une sorte de cercle vicieux ou de parasitisme littéraire, par
goût de ne se nourrir que de sa propre substance, la Décadence
tend à travailler éternellement sur la même écriture . . . écriture
parcellaire et rhapsodique, utilisant sans vergogne la seconde
main, incorporant à sa propre substance des éléments venus
d'ailleurs et faisant de l'hétérogène sa loi" (De Palacio 1994b,
196, 202).

Seule la mort parviendra à mettre un terme à ce "dilemme,"[16]
à cette lutte acharnée entre l'écriture et le silence: terrible ironie
du sort, un cancer de la gorge empêchera Huysmans de parler sur
la fin. Dans son effort toujours poussé plus loin pour atteindre
l'inaccessible—de *Sac au dos* à *En route* en passant par *En rade*
et *Là-bas*, les titres du romancier désignent souvent le mouvement en direction d'un ailleurs constamment repoussé, sans
cesse redéfini—conscient que son salut ne se trouve ni dans
l'écriture ni dans le rêve et encore moins dans l'écriture du rêve,

Huysmans choisira finalement le silence absolu du cloître. En 1898, alors que l'auteur de *La cathédrale*, en quête d'absolu, se ferme définitivement au monde extérieur, le jeune Paul Claudel, lancé sur les chemins d'une brillante carrière internationale de Pékin à New York, rentre de Foutchéou avec un secret dans ses bagages: de manière ironique, en mandarin littéraire "peindre une peinture" se dit "écrire une peinture" (Leys 21). Huysmans, ayant peu voyagé, s'en doutait-il, lui qui ne cessa jamais de croire ni de répéter qu'écriture et peinture ne faisaient irrémédiablement qu'une?

Reed College

All the following illustrations are taken from *The Graphic Works of Odilon Redon,* with an Introduction by Alfred Werner. New York: Dover Publications, Inc., 1969. The dimensions are in millimeters, the first number indicating the height, the second number the width.

"**Dans mon rêve, je vis au ciel un visage de mystère**" (291 × 238). *Hommage à Goya,* 1885.

"La fleur du marécate, une tête humaine de triste" (275×205). *Hommage à Goya*, 1885.

"Un fou dans un morne paysage" (226 × 193). *Hommage à Goya*, 1885.

"Il y eut aussi des êtres embryonnaires" (238 × 197). *Hommage à Goya*, 1885.

"Un étrange jongleur" (199 × 190). *Hommage à Goya,* 1885.

"Au réveil j'aperçus la déesse de l'Intelligible au profil sévère et dur" (276×217). *Hommage à Goya,* 1885.

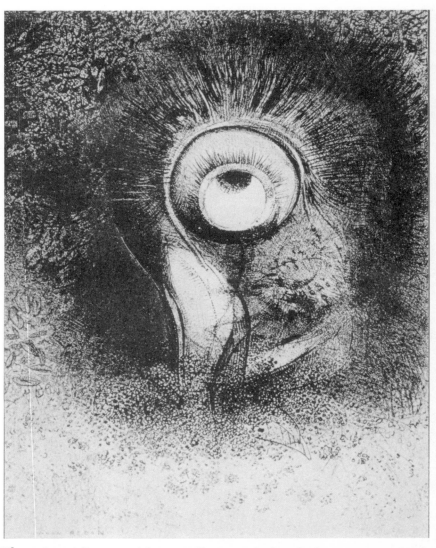

"Il y eut peut-être une vision première essayée dans la fleur (223 × 172). *Les Origines,* 1883

NOTES

1. Odilon Redon, *Hommage à Goya* (1885): album de six lithographies au fusain édité à cinquante exemplaires par Dumon puis à vingt-cinq exemplaires. Les dimensions sont en millimètres, le premier chiffre indique la hauteur, le second la largeur. Nous reprenons les numéros utilisés, en 1913, par André Mellerio dans son catalogue des oeuvres d'Odilon Redon.

No. 1: "Dans mon rêve, je vis au ciel un visage de mystère" (291 x 238): Mellerio 54.

No. 2: "La fleur du marécage, une tête humaine et triste" (275 x 205): Mellerio 55.

No. 3: "Un fou dans un morne paysage" (226 x 193): Mellerio 56.

No. 4: "Il y eut aussi des êtres embryonnaires" (238 x 197): Mellerio 57.

No. 5: "Un étrange jongleur" (199 x 190): Mellerio 58.

No. 6: "Au réveil j'aperçus la déesse de l'Intelligible au profil sévère et dur" (276 x 217): Mellerio 59.

2. La première édition des *Croquis parisiens* fut celle imprimée à Bruxelles fin mai 1880 par les soins de Félix Callewaert père et accompagnée de huit eaux-fortes signées Forain et Raffaëlli.

3. La nouvelle version du texte supprime les mots suivants: "auguste" (8:292), "et," "sombre," "m'" (8:293), "morne" (8:294), "de sueur froide" (8:295). Les mots entre crochets dans les citations sont ceux de la version de *La Revue Indépendante*.

4. Sur Odilon Redon voir: Huysmans 6:214 et 299–301; 10:135–38; et 7:96–98. Le cauchemar de des Esseintes se trouve dans 7:143–49; ceux de Jacques Marles dans 9:29–36, 9:99–111, 9:211–28. Sur Huysmans et Odilon Redon, je renvoie aux articles d'Annette Kahn, de Ruth B. Antosh et de Marc Eigeldinger. Sur les récits de rêve dans l'oeuvre de Huysmans, voir ceux de Michel Collomb, de Françoise Carmignani-Dupont, de Rose Fortassier et enfin d'Yves Vadé.

5. L'année suivante, dans un article consacré à Gustave Moreau, un critique d'art conseille aux artistes de "donner . . . une réalité plastique au rêve" (Renan 35).

6. Robert L. Delevoy s'interroge: "Illustrations cela? Légendes du texte, de l'image? Transcriptions? Traductions? Analogie? Chaque fois, en vérité, un texte verbal est investi par une écriture onirique où tout se livre à neuf. Où le rêveur du verbe invente sa propre grammaire graphique. Où les points d'adhérence de signifiant à signifiant sont aussi minces, qu'est tendue, violente, la distance entre signifiés et signifiés. Parce que entre les deux tout le matériel sexuel charrié par la rêverie est entré en action, véhiculé par l'énergie qui circule entre l'inconscient et le conscient (Delevoy 142).

7. Même si, à en juger les déclarations de Jacques Marles dans *En rade* de 1887, Huysmans demeure sceptique quant aux théories du rêve puisque "il est certain . . . que, quelle que soit l'opinion qu'ils professent, les savants ânonnent" (9:62), le carnet vert dans lequel l'écrivain consignait ses propres rêves témoigne de sa fascination pour la vie inconsciente. En voici un extrait daté de 1886: "*Rêves,*—cette nuit—descente par la cave dans les égoûts; aux abords sur terrains vagues—petites serres de jardinier, vitres au blanc d'Espagne—des

marches de cave—du noir—Eau noire battant les marches en courant" (Lambert 1). Sans prêter à ce passage toute l'attention qu'il mérite, notons simplement l'attrait qu'excercent sur l'auteur les impressions visuelles liées à la couleur, et l'emploi d'un terme appartenant au champ sémantique de la peinture. Huysmans rêve en noir et blanc (d'Espagne), à la manière des lithographies de Goya et de Redon. La similitude entre rêve et peinture est bien dans l'air du temps.

8. Huysmans 8:137. On trouve encore dans *L'art moderne* et *A rebours* la même phrase presque mot pour mot, exemple flagrant d'autocitation: "Puis des fusains partaient plus avant dans l'effroi des rêves tourmentés par la congestion" (6:299) et "puis des fusains partaient plus loin encore dans l'effroi du rêve tourmenté par la congestion" (7:96).

9. "il s'éveilla . . . suffoqué, glacé, fou de peur" (7:149), "Jacques . . . se réveilla . . . fourbu, mourant, trempé de sueur" (9:225).

10. François Chapon voit dans ce "frontispice volant, à joindre, si l'on veut, au livre de Huysmans" la marque d'un "grand précurseur de l'illustration moderne." Il aura seulement manqué à Redon les conseils avisés d'un mentor comme Mallarmé ou d'un éditeur pour qu'il sache "situer ses recherches dans le contexte typographique. . . . [Il] en aurait développé la portée en les intégrant à la magie du livre." (Chapon 27).

11. Mellerio 147. Dans son article, Mellerio décrète qu'"'on ne saurait trouver dans Redon l'habituelle manière d'illustrer un texte. Nous constatons une interprétation illimitément libre dans le domaine plastique. C'est moins l'expression d'une exacte conformité recherchée avec la pensée littéraire, que les idées et les émotions très personnelles jaillies au contact de tempéraments extériorisés dans un autre art. En somme, non la servilité ni même un accommodement large, mais un parallélisme corrélatif" (Mellerio 148).

12. Pour Huysmans, "M. Redon présentait des *traductions* d'Edgar Poe" (6:300); "il a cherché la *traduction* de cette phrase de Flaubert, dans *La tentation*" (10:135); "Odilon Redon semblait avoir *transposé*, dans un art différent, les mirages d'hallucination et les effets de peur [d'Edgar Poe]" (7:97); "c'est, en effet, une véritable *transposition* d'un art dans un autre" (6:300). C'est moi qui souligne.

13. Une autre alternative nous est fournie par l'exemple de Gautier cité par Micheline Besnard: "Or, comment rendre le visible mieux que par un art visuel? Pour Gautier qui, chaque année, *rend compte* du Salon, ce n'est pas l'écriture qui peut "*rendre*" la réalité, mais le dessin et la peinture. Aussi oriente-t-il son texte vers le présent du tableau. Il voit non seulement en peintre, mais pour ainsi dire, par les yeux des peintres qu'il admire, et plus particulièrement les Orientalistes. On connaît la technique si caractéristique chez Gautier, de la "transposition d'art": reproduire, par l'écriture, la vision du peintre, intégrer, dans son texte, le tableau." (Besnard 45–46; c'est moi qui souligne).

14. Les responsables des expositions, les auteurs et les éditeurs du livre d'art ou du catalogue d'exposition semblent avoir tiré profit de ces remarques si l'on en juge par la structure de quelques ouvrages récents consacrés au symbolisme. Voir le chapitre intitulé "l'ambivalence du désir et de la mort (1870–1900)" dans l'étude de Robert L. Delevoy. Ici les oeuvres de Redon, Knopff, Denis, Rodin, Klinger, Rops, Klimt, Lévy-Dhurmer, Munch, Beardsley et Gauguin sont accompagnés, pour tout commentaire, de poèmes de Rodenbach, Valéry, Maeterlinck, Jammes, Louys, Gourmont, Régnier, Mallarmé, Baudelaire, Verhaeren et Verlaine. Le catalogue de l'exposition *Le Symbolisme dans les collections*

du *Petit-Palais* tenue au Musée du Petit-Palais du 21 octobre 1988 au 19 février 1989, reproduit le même modèle. Là, des textes de Valéry, Montesquiou, Baudelaire, Hérédia, Régnier choisis par Thérèse Burollet accompagnent, au lieu de commentaires, les toiles de Moreau, Puvis de Chavannes, Redon et Lévy-Dhurmer, entre autres, dans la partie intitulée symptomatiquement "correspondances".

15. Au même moment, l'attitude de Zola me semble, elle aussi, révélatrice de cette incapacité: "je me permettrai d'emprunter à ce critique la description de la toile, car, franchement, je m'avoue incapable d'en écrire une semblable" (Zola 188). Valéry invoque les raisons de cet échec dans "Souvenir de J.-K. Huysmans": "Mais comment n'avoir pas recours à la recherche, aux figures continuelles, aux écarts voulus de la syntaxe, aux vocabulaires techniques, aux artifices de ponctuation quand l'on vient se joindre bien tard à un système littéraire déjà mûr et enrichi; et quand il s'agit de décrire encore, après un siècle de descriptions, après Gautier, après Flaubert, après les Goncourt?" (Valéry 755).

16. C'est le titre de la nouvelle publiée par Huysmans dans les numéros 5 et 6 de *La Revue Indépendante* en septembre et octobre 1884.

11

Piety and *Pourriture*: Huysmans's Women Terrorists

Renée Kingcaid

I⊤ comes as no surprise to any serious (or even casual) reader of Huysmans's novels that their author was a misogynist. In *J.-K. Huysmans: Novelist, Poet and Art Critic*, Annette Kahn aptly summarizes this charge against the father figure of the Decadence: "Many of Huysmans's works do not contain a female character of any consequence; this very omission reinforces the fact that Huysmans was scared of women, was disgusted by what he considered their stupidity, often despised them for the power they exerted over him, experienced trouble relating to them, and tried hard to live without them" (Kahn 33).

A great deal of Huysmans's misogyny is related to a horror of the flesh and its demands, a horror that devolves necessarily onto the figure of woman herself in her psycho-semantic (for example, in Huysmans's semes of his terrorized fantasy of woman) and in her spatial representations. In other words, misogyny in Huysmans's case takes the form of what psychologists call the "fight or flight" reaction of panic; for confirmation, we have only to look to Huysmans's spiritual confidant the abbé Mugnier, who reveals in his journal the depths to which Huysmans's horror of sexual temptation is really a defensive reaction against Huysmans's own propensity to the inevitable human vice of *luxure*. According to the abbé, who began his friendship with Huysmans during the period immediately preceding the latter's conversion to Catholicism, Huysmans's inborn melancholia and pessimism seem quite simply revolted by the fact that carnal pleasure should feel so good. Huysmans "repeated to me," writes Mugnier, "that the carnal question came down to this: the scabbard and the sword made for each other. Hence old and ugly women with whom younger men sleep with pleasure, because there is underground harmony. The young woman is the pod that opens" (16 February 1904: 145).

This inevitability of the sexual impulse leads in turn in Huysmans to a pre-Freudian concept of the conservation of libidinal energy: if it is denied outright sexual gratification, the libido will simply seek other outlets. "It is possible to be chaste," the abbé Mugnier once again cites Huysmans's opinion, "since there are chaste individuals. There are some in cloisters, but Huysmans adds, the devil does not lose anything, for one finds there the nastiness of aggressive old maids" (14 December 1903: 143).

So the sexual dam will break, and terror, like murder, will out: my purpose here is, thus, to examine woman as sexual terrorist in three of Huysmans's works that are not ordinarily spoken of in one breath: the 1881 *En ménage*, the 1898 *La cathédrale*, and what Huysmans's biographer Robert Baldick so aptly calls his "blood-and-pus" biography (Baldick 292) of *Sainte Lydwine de Schiedam* published in 1901.

I begin by taking issue with the notion that the *omission* of female characters from Huysmans's work is the first and most obvious sign of his misogyny. Indeed, Huysmans made much of his early reputation as a novelist with works in which women are represented, overall, in a rather sympathetic light: *Marthe, histoire d'une fille*, and *Les soeurs Vatard*.[1] This light, however, is far less sympathetic, and the figures of women much more menacing, in the novels with which we are concerned here: André Jayant of *En ménage*, Durtal of *La cathédrale*, and Huysmans the hagiographer of Saint Lydwina, find themselves surrounded by multiple manifestations of female sexuality. The effect is that of a hideous psycho-semiotic proliferation of the primordial obsession: in his dread of woman, the misogynist imagines women, women, everywhere. All three men, therefore, defend themselves against this sexual nightmare by a consistent strategy that assigns specific semes and spaces to the female in a desperate effort to confine this threat and thus control it: a semiotic and spatial strategy of "divide and conquer," one might call it, that responds to the original dilemma of the "fight or flight." There will, however, be no ultimate confinement of the female; throughout these works, the single sign "woman" will prove horrifyingly polysemic, polyspatial, and, finally, dreadfully recombinatory. "Woman," thus, will become tolerable only when Church-sanctioned misogyny releases her, in the case of Saint Lydwina, from the bonds of sex by releasing her also from the bonds of space.

En ménage, Huysmans's only novel of married life (it would be redundant to specify that it is of unhappy married life), is a classic illustration of the sorry adage that one can neither live with the opposite sex nor without it. Aghast at having discovered his wife *en flagrant délit d'adultère*, André Jayant flees his conjugal dwelling in favor of the familiar and more reassuring space of a bachelor apartment. In order to make sure that this new space indeed remains safe, providing the refuge from the unpredictability of female libido that originally chased him from his marital *ménage*, Jayant proceeds to orchestrate a careful division of the roles and spaces that he will now allow his various women to fulfill in his life and within his walls: they may not sleep under his roof, they may be maid or mistress or mother, but they may not be all of these at the same time and in the same place.

Thus, *En ménage* sets spinning what is, for Huysmans, a truly astonishing array of female characters. Berthe Jayant, André's faithless wife, is succeeded first by Blanche, the prostitute whom André insists on visiting only in her rooms and not in his, and then by Jeanne, André's former mistress, who will break through the spatial barrier—and eventually the semiotic one as well—by sleeping with André in his very own bed.

Before Blanche and Jeanne, however, the most important woman from André's bachelor days is Mélanie, the housekeeper whom he re-engages after he leaves Berthe. Mélanie's function in the novel pairs her with Mélie, the housekeeper with whom André's friend and fellow misogynist, the painter Cyprien Tibaille, eventually takes up lodgings in his own right. A disabused bachelor's ideal of the perfect mate, Mélie cooks, cleans, sews, shops, keeps the household books, and doesn't pester Cyprien for sex as long as he keeps his mouth shut about her drinking. She is, as Cyprien exults to André, "A dream, in short! . . . The comfort of marriage without the wife!" (Huysmans 4:67). Mélie is in fact more bovine than human, if we follow through with Cyprien's description of her: "I must add that Mélie . . . is a nice girl, that she has serious qualities, that she fulfills finally all the conditions of a last ideal that grew on me: to find a mature, calm, devoted woman without amorous needs, without coquetry, and without pretention, a powerful and peaceful cow, in a word."[2]

Cows aside for the moment, though, André wholly agrees with Cyprien's division of women into the sexual and the non-sexual, including the proviso that only the non-sexual should be allowed within the confines of the male living space. Accordingly, the women of *En ménage* all fall into one or the other of these cate-

gories: Berthe, Blanche, and Jeanne are sexual and thus excluded
from André's bachelor apartment (though, as I mentioned earlier,
Jeanne will break this pattern and confound the defensive reactions of the misogynist); Mélie and Mélanie, as non-sexual and
therefore non-threatening, are admitted into male space. It is
worth pointing out, moreover, that the sexual group of women
allows for far more individual differences among its members
than does the non-sexual. Berthe, for example, is frigid and hos-
tile, Blanche is professionally passionate, and Jeanne is ardent
but fickle. Mélie and Mélanie are virtually indivisible, to the
point of sharing almost the same name.[3] The relative indivisibil-
ity of the non-sexual group contrasts strongly with the variations
in the sexual group to suggest that only that which is thought of
as capable of being semiotically contained—the monosemic, as
opposed to the polysemic—may be safely brought within the
male domain. Indeed, as André says of Mélanie's function: "The
fire and lamps lit, clothes brushed and mended, dinner ready on
time and eaten, feet in my slippers, I am going to have all that
and respect as well for my thirty-five francs a month; I am
saved!" (4:67).

Yet this system is no sooner established than, predictably, it
begins to fall apart. Though she may be contained within the
house (and then only during the hours of her daily employment,
since she has her own husband to return home to each evening),
Mélanie is not containable with the single female signifier
"housekeeper." Ironically, she initially appears as a *ménagère en
moins* ("absent or negative housekeeper"), since she is barely
adequate to her assigned household tasks. André complains:

> As in the past, [Mélanie] was incapable of building a fire. . . . She
> also persisted in swiping the newspapers from him to cover the table
> and the sideboard of the pantry . . . broke the handles of cups,
> patched them up as best she could, . . . broke the pencils she swiped
> on the pretext of writing down expenses. . . .
> As in the past, she poured boiling water into the glasses and on
> the knives to wash them, and she was quite stupified when the for-
> mer cracked and the latter lost their edge; she regularly left in the
> sauces the tied bouquets of bay leaf and thyme, left, while sweeping
> the living room, her feather duster on a piece of furniture, every day
> forced her employer to remove the pile of newspapers and books that
> she collected in the bedrooms and piled on his desk in the very
> place he wanted to write. (4:116–17)

Mélanie's failings as a housekeeper, however, reveal her real
symbolic role for André, the second and more fundamental seme

of which he remains, apparently, unconscious. A *ménagère en moins*, Mélanie is actually *une mère en plus* ("an additional mother"). The repetition of "as in the past" in her long lists of faults suggests that Mélanie's consistency in error is of greater importance to André than would be her potential for better service. He accepts her and her failings as inevitable—exactly as one is stuck with one's own mother as primary caregiver, for better or for worse. Like Maman, Mélanie is simply a given in André's life. It does not even occur to him that a more competent housekeeper might be had for the asking, or for the right price. More importantly, Mélanie's unchangeable failings create for André the comfortable illusion of time stopped, if not actually turned back, so that the housekeeper's return to him is, in effect, his return to her: "[Mélanie's] rediscovered faults did not displease André. He expected them in passing, greeted them as acquaintances, was surprised, in spite of everything, to see them neither decreased nor increased. He noted with satisfaction that the stupidity of his maid had remained constant" (4:117).

This satisfaction is all the more surprising in that Huysmans's male characters, like their creator, are singularly dependent upon the competence of female care to insure the material comforts without which life would be even less tolerable than it already is (see Kingcaid 1993). So Mélanie's faulty housekeeping must indeed be less important to André than her ability to undo the passage of time. Surrounding him once again with a décor that had always been for him what it is now again, Mélanie returns André not only to bachelorhood but to boyhood itself: "at times it even seemed to him that he had always remained a boy/bachelor; . . . he no longer doubted that this fond dream: to cross out two years of his life, could, finally, become possible" (4:121). Mélanie's shortcomings, then, as well as her ability to turn back time strengthen the maternal role she plays for an André who naively supposes that her housekeeping alone allows him to "savor a child's joy when he was settled into his new lodging" (4:115).

The ultimate danger of which André remains unaware, however, is that maternity, whatever its unconscious figurations, is always a package deal: there is more to the cultural signifier "mère" than the material care to which he chooses to limit his already limited understanding of Mélanie. In Mélanie's case, jealousy is a particularly ominous part of this maternal package; wanting to be the only one allowed to care for André, Mélanie lives in fear that Madame Jayant, whom she believes to be ill and recuperating out of the country, will one day return to reclaim her man and her house. Mélanie, it must be repeated, is not (at least consciously) sexually jealous of André;[4] in this she conforms to the semiotic division assigned to her by her employer and figurative son, a division that Simone de Beauvoir so incisively characterizes in *Le deuxième sexe* as that between "bed service" and "household service" (2:280). However, the counterthrust of *En ménage*, the terror that the misogynist must seek constantly to surmount, is the libidinal energy arising not only from within himself, but from the female characters themselves.[5] Thus, Mélanie's overt renunciation of the sexual domain actually reinforces her maternal hold on André, along with her jealous dread that bourgeois marriage will eventually replace her with the one woman who can—indeed, who must—perform both "services."

This being the case, Jeanne's first night in André's apartment— a concession that she obtains by wisely threatening never to sleep anywhere with him at all—is the dramatic center of the novel. The emphasis in the scene is not on the reprise of a sexual relationship *per se*, but on the difficulties of its circumstances: when and where to make it happen, and how to live with the results.[6] Jeanne claims that her apartment is off-limits, as it is spied upon by friends of her rich *amant en titre*, while André claims to fear the gossip that Jeanne's comings and goings will be sure to generate in his building and his neighborhood.[7] Moreover, he professes grave economic scruples: how much housekeeping, after all, can one expect for thirty-five francs a month? For such a sum, he reasons speciously, "I cannot require [Mélanie] to share . . . her consideration and her brush strokes between Jeanne and me" (4:242).

These spatial and economic considerations are, of course, merely displacements of the larger Oedipal drama which André faces, that is, his fear of confronting Mélanie on the sexual grounds that remain implicit between them. André's, then, is the overwrought libido that pronounces itself guilty for actually *obeying* the incest taboo, since for him sexual fulfillment goes beyond rejection of the (unconscious) mother, to parade her replacement before her eyes. Surrounded by the maternal taboos personified by Mélanie, the episode of Jeanne's first "sleep-over" becomes André's timid if determined Oedipal defiance of the all-powerful mother, whose sexual jealousy (of the rival) and whose seductiveness (to the son) may be all the stronger for their being repressed. This Gordian knot can only be slashed by the

familiar phallic sword of *luxure*, and André, rather than not have
Jeanne at all, resolves to bring her home after all to sleep under
a roof that is physically his, but symbolically Mélanie's: "but I
am becoming an imbecile, he said to himself suddenly; there is
no batchelor who doesn't receive mistresses in his home and
their maids keep quiet. Mélanie will act as they do" (4:242).

The resulting confrontation between symbolic mother, invad-
ing mistress, and terrified misogynist reveals clearly the flaws in
the semiotic strategy of "divide and conquer" as a response to
the "fight or flight" of sexual anxiety. Although it is too long
to examine in full detail here, the episode is made to "work"
novelistically only by a radical split and redistribution of the
signifier "femme" into a number of its component signs: mother,
lover, and child. In the first place, Jeanne is given a fear of Mélanie that barely surpasses André's own: as the lovers lie together
in bed on their Sunday morning, they are nothing so much as
guilty children waiting to be caught. Jeanne's terror, in particular,
magnifies the warning signs of Mélanie's arrival in the apartment
and transforms the adult mistress into a cowering child, con-
sumed with shame:

> —A jingle of keys accompanied by the sound of footsteps in the
> dressing room completely frightened [Jeanne]; she would have liked
> to have been able to slip under a piece of furniture, to hide herself
> behind an armchair, to disappear, at all costs.
>
> Jeanne now no longer dared to enter the bathroom; she was afraid
> that the maid might open the connecting door; the slippers she heard
> shuffling in the kitchen made her dizzy and gave her palpitations;
> she almost regretted being up, thinking that if she had remained in
> bed, she would have buried her nose in the pillows at the maid's
> approach. (4:259)

At the center of this terror there exist already, however, the
recombinatory stirrings of female libido, a reassemblage of arti-
ficially divided semes into the single, monolithic signifier
"femme." In her fear of Mélanie, Jeanne becomes the bedroom
counterpart of the housekeeper; she fears Mélanie as the latter
fears Madame Jayant. When mistress and maid actually meet at
the luncheon table, Mélanie reacts to Jeanne's presence not with
opprobrium and blame but with an excessive display of maternal
sollicitude. To André's great and unanticipated relief, all seems
to remain well with his semiotic strategy: Mélanie behaves like
a proper housekeeper, who includes Jeanne in her ministrations
(and who charges André no additional fees for these services!);

on the psycho-sexual level she is the tender mother whose love runs pure and deep enough to extend to her victorious rival so that the son, in his Oedipal fantasy, is relieved of his guilt and permitted to function as a sexual being even *within* the physical space that he fundamentally perceives as belonging to the mother.

Such a reconciliation, however, is only the eye of the libidinal storm. For the predictable result of Andre's symbolic abdication of his roof to Mélanie and of Jeanne's subsequent penetration into male space is that André's affair with Jeanne breaks up. This is not accomplished suddenly, when, subsequent to the marriage of her *amant en titre*, Jeanne announces her imminent departure for England. Semiotically, the seeds of the rupture are sown within the reconciliation scene itself. Under the impetus of their common femininity, Mélanie and Jeanne refuse to remain within the strictly defined boundaries of meaning and behavior that a cowering André has laid out for them. As a "working-class woman" herself, Jeanne is embarrassed at being served as a lady by another woman of her own working class; worse, the probity of Mélanie's working life reminds Jeanne of the scandalous sources of her own additional income (4:262). It is only a matter of time before Jeanne and Mélanie strike up a comfortable woman-to-woman friendship from which André is entirely ex- cluded—he comes upon them suddenly in the dining room again one day, with Jeanne fitting a new dress on Mélanie—and before Jeanne also begins to speak of releasing Mélanie from her "housekeeping service" and of taking on both services of "house- keeping" and "bed" herself by moving in permanently with André.[8]

Jeanne's defection from the Oedipal triangle thus reveals the false premises of the maternally safe, sexually sure, and emotion- ally convenient *non-ménage* that André had taken such pains to establish between his mistress and his housekeeper (mother). He has made two mistakes, for which he pays, ironically, by re- turning to Berthe and the relative convenience of bourgeois mar- riage. War-weary, then, the misogynist opts for the most convenient arrangement possible for the unavoidable misery of life with the opposite sex, that which offers both *services* for the price (spatial and psychological) of putting up with only one woman.[9] André's first mistake had been to allow Jeanne into his own masculine space; his second had been to seriously underes- timate female desire and the recombinatory power of the signifier "femme." One cannot ultimately, André learns to his chagrin, break apart this signifier, this awesome force of female libido, into discrete and thus more easily manageable semes. Indeed, is this not what the misogynist already knows and shrinks from in horror: without the libidinal power of woman reaching out so compellingly to his own ambiguous combination of dread and desire, what would there in fact be to fear?

The spatial representation of sexual anxiety, and the problem of female polysemy come into even sharper relief in *La cathé-drale*. It is common in Huysmans criticism to read this novel, which is really an extended hymn of praise to the Chartres cathe-dral and its patroness, the Virgin Mary, as a religious resolution of the misogyny so evident in his earlier works.[10] If I argue that the opposite in fact is true—that, in effect, the Virgin Mary of Chartres herself is no less a sexual terrorist than Berthe, Jeanne or Mélanie—it will be once again on the basis of woman's rela-tionship to space. This time, that space is the space of the cathe-dral, a space that no longer contains or excludes either the male or the female, but which now expressly embodies the female. The woman here *is* the building, as Durtal expressly identifies the Virgin with the medieval stone architecture erected in her honor: "I," admits Durtal:

> who am not a visionary and who must resort to my imagination in order to [imagine the Virgin], it seems to me that I see her in the contours, in the very expression of the cathedral; her features are a bit blurry in the pale dazzling light of the large rose window that blazes behind her head, like a halo. She is smiling and her eyes, all lit up, have the incomparable brightness of those clear sapphires that illuminate the entrance of the nave. Her fluid body spills into a guileless flaming dress, crossed with fluting, corded . . . Her face has a whiteness that becomes pearly and her hair, as if spun by a spin-ning wheel of the sun, flies in golden strands. . . . The basilica in which She resides and which merges with Her is illuminated by her grace. (Huysmans 1930, 394)

Huysmans's religious conversion is extraordinary in that it im-posed few limits on the voices of authority to which Huymans felt obliged to respond. Submission to religious authority did not entail for Huysmans the renunciation of his own lights as thinker, critic and writer, even or again perhaps especially when he was threatened with inclusion by Rome on the Index of Pro-hibited Books. Rather, as I have argued elsewhere, conversion multiplies the occasions to make meaning by opening up new sign systems as languages in which belief in and devotion to God may be expressed (see Kingcaid 1987).

Thus, it would seem that La cathédrale, whose narrative line is a thinly disguised pretext for the interpretation of Christian symbols (the more obscure the better), also resolves the semiotic problem of polysemy which eventually got the better of the hapless André Jayant. As the characters of La cathédrale are only too happy to explain, no single representation can fill the sign to capacity or exhaust its power to generate meaning. Thus, the dove may variously signify the Virgin, the Holy Spirit, or the virtue of patience (Huysmans 1930, 336–37), while the lion and the eagle may stand in equally well for the Prince of Darkness and the Son of God.

Yet the great irony of this novel so thoroughly given over to exegesis—and, in my reading, the proof that La cathédrale begs rathers than sublimates the question of Huysmans's misogyny— is that Durtal fails to recognize, much less interpret correctly, the most obvious sign of all. The device of the woman-made-wall, that is, the physical identification of the Virgin with the stone building erected in her image, erects only a temporary dam against a still swift-running current of dread. It does so by offering Durtal a blind spot behind which to hide his sexual ambivalences: for Durtal, entering the cathedral is not—repeat not—in any way to be construed as symbolic of sexual penetration.

Another way to say this is that Durtal, who prides himself on having overcome his temptations to luxure at Chartres (Huysmans 1930, 29–30) but who chides himself at the same time for the tepidity of his new-found faith, for his state of "horrible spiritual anemia" (28), is, to put it bluntly, stonewalling. Woman-made-wall works so well as a blind spot for him precisely because it is so overloaded with sexual anxiety. Durtal may have claimed to have conquered luxure during his stay at Chartres, but in fact he has once again simply displaced it. It is all too evident that the beauty of the cathedral serves as an incarnation of the Virgin's physical beauty as woman, and that Durtal is just as attracted to this as he is to the cathedral's mystical aspects. Too schooled in art to do otherwise, Durtal does indeed let slip that his human love for the cathedral surpasses his aesthetic appreciation of it: "Now it is less [the cathedral's] soul that haunts me than its body. I wanted to study archeology, that miserable anatomy of buildings; I fell humanly in love with its contours and the divine side fled leaving nothing more than the earthly side. Alas! I wanted to see and I did a poor job of edifying myself [je me suis malédifié[11]]; it is the eternal symbol of Psyché which is beginning again!" (Huysmans 1930, 176).

Naturally, the blind spot has significant advantages for the misogynist; it allows him to beg the sexually charged question of space that resounded throughout *En ménage*. Durtal cannot see how entering the cathedral could possibly be equivalent to entering a woman, because if he looked for this interpretation, it would be all too evident and therefore intolerable. The advantage of the woman-made-wall, then—along with the "spiritual anemia" of which Durtal conveniently complains—is that it allows him not to look. That is, if woman is the building, she is neither within nor without it; she is not to be penetrated across the frightful obstacles of vagina and hymen. Nor does she threaten to penetrate male space. As a cathedral, then, Chartres is laden with signs to be interpreted, but as a cigar—well, it is just a cigar.[12]

Yet, just as we saw in *En ménage*, the stasis point of the male dread of female polysemy is only temporary and fragile; it is effected only through an elaborate and tenuous reunion of mutually exclusive signs. André Jayant was successful in his "divide and conquer" strategy so long as everyone kept to their pre-assigned spaces and semes: Mélanie as tolerant mother/house-keeper, and Jeanne as mistress. When the libidinal energy seeping out from Mélanie as mother began to stimulate Jeanne herself, André's careful compartmentalizations crumbled to pieces, resulting in the violence of his rupture with both women and his return to the original source of his terror: shared living space with his legal wife, Berthe.

In Mary, of course, are united the most extremely, mutually exclusive of female semes—virgin and mother; within this opposition there is therefore concentrated such a high degree of centrifugal polysemic force, that the compartimentalized semes are bound to fly apart—and reassemble into the dreaded monolithic signifier "femme"—with a most extraordinary potential for violence. It is thus not only the tedium of provincial life and the proddings of a reluctant vocation that finally drive Durtal away from the cathedral: it is the feared omnipotence, once again, of the female undivided and unconquered. Durtal's final speech of praise to the Cathedral's patroness offers telling glimpses of that violence, as of his fear: "even down to the bellicose aspect of some details of the sanctuary, that knightly turn recalling the Crusades, with the sword blades and the shields of the windows and the rose windows, the helmet of the gothic vaults, the coats of mail of the old church steeple, the iron lattice of certain window panes, . . . everything conveys that liberty that She possesses, when She wants, to be 'like an army drawn up in battle, terrible'" (Huysmans 1930, 394).

Finally, however, *Sainte Lydwine de Schiedam* paints, in a way that *En ménage* and *La cathédrale* could not, a new feminine ideal whose power to terrify can now actually—to Huysmans's great relief, if not necessarily ours—be praised. One of Huysmans's last works, *Sainte Lydwine* ties up the loose ends of misogyny, space, and polysemy as an expression of sexual anxiety that we have been following here, offering a Decadent corrective to the mysticism of the converted Huysmans and a Catholic underpinning for a still unrepentant misogynist.

When *Sainte Lydwine* appeared, Huysmans, as usual, proclaimed that he was entirely dissatisfied with the work. He complained to Adolphe Berthet in July 1901 that, "writing St Lydwina was an act of penance for me. . . . There were few opportunities for the artistic dimension to take off; it is the literary equivalent of fasting . . ." (translated and quoted from Beaumont 207). Yet like Durtal before him, Huysmans is betraying another blind spot; his treatment of Saint Lydwina, whose claim to fame is the life of living martyrdom she suffered in voluntary expiation for the sins of others,[13] owes much of its evocative force to the Decadent attraction to *pourriture* ("decay") as a source of feminine beauty. After the aridity of *La cathédrale, Sainte Lydwine* is almost refreshing in its merciless catalogue of the hideous afflictions which the poor woman suffered. The biography is vintage Huysmans, as the following lengthy, but entirely typical, passage demonstrates:

> the entire body of the unfortunate woman was raw; in addition to the ulcers in which colonies of parasites took root and were nourished without being destroyed, a tumor appeared on her shoulder which putrefied; then, it was the feared evil of the Middle Ages, the sacred fire or the illness of burning which started on the right arm and consumed the flesh to the bone; the tendons twisted and burst, except for one which held the arm and prevented it from detaching itself from the trunk; from then on it was impossible for Lydwine to turn to that side and she only had the left arm to lift her head, which in turn decayed. Horrifying neuralgias assailed her which bored, like a brace and bit, into her temples and struck her skull with violent mallet blows; her forehead cracked from the roots of her hair down to the middle of her nose; her chin came off under her lower lip and her mouth swelled; she went blind in her right eye and the other became so sensitive that it could not bear the least light without bleeding; she also experienced raging toothaches, which sometimes

lasted weeks and made her half-crazy; finally, after an exhausting
episode which suffocated her, she bled from the mouth, the ears, the
nose, in such quantity that her bed was dripping. (Huysmans
15:1:80–81)

If this is stylistic fasting, one could reasonably ask what Huysmans's idea of feasting is.[14] In fact, what is going on here is no
penance, no sublimation of misogyny at all, but rather, its ultimate gratification. In *Sainte Lydwine*, reverence turns so quickly
to complacency, and complacency so rapidly to delectation, that
we rapidly find ourselves embraced by a Church-sanctioned *volupté* of female-inspired terror—a holy terror, perhaps, but terror
nonetheless. Repressed sexuality runs rampant through Huysmans's continued description of woman's suitability for the role
of substitute expiatrice of others' sins, as he writes, "Add that in
virgins, the suppressed maternal love dissolves itself in the de-
light of the Spouse [Jesus] who doubles himself for them and
becomes, when they desire, the Child; . . . Despite their capricious side, and subjection to illusions, it is thus among women
that the Spouse recruits his preferred victims" (15:2:100–101).

It is not too much, then, to accuse the misogynist of outright
sadism (disguised as religious adoration) by the time he gets to
Sainte Lydwine. Under the dual aegis of Decadence and Catholicism, it becomes clear that mystical substitution is the best use
to which, in Huysmans's view, the female body and soul can be
put. Where the Decadent Huysmans sees the suffering woman
as deservedly punished for the ambiguous sexual stirrings she
elicits from him,[15] the Catholic sees a martyr for his sins. Thus
Huysmans can finally write about woman in a convenient combination of good and bad faith: he adheres to Church tradition on
the natural inferiority of woman the temptress and, relying on
that tradition, he does not have to account for his own intentions
in this work of pure piety, in this "stylistic equivalent of fasting."
For the incorrigible misogynist, *Sainte Lydwine* is a win-win
situation.

Lydwina's ideality is ultimately confirmed by her relationship
to space. Though confined to her bed, Lydwina is blessed with
the extraordinary spiritual gift of bilocation; able to be simultaneously here and there, in and out, Lydwina is uncontainable,
unenclosable, neither to be banned from male space nor pos-
sessor of her own foreign space. Released from the laws of space,
Lydwina is also exempt from the sexual interpretation of those
laws. It is of no little significance that Huysmans concludes his
hagiography with the tale of his fruitless search for the remains
of Lydwina's house in Schiedam. For all practical purposes, Lydwina and her house have disappeared from her native town: "As

for the house she occupied, it is the subject of numerous contro-
versies. . . . Except for those bones and her memory which shines
brilliantly in that city, nothing, alas! remains here of Lydwina,
other than her headstone" (15:2:144–45).

The "alas!" of course, is that of the pious pilgrim in search of
relics, but in the light of *En ménage* and *La cathédrale,* it cannot
help but ring to the reader's ears with a resounding note of relief.
"It is difficult for a novelist to be chaste," the abbé Mugnier again
relates Huysmans's opinion, "because of the images with which
he is obsessed" (Mugnier 18 June 1891: 61). Though this is
clearly a chicken-and-egg argument (not all novelists have the
same obsessions, and a certain amount of sheer obstreperousness
would seem to constantly steer Huysmans's conversations with
the abbé into the murky waters of the bizarre sexual practices of
such writers as Maupassant, Flaubert, Paul Bourget, and even
Victor Hugo who, as Huysmans assured the abbé, was not above
picking up young girls on city buses!). Huysmans was at least
aware of the usefulness of religion in the ongoing battle against
sexual temptation. "Yesterday," writes the abbé Mugnier in November 1989, "Huysmans repeated to me that chastety is not
possible outside the religious idea. If he had not sincerely come
back to God, he would find pleasure in carnal dealings with
women" (Mugnier 110–11).

It appears clear, then, that whatever uneasiness conversion
may have evoked in the sexually anxious conscience of the confirmed misogynist who is nonetheless drawn to the flesh pots of
Babylon (he will remain a *littérateur* who must then, by definition, struggle with temptation until the end of his life[16]), Huysmans can be both gratified and relieved by the existence of Saint
Lydwina, who accepts *as woman* the extreme chastisement due
all women for their sexual attractiveness, now destroyed in the
combination of piety and *pourriture* ("decay") exemplified in the
saint. Of all the sinners Lydwina's sufferings save, then, it would
seem that Huysmans considers himself far from the last in line;
it is, after all, not her tale of fight or flight from the battle of
concupiscence that he tells—it is, to all extents and purposes,
his own.

Saint Mary's College

NOTES

1. The sympathetic portrayal of these feminine characters, of course, may
have more to do with the desire to *épater le bourgeois* that was part and parcel

of Huysmans's adherence to the Naturalist creed at the time of their composition, than with a real attempt to present woman in a positive light for her own sake. Annette Kahn, for example, compares the representations of women in these novels to Huysmans's art criticism of Degas and Forain, suggesting, first, that the novelistic descriptions of the women represent exercises in the *transposition d'art* in Huysmans (Kahn 40, 43), and, second, that the similarities between his descriptions of women in his novels and in his art criticism "shows the extent to which his preoccupation with women affected his whole descriptive code" (Kahn 44). For us, the most important part of Huysmans's description code will be that found in—or omitted from—*La cathédrale*.

2. Huysmans 4:337–38. While this description of Mélie is hardly flattering, Mary Donaldson-Evans's reading of *En ménage* as "Huysmans's Roman-Abattoir," makes it downright sinister. Donaldson-Evans reminds us that André Jayant is a frustrated novelist who had originally (if inadvertently) given his wife her opportunity to entertain her lover by his early-morning visit to a slaughterhouse, where he had hoped to obtain documentation for a novel. Donaldson-Evans's analysis of the importance of the slaughterhouse bodes ill for both André and the bovine Mélie (among whose duties are the medical ones of cleaning up after Cyprien's digestive and sexual illnesses). André's novel, she writes, is "never written, but the allusion [to the slaughterhouse] is not gratuitous, for his own fictional existence is hardly less instinctual—or more enviable—than that of beasts being led to the kill. Furthermore, despite this apparently deterministic subject, *En ménage* is not a *roman-laboratoire*, but a *roman-abattoir*, mercilessly slaughtering all the sacred cows of late nineteenth-century France with its 'bursts of sinister gaiety and expressions of ferocious wit'" (Donaldson-Evans 208). The quote within the quote (Donaldson-Evans adds) is from Huysmans himself, given in translation in Baldick (59).

3. Mary Donaldson-Evans, again, traces this name to the Greek word for "honey," *meli*, and notes that honey was often a basis for medical elixirs in the nineteenth century. Thus she reinforces the care-taking functions of Mélanie and particularly Mélie, whom Cyprien took on primarily for her nursing functions (Donaldson-Evans 206). One can note, moreover, the irony of these names for the English-speaking reader, for whom "Honey," of course, is a traditional term of sexual endearment.

4. Mélanie's jealousy of Berthe is based primarily on her aversion to letting anyone else see to André's material needs. She herself marks the difference between sexual jealousy and its domestic variation in her opinion of André's relationship to Blanche: "Well, she said, since Monsieur's lady is still sick, Monsieur must indeed frequent another" (4:207). Her fear and relief are palpable—and thus prepare the reader for the comradeship that will develop between housekeeper and mistress—when Mélanie learns that Jeanne is not Madame Jayant: "Mélanie's stupor increased, but she smiled nonetheless and left relieved, still preferring the arrival of any mistress to the return of the legitimate wife" (4:244–45).

5. Like Huysmans's monks who work off their sexual tensions in aggressive bickering, woman will not be denied either without compensatory effects.

6. In this, the scene corresponds roughly to Durtal's preparations for receiving Mme de Chantelouve's first visit in *Là-bas*. All of these preparations focus on the space of the visit. Durtal is embarrassed that the globe of his lamp is dirty and readjusts the shade so that the defect will pass unnoticed. More

importantly, he regrets that his salon has no sofa. For a first assignation, he is not convinced he should lead her directly to the bedroom, and thus wonders whether "I ought to lay her right on the rug" (Huysmans 1908, 143).

7. "The idea of bringing Jeanne to his home astounded him. He saw the bourgeois house he was living in stirred up, the concierge picking quarrels with the girl, yelling at her to wipe her feet, asking her, every time, where she was going; Mélanie, outraged, ranting about Jeanne, grumbling, complaining, refusing to greet her and to serve her; he saw all of a sudden the tranquility of his interior going to ruin, replaced by a real hell of gossip and fights" (OC 4.237).

8. It is among the most delicious ironies of this novel, of course, that the male characters are almost invariably happier *out* of *ménage* than they are within it.

9. It is certainly not through a new-found burst of physical passion that André returns to his wife; it is simply easier on the male libidinal/nervous system to accept a bourgeois marriage that permits, in fact requires, that one woman provide both "services" of bed and housekeeping. André, then, "expected nothing good from that ease with which Berthe had let herself be conquered . . . then consoled himself at the prospect of leaving that odious bachelor's life, with its abundance of female crises and maid's swipings, to settle again into a well organized household, perhaps finally to live in peace" (4:378). There is no guarantee at the end of the novel, however, that this new version of an old *ménage* will indeed be "well organized" (André and Cyprien are both pessimistic but resigned about the prospect of life with women again), but Huysmans offers André at least one note of optimism. André buys Berthe a new house in the country; though the deal can easily be construed as blackmail by her family to reunite them, the house purchase nevertheless represents a new space for their new beginning. On the importance of the "skirt crisis," or the dreaded imperative to sexual gratification, see Baldick, who quotes (in translation) Huysmans's own third-person appraisal of his innovation in *En ménage:* "Note how accuractly this crisis is represented [in *En ménage*], and remember that Huysmans was the first to discover this minute district of the soul" (Baldick 59).

10. See again Annette Kahn, for example, who discusses "sublimation" as part of Huysmans's attitude towards the cathedral, writing about the 1898 novel: "All physical urges have been sublimated into a love of the Virgin Mary, who finally fulfills the quest for an ideal woman. This love of the Virgin Mary is manifest in . . . the adoration of the Chartres Cathedral itself, which Huysmans describes in female terms . . ." (Kahn 60). Yet Kahn is perceptive enough to recognize that this may not be the entire picture: "After his conversion to Catholicism, Huysmans's obsession with women is less openly expressed. His sexual urges are frequently sublimated in his enthusiasm for certain religious works of art and his ambivalence towards women continues to be a tension in his work" (Kahn 34). As shall be seen, I read more tension than sublimation in Huysmans's approach to the Virgin of the Chartres cathedral; in fact, as shall be seen, I am not sure that Huysmans ever arrives at sublimation of his misogyny, even—or especially—in his hagiography of Saint Lydwina.

11. The pun on "malédifié" sounds almost intentional: architecturally and spiritually, Huysmans is poorly "edified" according to his own plans for his study of the cathedral.

12. It is certainly not insignificant in this context that Huysmans's favorite

part of the cathedral is its womb-like crypt. This preference again, however, begs the question of sexuality in the cathedral by attempting to create a pre-sexual identification between mother and as-yet unborn child. Naturally (for example, when one is not dealing with a virgin mother), the child arrives in the womb in the first place through sexual penetration, but this is a fact of which he is allowed to remain—indeed, is expected to remain for quite some time—blissfully unaware!

13. This doctrine of mystical substitution is developed at great length in the biography. Huysmans's belief in this doctrine is usually traced to the combined influences upon him of Léon Bloy (particularly in Le désespéré), and of the defrocked priest/occultist whom Huysmans consulted for Là-Bas, the Abbé Joseph-Antoine Boullant (see Baldick 214, and Cogny 200). Huysmans conceives of mystical substitution as a means of redressing the balance of good and evil upon the earth, as he explains in Sainte Lydwine: "In order to right the crimes of some, [God] demands the mortification and prayers of others; . . . Through the ages, he has always found saints who have agreed to pay, through pain, the ransom of sins and mistakes" (15:1:37). It is hardly coincidental for Huysmans that the "some" ("des uns") that God finds for mystical substitution are more usually "women" ("des unes"), for, still in Sainte Lydwine, we read: "The truth is that woman's soul, and her temperament, are more loving, more devoted, less selfish than man's; . . . therefore Jesus finds a more zealous welcome in her; she has attentions, refinement, little caring acts that a man, when he is not Saint Francis of Assisi, does not know" (15:2:100–101).

14. In his discussion of Sainte Lydwine, Pierre Cogny is willing to take Huysmans at his word on the question of fasting vs. feasting. Cogny writes that in this biography, "art, for the first time, is relegated to the background, the hagiographer is aware of it. . . . The writing so characteristic of Huysmans has completely changed! Here, no authorial coquetry, but a reporting without smugness: he was trying neither to move nor to surprise, but to inform, almost dryly, and he gives the impression of having systematically put aside every rhetorical form, convinced that the quasi-clinical presentation of facts is the only way to convince and that the subject itself precludes the slightest verbal fantasy" (Cogny 207, 208–9). Rather then reveal a change in Huysmans's methods of writings, I would suggest that Cogny's own terms bring us back to Huysmans's earlier roots in the clinical observation of fact—which is, of course, its own form of rhetorical presentation—that characterizes his Naturalist and Decadent writings!

15. A convincing argument can be made, of course, for the synonymity of "decadent" and "misogynist," and not only in Huysmans's case.

16. In all fairness to Huysmans, it must be pointed out, as it has been so many times before, that this life finishes in a most exemplary and expiatory manner itself, in his virtually intolerable sufferings from the throat and mouth cancer of which he eventually died.

12

L'homme sans nom et la terreur littéraire

William Paulson

L'on se souvient de *L'homme sans nom* de Ballanche avant tout comme "source" ou "inspiration" de l'épisode du Conventionnel G. dans *Les misérables*. C'est chez Ballanche que Hugo a vraisemblablement déniché la figure d'un ancien représentant du peuple, désormais retiré du monde en signe d'expiation de son vote en faveur de la mort de Louis XVI. *L'homme sans nom* mérite pourtant de son propre chef une place dans un recueil sur la littérature et la terreur au dix-neuvième siècle, non seulement parce que c'était en effet une oeuvre connue à l'époque et une pièce maîtresse dans le dossier du sacrifice expiatoire chez Ballanche, mais parce qu'elle conjugue la Terreur de 93 et la terreur littéraire, innovation romantique dont Jean Paulhan se fera le théoricien dans *Les fleurs de Tarbes*. En Ballanche et en son personnage, l'Homme sans nom, se confondent deux figures que Paulhan sépare: le critique terroriste qui dénonce le pouvoir des mots et le rhéteur qui, selon le premier, y cède. *L'homme sans nom* est donc un apologue de la parole à l'époque de l'imprimé autant que de la violence et du sacré à l'époque des lumières démocratiques.

Réédité à l'occasion du bicentenaire de la Révolution de 1789, discrètement mis en valeur dans ces milieux intellectuels où l'on n'en finit pas de déplorer 1793, *L'homme sans nom* appartient à la première moisson d'écrits politiques de Ballanche sous la Restauration, avec *Le vieillard et le jeune homme* et surtout l'*Essai sur les institutions sociales*. Dans ces trois textes, l'imprimeur devenu écrivain prône une Restauration modérée, réconciliatrice, comme synthèse de deux grands courants ou formes de pensée, l'un ancien et l'autre moderne, qui ont le malheur ou du moins la particularité d'exister simultanément dans la France post-révolutionnaire. Des trois, *L'homme sans nom* est sans doute celui qui conforte le plus les "archéophiles" (prémodernes en passe de devenir antimodernes) et laisse les "néophiles" (modernes, hommes des lumières) insatisfaits.

Le texte se présente comme le récit d'un épisode de voyage. Traversant les Alpes en août 1814 (dans un décor dont Balzac a peut-être profité pour *Le médecin de campagne*) le narrateur arrive dans un hameau misérable, où on lui indique, à l'écart des autres habitations, "la maison du Régicide" (Ballanche 1989, 38), ancien conventionnel qui n'utilise plus d'autre nom que cette épithète. Le narrateur décide aussitôt qu'il lui faut "voir et entretenir" cet "être singulier" (39). Aussitôt dit, aussitôt fait. La première partie de l'ouvrage est dominée par le récit de l'Homme sans nom. Dans la deuxième partie, le narrateur, de retour au hameau, apprend la mort du Régicide et les derniers épisodes de sa vie; il recueille enfin et offre au lecteur des notes retrouvées dans sa maison après sa mort.

Dans la première partie il devient vite évident que la terreur au coeur de *L'homme sans nom* est celle que subit le Régicide lui-même au sein de la Convention. Terroriste malgré lui, il est avant tout victime d'une terreur langagière. Son récit est celui d'une jeune personne séduite par le pouvoir des mots, perdue par la sensualité grisante des paroles de la foule. J'use à dessein du féminin grammatical de *jeune personne séduite*. Dans un passage qui rappelle étonnamment le régime discursif des *Liaisons dangereuses*, le Régicide explique que ses premières concessions aux partisans de la condamnation, qui faisaient partie d'une stratégie de défense naïve et erronée, ont entraîné infailliblement sa perte, c'est-à-dire son vote contre son roi: "nous voulions nous réserver tout notre courage pour le moment où il s'agirait de l'application de la peine . . . je me laissai entraîner à ces premières lâchetés, gage assuré de la dernière; car d'un instant à l'autre les circonstances devenaient plus menaçantes, le poste plus périlleux. Etrange position que celle d'admettre des principes dont on se promet de repousser ensuite les conséquences, comme si les conséquences n'étaient pas toujours forcées et inévitables!" (Ballanche 1989, 49). On croirait entendre la Merteuil expliquer à la petite Volanges qu'en s'arrangeant pour recevoir le courrier de Danceny elle avait passé le contrat qui livrait son corps à Valmont. Le Régicide traite son vote de faute morale, et s'accuse d'avoir été entraîné par de mauvaises influences, une atmosphère malsaine et un paysage moral où tout ce qui était solide se liquéfie, mais surtout par la complicité de sa propre chair:

[les discours] me subjugaient moi-même malgré toute l'antipathie que j'opposais, et me plongaient tout entier dans le bain mortel d'une funeste et délirante contagion. (Ballanche 48)

[je fus] une pauvre créature délaissée . . . une parole inconnue . . . vint se placer sur mes lèvres iniques . . . j'étais un être sans moralité. Ma bouche, devenue le plus vil instrument . . . une voix étrangère qui mentait à ma pensée, qui immolait ce que j'avais de plus cher en moi. D'ailleurs n'avais-je pas vu, malgré tout le désordre de mes sens, cette joie atroce et convulsive . . . le crime de mes lèvres. (Ballanche 51)
la profonde abjection où j'étais tombé n'avait pas achevé de me pervertir. (Ballanche 53)

Le corps et la parole de l'homme sans nom travestissent sa personne et sa pensée pour donner lieu au mot figé, écrit, qu'est sa voix acquise aux partisans de la mort du roi.

Or Ballanche lui-même prétendra n'avoir d'abord publié *L'homme sans nom* qu'à son corps défendant: "je ne voulais livrer la pureté de ma pensée, et j'oserais dire la pudeur de mes sentiments" (Ballanche 28). Telle est l'explication qu'il donne après-coup, en 1828, pour justifier la publication quasi-confidentielle de *L'homme sans nom*, paru en 1820, sans nom d'auteur et tiré à cent exemplaires. Cette réticence est d'ailleurs habituelle chez lui, au moins à partir de 1811–1812, date à laquelle il fait ses premiers projets de publication confidentielle. Le 14 septembre 1811, il se déclare prêt à tirer *Inès de Castro* à vingt-cinq exemplaires. Le 17 novembre 1812 il écrit à son ami Beuchot: "Je veux imprimer à cent exemplaires seulement un ouvrage qui aurait pour titre: Antigone. / Inès de Castro. / Fragmens."[1]

En outre, sa pratique de l'écriture et de l'impression montre clairement qu'il considère la publication (et dans une moindre mesure l'impression) comme un tournant décisif où se fige irrémédiablement un processus d'écriture qui va des brouillons aux épreuves. Il en va généralement ainsi dans la culture de l'imprimé, mais Ballanche en est particulièrement conscient, et très explicite dans ses réflexions à ce sujet. Ses pratiques d'écriture et d'impression en témoignent également. Il corrige énormément ses épreuves; les dossiers de la Bibliothèque municipale de Lyon contiennent des cahiers imprimés à part, et dans la Préface à la seconde édition de *L'homme sans nom* il avoue, "si une fois je m'étais mis à faire autre chose qu'une réimpression pure et simple, je ne sais plus où je me serais arrêté" (Ballanche 33).

Dans son explication, en 1828, de la demi-publication de
L'homme sans nom en 1820, Ballanche déclare encore n'avoir
pas voulu contribuer au délire collectif qui suivit alors l'assassi-
nat du Duc de Berry. Ce meurtre est pour les ultras une reprise
de l'exécution de Louis XVI: Ballanche, modéré, ne manque pas
de noter ce rapport, mais dénonce également le parallèle entre
le délire régicide de la Convention et le délire anti-républicain
des ultras de 1820. Ne pas publier ce qui pourrait réconforter
les ultras dans leur affolement, c'est donc résister à la séduction
terroriste qui a perdu le Régicide. Et les signes de rapprochement
entre Ballanche et l'Homme sans nom se multiplient. Au début
de l'*Essai sur les institutions sociales*, Ballanche se décrit
comme un solitaire au milieu de la foule (Ballanche 1833, 2:16),
trait qu'il prête à l'assassin du duc de Berry dans l'*Elégie* (Ballanche 1833, 3:338) et à deux reprises au régicide de *L'homme sans
nom* (Ballanche 1989, 62, 81).

Ce ne sont pourtant pas les indices les plus flagrants de cette
identification de Ballanche avec le Régicide et ses semblables.
Dans sa préface Ballanche affirme en un étrange démenti que "la
plupart des expressions que je mets dans sa bouche ne doivent
point m'être attribuées" (Ballanche 1989, 29). Comment un lecteur tant soit peu averti de la distinction entre un auteur et le
récit d'un personnage aurait-il pu songer à attribuer à Ballanche
les expressions sortant de la bouche du Régicide, si Ballanche
ne l'avait pas mis sur cette voie lui-même par la véhémence de
son démenti? Evidemment, on peut considérer que Ballanche
explique ici qu'il ne prétendait pas innover ou inventer en cam-
pant son personnage, mais au contraire qu'il voulait donner voix
(ou plutôt donner écriture imprimée) à certain discours consacré
sur la mort du roi, la Convention et les régicides. Mais cette
explication, partiellement convaincante, renvoie elle-même au
premier indice repéré tout à l'heure d'une identification entre
l'auteur et le Régicide, car il s'agit d'avouer, pour la énième fois,
que l'auteur moderne, tout comme le votant de 93, ne détient
pas une parole singulière mais qu'au contraire, il matérialise et
signe une parole en circulation, banale même lorsqu'elle délire,
car elle délire collectivement, faisant des hommes de la Convention des monstres ou de l'assassin du Duc de Berry, Louvel, un
représentant d'une vaste et, selon Ballanche, inexistante
conjuration.

On analysera ici les traces du rapport entre Ballanche et son
personnage dans deux contextes: d'abord, une spéculation d'or-

dre psychocritique, et ensuite, la terreur littéraire et la parole matérialisée de la culture de l'imprimé.

Ballanche adolescent aurait-il connu, à la mort de Louis XVI, une joie analogue à celle attribuée par Stendhal à l'enfant Henry Brulard? L'on connaît la phrase célèbre de *La vie* de ce dernier: "Je fus saisi d'un des plus vifs mouvements de joie que j'aie éprouvés en ma vie" (Stendhal 1955, 128). Il faut également songer à l'exemple du premier Chateaubriand, jeune noble "voltairien" et "rousseauiste," dont on trouve des traces dans *Les Natchez* (Chactas à la cour de Louis XIV), dans *Atala* ("Périsse le Dieu qui contrarie la nature! Homme, prêtre, qu'es-tu venu faire dans ces forêts?" [Chateaubriand 1969, 76]) et dans le *Voyage en Amérique* ("Liberté primitive, je te retrouve enfin!" [Chateaubriand 1969, 703]). Il y a quelques indices d'une phase analogue chez le jeune Ballanche, notamment l'influence de Rousseau et l'absence de pensée contre-révolutionnaire dans *Du sentiment*. Plus significative encore est sa grande "lettre testamentaire" de 1847, où il évoque les espoirs progressistes de sa jeunesse: "Enfant, j'ai d'abord senti sur moi le souffle des plus enivrantes illusions: je n'en pouvais avoir la conscience . . . Autour de moi, je n'entendais que des paroles dont le sens mystérieux pour moi seul me prédisait un siècle beau entre tous les siècles. . . . Hélas! hélas! qu'a été ensuite mon adolescence? . . . mon imagination prématurément obsédée par tout ce que l'on peut concevoir de plus odieusement douloureux. . . . De cruelles souffrances heureusement sont venues me distraire de tant de calamités" (Paulson 32). Ostensiblement, et sans doute sincèrement, ce passage évoque la cruelle déception de la Terreur lyonnaise, les dangers et revers trop réels effectivement encourus et subis par la famille Ballanche. Comme tant d'autres, à cette époque, le vieillard évoque son adolescence en identifiant l'histoire de sa vie à celle de son pays. Or voici que réapparaît, sous sa plume, la figure d'une conscience naïve ou faible enivrée par le souffle des paroles, entraînée malgré elle dans un enthousiasme progressiste, voire révolutionnaire. Et il s'accuse d'avoir été *seul* à ne pas comprendre, comme si, dans son entourage, les autres disaient déjà, à un moment: "non, de toute cette agitation révolutionnaire il n'en sortira rien de bon", alors que le jeune Pierre-Simon, lui, y croyait encore. N'oublions pas la chronologie: au début de 93, Ballanche aurait pu garder, en son for intérieur, la foi révolutionnaire. Il aurait pu tressaillir de joie à la mort du roi, pour ensuite changer d'avis lorsque sa famille s'est vue menacée et dépossédée par la Terreur lyonnaise à la fin de l'année.

Un revirement si douloureux et si nécessairement culpabilisant expliquerait mieux que de simples dangers et ennuis réels mais extérieurs cette "obsession" de l'"odieusement douloureux," pour reprendre ses termes. C'est à un esprit en proie à ses obsessions odieuses, et non pas à un adolescent qui traverse avec sa famille une époque violente et dangereuse, qu'il appartient d'être "heureusement" distrait par les "cruelles souffrances" de la maladie. Comme si Ballanche avait renversé avant la lettre le mot d'Oscar Wilde pour s'écrier, "Mon dieu, envoyez-moi les douleurs physiques, car les douleurs morales, je ne peux plus m'en charger."

L'hypothèse d'un Ballanche régicide fantasmé, pour outrageante qu'elle soit, serait analogue au rapport auteur-personnage dans *La ville des expiations*, où le nouvel hiérophante expie un crime qu'aurait fantasmé Ballanche. L'hiérophante a tué un rival qui avait intrigué pour qu'il soit refusé par les parents de la jeune fille qu'il voulait épouser; Ballanche, lui, s'était vu rejeté par les parents de la seule fiancée de sa vie, de sorte que l'expiation la plus remarquable accomplie à la Ville est celle du crime que Ballanche aurait commis si le plus grand traumatisme de sa vie affective l'avait poussé au crime, au moins en imagination. La *Ville* se trouvant à la fin de la *Palingénésie*, on peut dire que cette grande oeuvre se clôt par la réconciliation entre deux Ballanche, celui qui s'est résigné à la douleur, ou s'est laissé distraire par elle, et celui, fantasmatique, qui aurait choisi la révolte. Ce genre de spéculation peut donc éclairer les origines de la doctrine ballanchienne de l'expiation et du progrès, sa synthèse des principes révolutionnaires et monarchistes.

"L'on appelle *Terreurs*," écrit Jean Paulhan dans *Les fleurs de Tarbes ou la terreur dans les lettres*, "ces passages dans l'histoire des nations . . . où il semble soudain qu'il faille à la conduite de l'Etat, non pas l'astuce et la méthode, ni même la science et la technique—de tout cela on n'a plus que faire—mais bien plutôt une extrême pureté de l'âme, et la fraîcheur de l'innocence commune" (Paulhan 61). Paulhan définit ainsi la terreur afin d'élaborer une théorie de ce qu'il dénomme la terreur littéraire ou critique: l'ensemble de doctrines et de pratiques qui prédominent dans la littérature romantique et moderne et qui dénoncent l'astuce et la méthode—la rhétorique, en somme—en faveur de la révélation incessamment renouvelée d'objets et d'expressions neufs. A première vue, on est très loin de Ballanche et de 93.

Et pourtant. La critique terroriste prétend prendre l'auteur en flagrant délit de céder au "pouvoir des mots," malsaine puissance de séduction qui réside dans tout langage "tout fait" et qui invite à l'abdication de la pensée. Munis de leur pouvoir, les mots traînent à leur suite "une pensée honteusement résignée" (Paulhan 56). "L'auteur de lieux communs *cède* à la puissance des mots, au verbalisme" (Paulhan 57; je souligne). Celui qui n'échappe pas à la "griserie des mots" est, toujours selon les terroristes, un "auteur lâche" (Paulhan 60). La terreur littéraire récuse une faute morale, l'esprit qui s'abandonne à la bassesse charnelle de la lettre.

Or ce sont les termes mêmes de la confession du Régicide. L'homme sans nom, retiré dans son chétif hameau, s'accuse en terroriste d'avoir été autrefois victime consentante d'une terreur, qui s'appelle en langage paulhanien pouvoir-des-mots. Il fait donc exception à cette règle énoncée par Paulhan, que le pouvoir-des-mots se trouve toujours chez l'autre, jamais chez soi: *mes* mots et même *mes* clichés, pense maint littéraire, ne sont jamais un appareil séducteur et creux auquel je succombe, mais bien au contraire l'expression la plus candide de ma pensée; ce sont *vos* mots et *vos* clichés qui vous égarent. Mais le Régicide se dédouble, devient un autre pour lui-même. Héautontimorou-ménos, l'Homme sans nom se fait victime et bourreau, plaie et couteau, et cela sur le plan littéraire aussi bien que sur le plan politique ou religieux.

Ce double rôle chez un personnage qui, nous l'avons vu, fait figure de double projeté de l'auteur, correspond vraisemblable-ment à la profonde ambivalence de Ballanche vis-à-vis non seu-lement de la Révolution mais de la culture de l'imprimé, au sens que Marshall McLuhan et surtout Walter J. Ong ont donné à "print culture." Car il n'est pas difficile de montrer que les phé-nomènes littéraires et critiques disséqués par Paulhan sont juste-ment ceux de la culture de l'imprimé dans sa maturité, c'est-à-dire, dans le contexte français, à partir de l'époque romantique. Il s'agit grosso modo du rapport au langage créé par la distance entre auteur et lecteur qui accompagne le livre imprimé devenu bien de consommation dans un marché développé. La disponi-bilité de l'imprimé fait que l'on ne supporte plus la formule ou l'épithète, autrefois partie intégrante du récit oral et de la mémo-risation; désormais la littérature appareille de sa rhétorique na-tale pour se lancer dans une dialectique d'innovation, d'auto-dépassement formel. Le feu trésor communautaire de la langue poétique et éloquente perd sa richesse et sa vitalité en se maté-rialisant. Désormais on attend de chaque auteur qu'il outrepasse le donné littéraire pour livrer un sens inédit, plus-value qui seule puisse justifier l'achat ou la lecture du livre; faute de quoi, on accuse l'auteur d'abandonner le sens pour voler des bouts de parole qui ne valent rien.

Or Ballanche est lui-même imprimeur, fils d'imprimeur et surtout théoricien (notamment dans son *Essai sur les institutions sociales*) du rapport langage-pensée et de la tension entre les institutions anciennes et nouvelles de la parole. Ses "archéophiles" se réclament de la Parole comme institution sacrée, révélation du sens, tandis que ses "néophiles" se rangent volontiers sous la bannière de l'imprimerie et de l'arbitraire du signe. Dans un "Essai sur la propriété littéraire," inachevé et inédit de son vivant, Ballanche dépeint l'homme de lettres de son époque prenant ses pensées "dans ses lectures, combinant ses phrases, choisissant ses expressions, faisant enfin un ouvrage d'imagination ou d'esprit comme on fait un ouvrage d'orfèvrerie" (Ballanche 1985, 14). C'est le promeneur du jardin de Tarbes pris en flagrant délit de cueillir des fleurs, mais c'est aussi, les états d'âme et l'angoisse en moins, l'Homme sans nom récoltant son suffrage régicide dans la jungle discursive de la Convention. Ailleurs, dans son *Essai sur les institutions sociales*, Ballanche ajoute l'accusation d'*impudeur* à l'image platonicienne de l'écriture comme jeune fille qui se promène sans la protection de son père (Ballanche 1833, 2:337), ce qui rejoint l'auto-condamnation du régicide, dont la parole, qui lui est arrachée dans un flot de paroles impudiques, se fige aussitôt en chiffre de vote, aussi irréparable que l'imprimé livré au public.

Si le vieux dictionnaire de rhétorique auquel Hugo prétendra avoir mis le bonnet rouge est aristocratique, et si son geste terroriste se veut donc révolutionnaire, Ballanche nous donne, au contraire, et plus secrètement, l'exemple d'un proto-terroriste qui s'acharne contre la terreur révolutionnaire tout en s'identifiant avec elle. Le Régicide est tantôt la figure de l'auteur moderne effronté, qui trahit la parole en se l'appropriant et en la matérialisant, tantôt la figure de l'auteur moderne réticent, Ballanche luimême, dévoré de nostalgie et de remords, rejouant une scène de l'oralité perdue. Un portrait, somme toute, de l'écrivain en victime coupable, en bourreau récalcitrant.

University of Michigan

NOTE

1. Bibliothèque Nationale, Nouv. acq. fr. 5196:248, 5197:39.

Part 3
Resolution?

13

Masters and Slaves in *Le rouge et le noir* and *Indiana*

HOPE CHRISTIANSEN

CONTEMPORARY by date, but not often considered together, Stendhal's *Le rouge et le noir* and George Sand's *Indiana* might on the surface seem to have relatively little in common, yet they share at least one intriguing feature: a pervasive play of master/slave imagery.[1] One might even say that the tension between these two extreme modes of behavior drives the plot in key parts of each novel. Both Julien and Indiana test the master/slave dynamic in their relationships with members of the opposite sex, but ultimately, it is only when they abandon it that they achieve happiness and, at the narrative level, that their stories come to an end.[2]

It is important to acknowledge at the outset that the subject of master/slave relationships is very complex. In *Le rouge et le noir* it is intertwined with questions of social hierarchy; Julien's behavior with Mme de Rênal and with Mathilde de La Mole is often described by a master/*servant* vocabulary. In *Indiana*, on the other hand, the master/*slave* dynamic is inseparable from gender issues: it exists precisely because women have so little power—and men have so much—under the Napoleonic code. While these broader contexts are of interest in their own right, the focus here will be limited to master/slave imagery as it figures in love relationships, primarily those between Julien and Mathilde and between Indiana and Raymon.

In order to appreciate the complexity of the master/slave dynamic in *Le rouge et le noir*, one might consider a scene from Part I where Julien's interaction with Mme de Rênal not only prefigures the relationship with Mathilde, but also announces his *prise de conscience* at the end of the novel. The scene in question takes place several months after Julien's arrival in the

Rênal household, where Mme de Rênal enjoys literal power, or "mastery" over Julien; Julien's goal—in large part *because* of that power—quickly becomes that of "mastering," or subjugating, her, as if she were the enemy in a military campaign. This struggle is further complicated by the fact the two have gradually come to love each other. In this passage (which precedes the celebrated seduction scene), Julien, in the presence of the sub-prefect, touches Mme de Rênal's foot, causing her to drop her scissors and to warn, "—Be careful, I order you" (Stendhal 1964, 107). He instantly takes offense at Mme de Rênal's choice of terms: "she could say to me *I order you*, if it were something relating to the children's education, but in responding to my love, she assumes equality. One cannot love without *equality*" (107). Julien's statement at this early stage is but a preview of the lesson offered ultimately by both *Le rouge et le noir* and *Indiana*—that there is no place for real love as long as the relationship is based on a disparity of power, whether it be real or figurative.

If this basic dynamic were not complicated enough, given the intermingling of master/slave and master/servant vocabulary, there is also a tendency on the part of Julien and Mme de Rênal to play *both* roles (a pattern of behavior which will resurface later in the novel in the relationship between Julien and Mathilde). Shortly after Julien and Mme de Rênal make love for the first time, for example, it is the latter who instructs the hero ("That education in love, given by an extremely ignorant woman, was a pleasure" [118]). She wields a power—albeit a loving one—over him that closely resembles, as the narrator affirms, her authority over her children (119). "A moment later," however, "she admired him as her master" (120). Julien, too, tests both roles; later, in the final pages of Part I, while hiding in the Rênal house just before his departure for Paris, he sees Mme de Rênal at once as a "truly superior woman" (236), because of her child-like gaiety and her expertise in orchestrating visits to his room, and as a women whose heart has become his "kingdom": "ah! there is a heart in which it is glorious to reign" (236). Elena Russo views Julien's adoption of this sort of slave-like posture as a rather painful, but ultimately productive, means of self-motivation: "that feeling of inferiority makes him experience 'horrible torments,' but it is also the principal motive that pushes him beyond himself and gives him the desire to take hold of the place of the master."[3]

Assuming that Russo's interpretation of Julien's behavior is valid, one could say that his interaction in Part II of *Le rouge et le noir* with the aristocratic Mathilde only intensifies that process of self-realization through the master/slave dynamic. It becomes obvious very quickly that many of the same patterns of behavior manifested in the Julien-Mme de Rênal relationship will also figure in that between Julien and Mathilde. In describing one of their early encounters at a ball, for example, the narrator again uses a mix of master/slave and master/servant vocabulary which reveals the two distinct, yet inseparable, types of relationships featured in the novel: "[Julien] did not deign to raise his eyes to Mathilde. She, with her beautiful eyes, opened extraordinarily wide and fixed upon him, appeared to be his slave. Finally, as the silence continued, he looked at her as a valet looks at his master, to receive his orders" (Stendhal 300–301). The narrator's choice of terms is revealing: while Julien is, literally, the "valet" for the La Mole family, and Mathilde, consequently, the literal "maître," she already imagines for herself the more figurative role of "esclave." Moreover, the use of the expression "to appear" suggests Mathilde's tendency to play a role rather than be herself; she may never truly *be* Julien's slave, but she can *appear* to be.

What this brief passage shows is that the play of master/slave is just that for both Julien and Mathilde, a *game*, albeit with real, serious consequences, in which both attempt to reverse their respective roles. Mathilde will increasingly "play the slave" because it corresponds to a romanesque ideal that introduces a sense of meaning into her otherwise boring life, in which she is, paradoxically, "enslaved." Julien, in turn, not only has much to gain in a real sense by "mastering" the aloof, aristocratic Mathilde, but he, too, models his behavior throughout the novel (and particularly in the context of love relationships) on a self-imposed sense of duty.

Once established, this basic pattern of behavior is recycled, with increasing intensity, over and over again. Recognizing that Julien might help realize her fantasy of imitating the story of her glorious ancestor, Boniface de La Mole, Mathilde initially assumes the role of master, in order to verify that Julien is "worthy" of her. In the seduction scene, for example, she tells him first how to use a ladder to reach her room, then how to ease it to the ground by rope; she gleefully informs him, once he obeys her commands, that he will, later, be obligated to use a more direct means of transit—the door. Ironically, his willingness to "lower" himself by following her orders has the effect of elevating him, in her eyes and in his own, to her level, as Mathilde herself expresses: "Ah! how this man is worthy of all my love!" (Stendhal 345). It is paradoxical that once Julien proves his worth, she almost immediately regrets having surrendered the dominant role; she is furious, "shocked by [his] air of triumph. So he is my master, she said to herself" (347). Yet on the very next day she revels in his "masterly" gestures, such as when he impulsively brandishes a sword, as if ready to kill her: "Mademoiselle de La Mole, delighted, could think only of the happiness of having been on the verge of being killed. She went so far as to say to herself: he is worthy of being my master, since he was about to kill me" (353). The constant oscillation in her reactions, from scorn to submission, is matched by corresponding behavior on the part of Julien, who shifts from anguish, even "crazy ideas" (354), to aggression, treating Mathilde as "the enemy" (423) or even "a demon" (424).

Ultimately the very playing out of the master/slave dynamic becomes the relationship's only reason for being. As René Girard suggests, neither Julien nor Mathilde desires the other directly, but rather through the image of what the other should be:

> Like two dancers obeying the baton of an invisible conductor, the two partners observe a perfect symmetry: the mechanism of their desire is identical . . . In double mediation each one stakes his freedom against the other's. The struggle ends when one of the partners admits his desire and humbles his pride. Henceforth no reversal is possible, for the *slave's* admitted desire destroys that of the *master* and ensures his genuine indifference. This indifference in turn makes the slave desperate and increases his desire. The two sentiments are identical since they are copied from each other; they exert their force in the same direction and secure the stability of the structure. (Girard 1965, 109–10)

The word *stability* is critical, for it captures the essence of the Julien-Mathilde relationship: as long as they are driven to play out the master/slave dynamic, there can be no resolution, no equality—indeed, no true self-realization—just a constant, increasingly intense, rotation of roles.

One scene in particular illustrates just how perverse the dynamic can become. During the reconciliation phase of a typical cycle of behavior, Mathilde dramatically begs to be punished: "—Punish me for my atrocious pride . . . you are my master, I am your slave, I must beg your forgiveness on my knees for having tried to rebel. . . . Yes, you are my master . . . reign forever over me, punish your slave severely when she tries to rebel" (363).

She then cuts off one side of her hair, offering the following explanation: "—I want to remember . . . that I am your servant: if a dreadful pride ever comes to lead me astray, show me this hair and say: it is no longer a question of love, it is not a matter of the emotion that your soul may feel at this moment, you have sworn to obey, obey on your honor" (363). Shortly thereafter, just after Julien has descended the ladder, he feels something fall on his hands; Mathilde has dropped her shorn hair, declaring: "There is what your servant sends you . . . it is the sign of an eternal obedience. I renounce the exercise of my reason, be my master" (364). That the relationship is based on artificial behavior is revealed by Mathilde's need to *remind* herself of her role as slave. More important, she substitutes for "slave" the term "servante"—which corresponds to Julien's actual role of "valet" mentioned earlier—a role which is literally impossible for the aristocratic Mathilde, but which indicates her desperate need to push to a new extreme her enactment of submission. Here she tries to *be* his *servante*, whereas earlier she only *appeared* to be his *esclave*.

While Julien may for a time derive pleasure from the *role* of master, he will eventually come to realize that it does not represent true happiness. It is only in prison, condemned to die after shooting Mme de Rênal, that he is able to recognize the duplicity of his power struggle with Mathilde and the potential for a simple and honest relationship with Mme de Rênal. Master/slave vocabulary virtually disappears in the final pages of the novel, as Julien and Mme de Rênal discover a peaceful state of equilibrium: "For Julien, except in the moments usurped by Mathilde's presence, he was living on love and almost without thinking about the future. Through a strange effect of that passion, when it is extreme and without the slightest dissimulation, Mme de Rênal almost shared his carefree attitude and his gentle gaiety" (496–97). Julien's conclusion that "man has two beings in him"[4] suggests his new awareness of the difference between the "inauthentic" self caught in the cycle of master/slave behavior, and the "authentic" one who finds love and happiness precisely because he ultimately considers Mme de Rênal his equal.[5]

A strikingly similar sense of duality quickly comes to the fore in Sand's novel as well, once again in the context of the master/slave dynamic. *Indiana*, still much less widely read than *Le rouge et le noir*, may be memorable above all for its complicated plot which includes nocturnal, mist-shrouded rendez-vous, dangerous ocean crossings, and a plan for a suicidal plunge into a waterfall. It tells the basic story of a woman who, trapped in a loveless marriage, first becomes involved in a troubled relationship with Raymon de Ramière, and then finds a fulfilling bond based on equality with her cousin Ralph. From the very start it is clear that "masters" have shaped the heroine's life—Indiana's husband, Delmare, "an excellent master before whom everything trembled, wife, servants, horses, and dogs" (Sand 49), only takes over where her domineering father left off. Yet Indiana also possesses "two beings in [her]," to use Julien's phrase: in addition to the submissive one, there is another, which manifests itself as "an iron will, an incalculable force of resistance against everything that tended to oppress her" (Sand 88). She possesses, in short, an inner strength that belies—and is in fact a consequence of—her subservient position. Just as Julien's early comment "One cannot love without equality" effectively expresses, as it turns out, what he is to discover through his relationship with Mathilde, this emphasis on Indiana's strength forecasts the ultimate resolution of the master/slave dynamic in Sand's novel.

The ambiguity inherent in Indiana's nature shows itself from the very beginning of her relationship with Raymon. While she initially seems to play the role of slave, and Raymon that of her liberator, the reader soon realizes that neither role is as stable as it first appeared. The narrator's pointed suggestion, "Had she not been born to love, this slave woman who was waiting only for a sign to break her chain, for a word to follow him?" (Sand 90), suggests that Indiana, once freed from Delmare, might enjoy a more equal relationship with Raymon. However, from the moment Raymon recognizes that Indiana loves him, his role shifts to that of subjugator: "He did not need to see the joy that was shining through her tears to understand that he was the master and that he could dare" (93). His desire to control the relationship is further illustrated when, in the same dramatic scene, Raymon makes an impassioned speech in which he explains how his love would differ from that of Delmare, how he is prepared to position himself, as he says to Indiana, "at your feet, keeping you as a jealous master, serving you as a slave . . ." (95). Even if he casts both roles in a positive light (the jealous master protects, and the slave serves willingly), he exercises his authority by effectively denying Indiana a role at all, designating himself both master *and* slave.

Yet in spite (or perhaps because) of Raymon's appropriation of the more dominant role, Indiana herself shows signs of "masterly" behavior, articulating that very strength of character revealed through the narrator's voice in the early passage. In an important conversation between the two after the death of Noun (Indiana's companion who, unbeknownst to the heroine, was also involved with Raymon) Indiana outlines what Raymon must do if he is to be her lover: "You must love me without sharing, without change of heart, without reserve; you must be ready to sacrifice everything to me, fortune, reputation, duty, business, principles, family; everything sir, because I will put the same devotion on to the scales and I want them to be equal" (148). Indiana clearly envisions, even this early, an equal distribution of power, one similar to that shared by Julien and Mme de Rênal at the end of *Le rouge et le noir*, but which proved impossible between the hero and Mathilde.

Further evidence of Indiana's authority and independence is revealed shortly thereafter when she participates in the hunt, a striking scene which foreshadows later developments in the master/slave dynamic with Raymon. Indiana's strength in this passage actually frightens and revolts Raymon, who obviously cannot conceive of her in a "masculine," or "masterly," role. As the narrator explains, "Men, and lovers especially, have the naive self-conceit of wanting to protect the weakness rather than admiring the courage of women" (162).

This passage establishes a cycle of behavior which turns out to be very similar to that seen in *Le rouge et le noir* between Julien and Mathilde: once Raymon recovers from the initial shock of discovering Indiana's aggressive side, his desire to "master" her grows in direct proportion to her displays of strength and lucidity. Evidence of this can be found in what may very well be the most dramatic scene of the novel, when Indiana, after finally agreeing to receive Raymon in her room, decides to "test" him in order to resolve her suspicions about his relationship with Noun. Indiana offers him a mass of hair which he assumes is her own, until he realizes that it was cut from Noun's head after her suicide. This represents a turning point for Raymon: after hearing Indiana speak of equal roles, witnessing first her physical strength and then her calculating behavior, he decides that he no longer loves her. For him, interaction with Indiana now becomes an outright war: "Then he swore, in his bitterness, that he would triumph over her; he no longer swore it out of pride, but out of vengeance. It was no longer for him a question of winning a pleasure, but of punishing an affront; not of possessing a woman, but of subduing her. He swore that he would be her master, even if for only one day, and that he would then

abandon her to have the pleasure of seeing her at his feet" (200).
Raymon can only be satisfied with a relationship that leaves Indiana conquered, punished, possessed, "reduced."

His plan to seize definitively the role of master by "playing
the slave" recalls the dynamic between Julien and Mathilde in
Le rouge et le noir. Immediately after deciding to "conquer" Indiana, Raymon declares himself once again "worthy" of her and
begs her forgiveness, pledging, in terms that bring to mind those
of Mathilde, to be her slave: ". . . command, Indiana! I am your
slave, you know it well . . . I will be submissive! . . ." (201). While
Raymon pretends to be something he is not, Indiana remains
honest; when she does escape from Delmare, planning to hide
in Raymon's apartment until her husband leaves for l'île Bourbon, she calmly tells Raymon: "Today, I come to get the reward
for my faith; the time has come: tell me, do you accept my sacrifices?" (216), as if to remind him once again that he, too, will
have to make sacrifices. Renowned for his eloquence, Raymon
comes to rely on inflated rhetoric in his efforts to reassert his
mastery, lauding Indiana's superiority, her divine, otherworldly
nature, while simultaneously depicting himself as a mere mortal,
enslaved by his natural instincts: "You were too perfect to play
in this world the same role as we, vulgar creatures, subject to
human passions, slaves of our coarse makeup" (240). It is, of
course, the height of irony that Raymon speaks the truth about
his own nature while being utterly hypocritical.

The growing tension apparent in the master/slave dynamic between Indiana and Raymon also characterizes the relationship
between the heroine and her husband, as is revealed by a decisive
confrontation just after Indiana's aborted suicide attempt. Indiana, now back with Delmare, defends her view of the two roles
of master and slave; acknowledging her legal servitude to her
husband, she nevertheless affirms her moral independence: "—
I know that I am the slave and you the lord. The law of this
country has made you my master. You can tie up my body, bind
my hands, control my actions. You have the right of the strongest,
and society confirms it; but you can do nothing about my will,
sir, God alone can bend it and reduce it. So find a law, a prison
cell, an instrument of torture, which will give you a hold over
me! It is as if you wanted to handle air and seize the void" (232).
When Delmare attempts to silence her, she replies: "You can
impose silence on me, but not prevent me from thinking" (232);
and then, when the quarrel reaches a peak of intensity, "I have
spent a few hours free from your domination; I went to breathe

the air of freedom to show you that you are not morally my master and that I depend only on myself on earth" (233). Thus Indiana not only confirms the dual nature of slavery, but also shows, ironically, what Raymon's behavior has already revealed, that "outward" servitude has nothing to do with "inward" freedom.

Indiana's speech serves effectively as a declaration of her independence and self-liberation from Delmare. After orchestrating her escape and surviving a treacherous sea voyage from l'île Bourbon back to France, she arrives at the house which Raymon now shares with a wife, Laure. Surprising him and falling at his feet, Indiana declares: "It is I, it is your Indiana, it is your slave, whom you called back from exile and who have come three thousand leagues to love you and to serve you; it is the companion of your choice who has left everything, risked everything, braved everything, to bring you this instant of joy! . . . I come to bring you happiness, to be all that you want, your companion, your servant, or your mistress. . . . I have come three thousand leagues to belong to you, to tell you that; take me, I am your possession, you are my master" (296–97). Unlike Raymon, who used strikingly similar terms to *act* the part of slave, Indiana resolves to *be* the slave. Instead of indicating weakness, Indiana's words and behavior in fact represent her determined pursuit of the dream of a life based on equality with Raymon, and as such are cast in a positive light. Indiana may be terribly mistaken about Raymon's nature, but she shows courage and sincerity in trying to turn the posture of slave into something meaningful. One need only remember that whatever her sacrifices, she expected an equal number from him.[6]

The lesson that true happiness lies beyond the master/slave polarity is illustrated by the contrasting fates of Indiana and Raymon. Indiana will go on, in the novel's rather unrealistic conclusion, to find a fulfilling relationship with her cousin in a peaceful, idyllic setting.[7] This relationship, unlike that with Raymon, is founded on equality, an equality that is expressed by the couple's commitment of the rest of their lives to freeing slaves.[8] Raymon, in contrast, seems destined to continue acting out the struggle for power. He has apparently met his match in the woman he marries, Laure de Nangy, who intends to play with Raymon the way he did with Indiana, as the narrator explains: "Less generous than madame Delmare, but more clever, cold, and flattering, vain and calculating, she was the woman who was to subjugate Raymon; because she was as superior to him in skill as he himself had been to Indiana . . . she derived a malicious pleasure in using that liberty which still belonged to her, and in making her authority felt for some time over the man who aspired to take it away from her. . . . for her, life was a stoic calculation . . ." (289–90).

It is ironic that Laure, whose attitude calls to mind that of Mathilde, should see *liberté* as a product of subjugating Raymon, for if the "lesson" learned by Julien and Indiana is taken to be true, then such "freedom" must undoubtedly be just an illusion. *Subjuguer*, the verb attributed to Laure here and elsewhere to Raymon, is also used repeatedly by Stendhal to describe Julien's attitude toward women until he finally abandons the role-playing, having realized that fulfillment comes only by "improvising" and treating the other as an equal.[9]

Given the dénouements of both novels, it is clear that a resolution of the tension between master and slave is difficult to achieve in the "real" world; after all, Julien finds happiness with Mme de Rênal only under a death sentence; Indiana with Ralph only after nearly committing suicide, then living an isolated existence on an island. But in the final analysis, both Stendhal's *Le rouge et le noir* and Sand's *Indiana*, two novels which seem on the surface to have so little in common, offer, within an intricate play of master/slave imagery, the same important message—that it is perhaps not the degree or the duration of the freedom which matters most, but rather, that freedom is tasted at all, and under what conditions. Julien and Indiana, in a word, become "masters" of their destinies by refusing to become "slaves" to the ultimately unfulfilling struggle for power and authority which so permeates the worlds in which they live.

University of Arkansas

NOTES

1. Similarities between *Le rouge et le noir* (1830) and *Indiana* (1832) were noted as soon as the latter was published. David Powell, discussing the public's reaction to *Indiana*, states that some readers made favorable comparisons of Sand's novel to *Le rouge et le noir* and Hugo's *Notre-Dame de Paris* (Powell 29); Curtis Cate shows that Sand did indeed meet Stendhal, in Venice (Cate 280), and explains that Henri Boussuge, a noted critic of the period, compared Raymon de Ramière to Stendhal's Julien Sorel, adding that *Indiana* displayed an "immense superiority of style" over *Le rouge et le noir* (Cate 203); Joseph Barry also refers to a critic who found *Indiana* "unjust" and "bitter," but who praised Sand's talent, "placing 'his' [it was assumed that the work, published

under the pen name J. Sand, had been written by a man] novel alongside Stendhal's recent *Le rouge et le noir*" (Barry 133). Marie-Jeanne Pécile, in her article on Sand's literary encounters, mentions Balzac, Hugo, and other important figures, but not Stendhal, except to say that "In her time, [Sand] was more famous than Stendhal and Flaubert and she was considered the equal of Balzac and Victor Hugo" (Pécile 52) and that Sand did not like Stendhal's "coarseness" (Pécile 61). In her preface to *Indiana*, Béatrice Didier suggests George Sand's familiarity with *Le rouge et le noir*: "One senses that she was nourished by Balzac. One can also think that she remembers Stendhal and that she knows *Le rouge et le noir* well. For her, as for Stendhal, the novelist is a mirror" (Didier 15–16). Nancy E. Rogers, in her article on stylistic similarities between Sand and Balzac, mentions in passing that the Sandian narrator's observations and personal commentary are in the manner of Stendhal, but lack his irony (Rogers 134); Marie-Jacques Hoog discusses parallels in character and theme; and Kristina Wingard shows that "There is in [Sand] . . . a narrative voice as characteristic as in Stendhal, although entirely different" (Hoog 392–93). Finally, after explaining that the publication of *Indiana* sparked renewed interest in *Le rouge et le noir* because of the striking parallels that critics perceived between the two novels, Sandy Petrey posits that since 1832, both traditional and feminist criticism have effectively disconnected *Indiana* from the realist texts with which it was initially equated (Petrey 133). "The reasons *Indiana* and *Scarlet and Black* were originally put together," he continues, "are the same as those subsequently invoked to set them apart" (Petrey 134).

2. Other critics have noted the presence of master/slave imagery, especially in *Indiana*. See for example, Rogers 1979; Massardier-Kennedy, who sees the "circular room" as a trap, and discusses "the enslaving effect of interior places" (Massardier-Kennedy 68); Haig, who considers the addition of slavery to the scene in the "circular room" "not as a veneer of concern or a contrived dénouement, but rather as an integral part of George Sand's sorrowful vision of love, irrespective of her feminist program" (Haig 1987a, 37); and James M. Vest, who explores similarities between *Indiana* and romance tradition: "As in the older romances, the heroine is exquisitely attractive, a superior woman reduced to the position of slave" (Vest 41). More generally, one might also relate the master/slave dynamic in the novels (particularly in *Le rouge et le noir*) to the Hegelian master/servant dialectic, as René Girard has done (Girard 110).

3. Russo 8. Russo links the struggle against authority to what might be called a literal building of character: "it is in struggling against all forms of power that the character establishes himself as such, that he is able to shape himself into a character . . . it is in protecting oneself against an arbitrary will that one discovers oneself as 'other,' a different and unique being" (Russo 1).

4. Stendhal 1964, 479. Victor Brombert has written at length about Stendhal's tendency to "experience everything in terms of opposites" (Brombert 1968, 77) and explains such polarities as "all part of a mechanism of action and reaction in which notions of offensive and defensive are essential movements of a psychological duel. These tensions . . . activate at every point a sense of projection into the as yet unlived moment" (Brombert 84).

5. Russo highlights this significant moment, affirming that in *Le rouge et le noir*, "the relationship between equals is very rare, occurring at privileged moments" (Russo 8).

6. Highlighting the ambiguity of Indiana's attitude, Petrey states: "The end of juridical subservience to Delmare would do nothing about moral subjection

to Raymon, as the text emphasises by repeating the key terms of Indiana's protest against being one man's wife in her abject plea to become another man's lover . . . Gender is an internal mystification as well as an external constraint, and the parallel between Indiana's pleas for freedom and for slavery pointedly define her womanhood as something she enacts as well as endures" (Petrey 143). Béatrice Didier's interpretation of Indiana's behavior here, on the other hand, is far more negative; she believes that the heroine is actually more enslaved by Raymon than by her husband: "The lover . . . is even more disappointing than the husband, to the extent that the heroine expected more from him. And society is such that when she is without a husband and without a lover, really alone, woman is reduced to nothing . . . The portrait that [Sand] gives of Indiana is, all in all, rather severe. She denounces her as eager to exchange one enslavement for another, ready, once liberated from her husband, to submit to all the humiliations on the part of her lover, incapable of living her freedom . . ." (Didier 1984, 26). Didier goes so far as to suggest, furthermore, that Indiana often derives pleasure from being mastered, and that "it is not difficult to find in the text a whole interplay of sadomasochistic images" (Didier 1984, 27).

7. Vest also emphasizes the positive turn of the plot for Indiana, stating that "both structurally and thematically, the central movement of *Indiana* is away from the confines of civilization toward a personal realization of individual freedom" (Vest 40).

8. Schwartz argues, in contrast, that "Indiana has an equal mature relationship with no one—she is Delmare's slave, Raymon's toy (or prey), and Ralph's 'child'" (Schwartz 72–73).

9. For an interesting discussion of the role of Laure in the novel, see Petrey 140–42. He cites the following passage where Laure revels in her feelings of superiority, "secretly triumphing from the inferior and dependent position in which this incident had just placed her husband in relation to her" (Sand 298), and concludes: "The tableau created when Indiana is at Raymon's feet and Raymon under Laure's thumb encapsulates substitution of gender for sex in Sand's first novel . . . Two characters—Indiana and Raymon, a woman and a man—take the feminine 'position of inferiority and dependence.' Two characters—a man and a woman, Raymon and Laure—take the masculine role of 'subjugating' their partners" (142).

14

Literature and Suicide

J. A. HIDDLESTON

THE subject is vast and extremely complex, from Achitopel and the Old Testament suicides, to those of classical drama, down to the bizarre demise of Tiffauges in Tournier's *Le roi des aulnes*. To limit the discussion to the nineteenth century might at first appear an arbitrary means of making the subject more manageable or of meeting the requirements of a publication devoted to the period, were it not that the incidence of suicide in literature becomes increasingly frequent in that century and above all since there would appear to be a fundamental shift in the function that it fulfils, particularly in narrative fiction. It had of course been a preoccupation of such Enlightenment thinkers as Montesquieu, Voltaire, Rousseau, and Hume, who in their desire to free men from religious taboo sought to make of suicide a subject of rational discourse, realizing that it was not necessarily an act dictated by the devil or by insanity. Their concern stemmed from a kind of humanism which would proclaim in Baudelaire's words "the right to *depart*" (1976, 2: 306). And indeed it was to a large degree because of the influence of the "philosophes" that it was enacted in 1791 that suicide should no longer be held to be a crime. But the discourse of Romanticism in this matter is very different from that of Rationalism. True, there are writers who like Madame de Staël (1832) denounce what they consider a pernicious obsession or tendency and who extol the noble and morally superior death of Jane Grey. But they do so in order to counteract the baleful influence of works, such as *Werther*, Rabbe's *Philosophie du désespoir*, or Maxime du Camp's *Mémoires d'un suicidé*, which betray a Romantic indulgence and misguided vainglory in suicide. In works like these we are very far away from classical tragedy where the suicide of the hero or heroine so often supplies the reasonable "dénouement" of the play, reasonable because the protagonist's position

209

has become intolerable and he or she has no other way to act in order to make amends, to fulfill a patriotic duty, to remain faithful to some lofty duty or principle, or to avoid dishonour. The suicides of Brutus, Antony and Cleopatra, Othello, Mithridate, or Atalide in *Bajazet*, whether they stem from a philosophy of stoicism or from an impossible situation arising from a fault such as pride, jealousy, or ambition, which brings an otherwise good person down from "high estate to low," have of course, for all the pathos or catharsis they may provoke in the minds of the audience or reader, nothing sinister about them and are not seen as a transgression of human or divine law or as some kind of taboo. Nor are they seen as "the coward's way out," as the unthinking cliché goes, but most often as an honorable exit.

But Romantic and post-Romantic suicide concerns less a specific situation or aspect of a character than the totality of the character, and is linked much more closely and fundamentally to a view of the world affected by "mal du siècle" or some similar "Weltanschauung." It is linked in the first place to the notion that, whatever the circumstances, life is not worth living, very often because of the superior nature, intellect, insight, or sensibility of the protagonist. That most extraordinary of all literary societies, the Suicide-Club, whose membership was, necessarily and perhaps mercifully, very limited, and which gave places of honor to Goethe, Byron, Chateaubriand, and George Sand, proclaimed in article six of its constitution that "suicide may be sanctioned only by the disgust of life, considered bad and unworthy of being lived" (Maigron 341). This aristocratic detachment from the vulgar business of living was to find perhaps its silliest expression in Villiers de l'Isle-Adam's *Axël*, in which the hero and heroine reject the treasure which they had sought to merit with lofty disdain: "Live? the servants will do that for us" (Villiers 283).

Romantic suicide may also be linked to a morbid preoccupation with the satanic, or with the dark, unhealthy underside of things. Initially, it appears as part of a Romantic indulgence in what by contemporary lights was thought to be unnatural, and thus finds its place in the literature of the time alongside the themes of incest, madness, homosexuality, criminality, or the taking of the side of Satan against God. This was no doubt aided by what was long thought to be a Christian acceptance of the notion dating from Saint Augustin that in Hamlet's words the "Everlasting had fixed / His canon 'gainst self slaughter" (*Hamlet* 1.2). Since one's life is not one's own, but a gift from God, and since we do not choose to be born, we have no right to choose to die. In Canto XIII of the *Inferno* Dante reserves the most appalling fate for suicides, whom he condemns to the seventh circle of Hell, below heretics and murderers immersed in their river of hot blood, placing them in a dark wood where they grow for all eternity as warped poisonous thorns. In the trees harpies tear at the leaves, repeating the violence which the suicides had done themselves in life. It is the sin without remission, against hope and against the holy spirit, essentially an unnatural crime, the punishment for which is to be placed only two circles of hell from Judas frozen in the icy coldness of his own treachery.

The self indulgence which characterizes so much of Romantic suicide involves considerable posturing. René for example decides to rid himself of the burden of life, but is eager to delay the final moment in order to enjoy the spectacle and to admire the fine figure of elegant despair which he cuts: "I resolved to invest all my reason in this insane act. I had no reason to hurry; I did not set the moment of departure, in order to savor in long drafts the last moments of life and to gather my strength, as a classical man would have, to feel his soul escape" (Chateaubriand 1969, 131). The same inauthenticity of seeing oneself from the outside as an object of surprise and admiration presides over his impulse to stab himself to death in the convent in front of a large gathering at the moment when his sister Amélie takes her vows. In the event he wisely avoids such a definitive action, but executes an equally spectacular and dramatic gesture by wresting her from the symbolic coffin in which she is to say adieu to the world and pressing her to his heart before being taken away unconscious from the astonished assembly. In a similar though less histrionic vein Jean-Marc in *Mémoires d'un suicidé* fantasises that he is present at his own funeral, and Philothée O'Neddy has some excruciatingly macaronic verses in which he plans to kill himself in the loge of a theater in front of a suitably impressed audience:

> I will shut myself up alone in a barred loge;
> And when the violins, oboes, and trills,
> To the great contentment of many a dilettante,
> Accompany the aria of the basso-cantante,
> My eye raised boldly toward the resonant vaults,
> Of a sublime opium I will swallow one hundred drops.
>
> (Maigron 329)

This theatrical, visual, "iconic" element is nowhere more effectively present than in Henry Wallis's painting of 1856 of Chatterton ("the marvellous Boy, / The sleepless Soul that perished in his pride"—Wordsworth 236) with George Meredith as model. We see the body laid out, the right hand, of poetic creation, reaching to the floor, while the other is placed on his heart. The flower at the window is clearly meant to symbolize rebirth or continuity, while the open casement represents the freedom of the soul. Here is suicide made peaceful and beautiful, and one is made to feel the lure of being "half in love with easeful Death," the temptation to "cease upon the midnight with no pain." Chatterton, like Octave in Stendhal's *Armance*, has taken "some dull opiate" and sunk "Lethe-wards" (Keats 191). The means of suicide assures a peaceful end as befits the Romantic context. There is no place here for the realism of hanging as in Zola's *L'oeuvre* or Baudelaire's prose poem "La corde," or for the digestive obscenities of arsenic poisoning of which Flaubert spares us some of the worst features in *Madame Bovary*. Indeed Peter Ackroyd's description in his book on Chatterton of the appalling effects of arsenic helps us to measure the extent to which the painting is an idealization very far removed from the sordid reality of the young poet's demise. Through such an icon a transfiguration has taken place; the image and the gestures are eternalized, as if the suicide were not dead, but lived on, confirming the suspicion that Romantic suicide is accomplished not so much to die, but paradoxically to live on in some mode or other. There is in the scene a strong sense of a survival or immortality, as if the victim had acceded to some higher level of existence.

One of the most iconic deaths in nineteenth-century literature is, of course, that of Atala; the body is laid out on a bed of flowers, mimosa pudica, with a faded magnolia in her hair, and the emphasis falls heavily upon her purity to such an extent that she might be taken, we are told, for "the statue of sleeping Virginity" (Chateaubriand 1969, 89). The emphasis is also upon the peace of the scene, the certainty of eternal values, and the triumph of the Christian religion, as befits Chateaubriand's intention in the *Génie du christianisme* to show the superiority of Christianity over paganism and "le mal du siècle". Although Girodet's painting "Atala au tombeau" is in many ways different from the scene in the story, it clearly celebrates these same elements with its grotto opening up on to eternal light and the promise of redemption symbolized by the cross standing out against the sky and heaven. In both works death and suicide indicate a return to order and eternal values that replace the ephemera and illusions of earthly existence. In the story Atala is consoled by le Père Aubry, who tells her that earthly happiness is illusory: "Illusion, chimera, vanity, dream of a wounded imagination!" (Chateaubriand 82). Indeed, she is enjoined to thank God for having released her so early from the vale of tears of earthly existence: "you lose little, in losing this world" (81). But when one remembers that suicide is a crime for the Christian and that this is expressly stated in the book, then certain ambiguities arise and refuse to be resolved. Atala has taken a poison so deadly that even the Indians know no antidote, to avoid breaking the vow of virginity which her mother had imposed on her in gratitude for her safe birth; but her love for Chactas is so strong and her physical attraction so violent that she cannot trust herself to keep the vow. The ambiguity and inconsistency reside in this: how is it that she knows her act is a crime (she indeed confesses as much when she replies to the priest's question about what she has done) and yet the priest absolves her because she did not know that a Christian cannot take her own life? She would appear both to know and not to know that her act is a crime, and to be both innocent and guilty at the same time.

But there are even greater ambiguities which precede Atala's suicide and redemption, since in the eyes of Chactas who knows nothing of her vow she appears as an enigma, both transparent and mysterious, innocent and in a sense satanic. The circumstances of their first meeting, when he is about to be burned by the enemy tribe of barbarous hunters, "les Muscogulges," are crucial, since they set their relationship under a disturbing ambiguity. She appears out of Christian pity to release him and spare him a horrible death at the stake; but he thinks she is the "Virgin of last loves" (41) sent to comfort his last moments before his dreadful ordeal. Struck by her beauty, he asks significantly: "How can one mix death and life?" (42), so that from the beginning love, life, and death are intermingled in the tortured, ambiguous, and contradictory imaginary universe of the story.

Nothing would be more natural than that during their wanderings in the forest their innocent love should be consummated in what is portrayed as paradise before the fall; but at the thought Atala sees flames coming up from the earth, and imagines her mother's torment in her grave. At other times she would gladly yield to this satanic temptation: "I would have rolled from abyss to abyss with the remains of God and the world!" (77). For Chactas she is an exasperating mystery, arousing the most violent and contradictory emotions of adoration and hatred: "one had either to love her or to hate her" (58). In his and the reader's imagination she has both the purity of a saint and the irresistible attraction of the taboo virgin. As Mario Praz pointed out many decades ago she is linked to hell and the underworld. Love in *Atala* appears as an unnatural passion far removed from the healthy, rumbustious, and innocent love of Tom Jones and Sophie Western, and Chateaubriand's saintly virgin is made to join the ambiguous legions of madonnas and whores, "belles dames sans merci," and "femmes fatales," who figure so prominently in the *Romantic Agony*, where love, instead of being associated with life and the affirmation of health and positive values, is linked to the hidden underside of the good, with death, evil, waste, and destruction. It is little wonder that for the contemporary critic Chênedollé,[1] Chateaubriand, far from demonstrating the spirit of Christianity in the story, was in fact guilty of putting poison in the holy eucharist and of corrupting the imagination and literary values of a generation of young people.

It is perhaps now becoming clear how the suicide fits into the central preoccupations of the story and its ambiguous scheme of values. Although on a superficial level it may appear so, it is not a sudden and unprepared gesture, and is emphatically not merely a convenient way of rounding off the plot. On the contrary, since Atala is both aware and unaware of the gravity of her crime, it is intimately and inevitably linked to her first appearance as the *"Virgin of last loves"* and to the uncertainty about the values she represents during their abortive idyll in the forest. It goes to the heart of the ambiguities not just of the story itself but of Chateaubriand's novelistic universe in which, since a similar pattern is repeated in *René*, the explicit values of purity, measure, faith, and utility are constantly undermined by the anti–values of the "révolté," the misfit, the outsider, of all that darker side of the human imagination which Chateaubriand opened up almost unwittingly, just as he had cleared from the description of external nature the fauns, satyrs, and nymphs of Neoclassicism in order to "to return to the grottos their silence, and to the woods their revery" (Chateaubriand 1978, 719).

Although there is no actual suicide in *René*, it can be read as a pendant to *Atala* in which the same themes, preoccupations, and ambiguities appear in a different mode and setting. First, the births of the two protagonists are similar. Atala's was difficult; her mother, she tells us, "brought me into the world with great tearings of her womb: they did not expect me to live" (Chateaubriand 1969, 74), and it was of course this traumatic birth which was the origin of the fateful vow. René's story is even more dramatic for his mother died in childbirth: "While being born, I cost my mother her life; I was pulled out of her womb with forceps" (119). Both births are ill-fated, indicating something unnatural and baleful about the destiny of the protagonists.

Secondly, while the relationship between Atala and Chactas is clearly that of lovers, since she is the daughter of Lopez who is Chactas's protector and mentor, she is also a kind of sister to him. Their love points if not to any real incest, then at least to what might be called an imaginary or virtual incest. In *René* Chateaubriand approaches this taboo subject in the most delicate and discreet manner; but reader and protagonist are eventually left in no doubt that Amélie's unnatural passion for her brother is the reason for her taking the veil, and indeed, at least ostensibly, the aim of the story, as part of the *Génie du christianisme*, was to show how religion could provide the haven of the convent for those who are excessively buffeted upon the seas of life and of passion. Fittingly, Amélie finds her haven, with a suitable view out over the (real) sea, and wins thereby the admiration of the Père Souël. It is important that initially René should be unaware of his sister's feeling towards him. His status as Romantic hero and as "homme fatal" is thereby greatly strengthened. He is seen as the satanic figure whose very presence is a blight and arouses, unbeknown to him, an illicit and unnatural passion in the innocent bosom of his sister, the one person he loves and who understands his enigmatic nature. He is marked by a strange destiny which removes him from the natural order of things; like the figure in Goethe's "Harzreise im Winter" he is the man "dem Balsam zu Gift ward" (Goethe 51).

It is possible then to argue that the real suicide in *Atala* is paralleled by a virtual suicide in *René*, not just because, as we have seen, René himself is tempted by suicide on more than one occasion, but because Amélie's vows involve a "Service of the dead" in which, clad in a shroud, she has to pass through the grave and die to the world. Her actual death is even more significant; for, we are told, she dies, "a victim of her zeal and her charity," looking after the sick whose highly contagious malady she contracts. The Mother superior adds that in the thirty years she had been head of the convent "she had never seen such a sweet and even-tempered nun, nor one who was happier to have quit the tribulations of the world" (Chateaubriand 1969, 144). There is here a suggestion of suicide, as if Amélie de la Miséri-

corde had sought out her own death on purpose as a release from
the sorrows of her existence.

Ostensibly, René's story shows the ravages of "le mal du siècle"
and the absence of religious belief. The hero is roundly condemned by le Père Souël: he is not a superior individual because
he sees the world in an odious light; solitude in the wilderness
is bad for those who do not live with God; René is "a young man
persisting in wild dreams, displeased with everything, and who
has shirked his responsibilities to society to devote himself to
useless dreams" (144); nothing in his story justifies the pity that
has been shown to him. What remained from the story, however,
was not the moral lesson, but, to the great annoyance of Chateaubriand himself, the prestige of the "homme fatal" who in Flaubert's words in *Par les champs et par les grèves* was to fill "half
a century with the clamor of his grief" (Flaubert 1923–36,
13:325). It was the prestige of the misfit, the outsider, of the
young man out of harmony with both society and the natural
world. It brought about the cult of introspection, of extreme emotions, of the contradictions in thinking and feeling in place of
balance, measure, and the perspicacity of the golden mean. It
was thought to be preferable to be uniquely misguided than to
be mediocrely right, so that madness, illness, criminality, and the
destructive power of emotion were thought to constitute more
alluring values in a literature which increasingly glorified the
outcast, the pariah, ancestors of the twentieth-century popular
figures of the "rebel without a cause" and "the crazy mixed-up
kid." In these new circumstances the notion of sincerity under-
goes a fundamental and lasting transformation which has affected our manner of looking at the world and the popular
perception of values. An observation such as "John is misguided
but so sincere" has its origin in this shift. To a Molière the remark
would be comic, since the "sincerity" would serve to aggravate
the wrongheadedness and there would be something perversely
ludicrous in being so entire in one's waywardness. But for Chateaubriand and his descendants sincerity and intensity have become values in themselves independent of what in former times
would have been thought the necessary concomitants of balance
and clearsightedness.

Similarly, the return to order and to true Christian values at
the end of *Atala* is equally problematic, or illusory; for what
remained was not the prestige of the saint, but the unwholesome
appeal of the heroine as sister of the "femmes fatales" of gothic
and romantic fantasies and the ancestor of the decadent creations

of Flaubert, Barbey, and Huysmans. Suicide in Chateaubriand appears as a supremely unnatural act. With its extolling of death and the whole reversal of values which it implies, it is the ultimate negation and appears as the very emblem of a certain form of Romanticism and Decadence. It would appear then to be a reasonable proposition that the literary obsession with suicide, like the emergence of autobiography and the espousal in the name of "sincerity" of the anti–values of intensity, outsiderishness, and "excess," is part of a radical change in our western consciousness. But another much more radical proposition, which is the principal contention of this article, suggests itself from our reading of Chateaubriand: that suicide is not just a peripeteia of the plot or its resolution, but that it reveals the central concern of the narrative in which it takes place and beyond that, more astonishingly, the ambiguities and inconsistencies in the mental universe and outlook of the writer.

I should like now to try to test this second proposition against some other major nineteenth-century novels. The enterprise would require considerable research and an extended analysis of the works in question, together with a definition of the novelistic world of their authors. All that can be achieved within the compass of a brief article is a preliminary staking out of the terrain and an indication of the broad lines of future inquiry. I propose do this by some sketches or vignettes of three major works of the period.

The suicide, in a ship off the coast of Greece, of Octave de Malivert in *Armance* is recounted not without hint of irony in the last paragraph of the novel: "The name of Greece awoke Octave's courage: I greet you, he said to himself, O land of heroes! And at midnight, on March 3, as the moon was rising behind Mount Kalos, a mixture of opium and digitalis he had prepared delivered Octave gently from this life which had been so troubled for him" (Stendhal 1962, 245). The very discreet, almost imperceptible, irony lies in the deadpan narration. After all he had gone to fight in a battle, presumably on the Greek side though the cause of the war seems to be a question of complete indifference to him, and to make himself worthy in his own and in his father's eyes of his warlike ancestors and his noble medieval name. It is to say the least highly ironic that he should commit suicide before setting foot on Greek soil. Octave dies ostensibly because he erroneously believes that Armance does not really love him; but also because he is an aristocrat "en rupture de classe" in the age of the steam engine when a title is an absurdity, and because he had not found the values whereby to live and resolve the contradictions within his character of sensibility and cruelty, spontaneity and calculation, placidity and uncontrollable rage, physical weakness and strength, the call of the priesthood and a career in science, aristocratic arrogance and the desire to pass incognito or to be his own valet. Furthermore, he is obsessed by a negative notion of duty which creates inhibitions rather than providing a means of effective action, and which is a major factor in his "impotence": "Instead of conforming my behavior to events I encountered in life, I had set myself up a rule prior to all experience" (176). His life consequently seems to be oriented towards failure and unfulfillment and the suicide which he ultimately and inevitably commits. One might be tempted to hasten to the conclusion that he dies because he has not had the good fortune to learn the lessons that Julien Sorel learns after the shooting of Madame de Rênal, when paradoxically he attains freedom in the prison house where he espouses the wisdom of living in the present and the values of naturalness, spontaneity, and that openness of spirit which Gide was later to call "receptiveness" (disponibilité). But the paradoxes and contradictions of Stendhal's moral universe cannot be resolved so readily, as is evident when we realize that, although Fabrice embodies those very values which Julien had discoverd, his quest for happiness is also doomed to failure. Whatever Stendhal's intentions in writing Armance, which may have been to write a scandalous work concerning a young man and the secret of his sexual impotence, what he has also given us is an introduction to the fundamental moral dilemma of his works, or to change the metaphor he has provided us with our first view of the basic architecture of his novelistic world. We find at every turn echoes of Julien and Fabrice, of the individual at variance with society and himself, a prey to contradictions in the uncertain and ultimately fruitless quest for happiness. And if Le rouge et le noir and La chartreuse de Parme contain no explicit suicide, it could be said that they end in quasi suicides; that of Julien through antagonizing the jury so that they can bring only one verdict, and that of Fabrice by his long, silent, and solitary withdrawal and ascesis in the Charterhouse, after the death of his son Sandrino, indicating that though he may be one of the "happy few," his line is not viable. At the end of each novel, we are left with ambiguities and contradictions about values and how to live and achieve happiness, of which the suicide of Octave might be said to be the emblem. His suicide, which appears almost gratuitous given that it is never satisfactorily explained, takes us beyond the particularities of the book to illuminate with its sombre light the later more sunlit works.

With Emma Bovary's suicide the ironies are initially at least more obvious, because of the arsenic poisoning with all the upset to the digestive system it involves and because the discrepancy between the dream of suicide and its appalling reality is truly grotesque. And yet the scene is one of the most moving of the book, especially in the account of the last rites, which Zola no doubt had in mind when describing the death of Angélique in Le rêve. But the scene is not just moving; it brings together three fundamental aspects of Emma's character which are important for our analysis, and which are all related to her suicide.

The first characteristic is one which is hardly ever commented on by modern critics though it was identified shortly after the first publication of the novel by Baudelaire in an article in L'artiste in October 1857. His paradoxical and astonishing argument is that because of her energy, ambition, and propensity to dream, "Madame Bovary remained a man" (Baudelaire 1976, 2:81). He points out her "sudden energy of action, rapidity of decision, mystical fusion of reasoning and passion" (2:82). Flaubert tells us that she remains "a pragmatic spirit in the midst of her enthusiasms" (Flaubert 12:54), and because of her extravagant imagination she has the essential Baudelairean qualities of "the hysterical poet" (Baudelaire 2:83). She provides a sharp contrast with the "feminine" Frédéric Moreau of L'éducation sentimentale, "the man of all weaknesses," whose impulses are puny and who remains incapable of grasping hold of time and events and imposing on them the patterns of his will. For all its ironies and willful exaggeration, such a view acts as a stimulating corrective to those critics who have stressed the weak side of her character, her passive dreams before windows or "plunging perspectives" (Rousset 127), and her inability to distinguish between illusion and reality. But it is not all vague yearnings; for her experiences of the outside world are internalized, transformed, romanticized. Baudelaire's view alerts us to what is active in her dreaming. Far from remaining passive, she imposes on the outside world and transforms it according to her vision. Rouen is not for her some dull provincial city but an "enormous capital, a Babylon which she was entering" (Flaubert 12:364). She sees Rouen as Babylon, just as Quixote sees windmills as giants; her revery is dynamic and hallucinatory, so that like the Don she is always summoned to action, precisely because at certain moments "action *is* the sister of dream" (Baudelaire 1975, 1:122; our italics), and the dream can be grasped by stretching out the hand. If reality does not conform to her desire, she bullies it into submission. Notice the rapidity with which she gets the power of attorney from Charles, how she fixes the rendezvous with Léon—"tomorrow, at eleven o'clock, in the cathedral" (Flaubert 12:328)—the ease with which she puts into action the desire to see Rodolphe early in the morning. No sooner does the idea occur to her than she sets off and arrives at his "château" "as if the walls, at her approach, had parted" (12:227). Passion endows her with "masculine" qualities and makes her intelligent (at least Baudelaire would have it so), clear-sighted, rapid in decision and action. The most striking example where passion, willpower, and temperament flow together in a curiously triumphal harmony and unison is perhaps both predictably and paradoxically when she decides on suicide. Gone are the sentimental and romantic dreams of a beautiful, languorous and spiritual demise: "Then her situation, like an abyss, became clear to her. She was gasping. Then, in a transport of heroism which made her almost joyous, she ran down the hill, crossed the cattle plank, the path, the alley, the market, and arrived in front of the pharmacist's shop" (12:432). After taking the poison she goes home, "suddenly appeased, and almost with the serenity of a duty accomplished" (12:434). Doubt, hesitation, vacillation are not part of her temperament, and she is much closer to Salammbô and Mâtho, than to Frédéric Moreau, who quickly abandons his puny effort to throw himself into the Seine, finding the parapet too high.

The second fundamental trait in her character is what might be called her selflessness, by which I do not mean to play down her selfishness as witnessed in her callous or unthinking neglect of her child. For all her very obvious faults Emma has much of that ability to lose herself in the objects of her contemplation in the outside world which is part of the mysticism and vision of Salammbô, Saint Antoine, and the saints of Trois contes. Saint Antoine for example would like, in an often quoted passage, to flow like water, vibrate like sound, shine like light, descend into the depth of matter, "to be matter" (Flaubert 15: 201), and Salammbô, though given to "abstinence, fasting, and purification" (Flaubert 14: 61), is led by a latent sensuality from a mystical identification with the natural world to a total loss of self and union with the goddess Tanit whose priestess she is: "I would like to lose myself in the fog of the night, in the flow of fountains, in the sap of trees, to leave my body, to be nothing but a breeze, a ray, and to rise up to you, O Mother" (14:60). Emma experiences similar states, though the description of them is more discreet than in the cases we've just mentioned. On going to ask Rodolphe for money after her affair with Léon, she finds herself through the operation of affective memory back with the same sensations as she had when first she fell in love with him "and her poor constricted heart dilated lovingly." But these feelings immediately dilate themselves *outwards*: "a warm wind was blowing on her face; the snow, melting, was falling drop by drop from the buds onto the grass" (12:426). Emma's revery, and it is one of the great charms of the novel, takes her (and the reader) out of herself till she merges with the landscape of sights and sounds, which seem to fascinate and beckon by the mystery of their presence and their "secret potentialities" (11:470). Significantly, such a moment occurs at her first idea of suicide when, after reading Rodolphe's callous letter ending their affair, she thinks of throwing herself down from the attic: "She was standing at the very edge, almost suspended, surrounded by a great space. The blue of the sky filled her, the air circulated in her empty head, she had only to give in, to allow herself to be taken" (12:285). There is perhaps a faint suggestion that this sense of loss of self is present at her actual death, when she feels that she has at last finished with all the betrayals, baseness, and desires which have afflicted her existence and when "a twilight confusion descended on her thought" (12:438).

The third characteristic is the most important of all; for it is in the death scene that is spelled out more clearly and tellingly than in any other part of the novel her fundamental confusion of love, sensuality, and religion, when "pressing her lips to the body of the Man-God with all her fading strength, she placed on it the most passionate kiss she had ever given" (12:446). The grotesqueness of the gesture is surreally hyperbolic, since with a mixture of monumental stupidity and blasphemy, she seems to see herself embarked upon a love affair with the Second Person of the Trinity, the real man at last who will not let her down. The intertextual resonances of the scene reach back to Valérie Marneffe in *La cousine Bette* who on her death bed and in full recognition of her past wrongdoings wrily reflects that her last coquetterie will be to seduce God: "I must *do the good Lord!*" (Balzac 1950, 6:507). But we can interpret Emma's gesture in another light and see it also as a manifestation of a quest for some absolute value, experience, or intensity, which, to use Baudelaire's expression from a rather different context, "has taken the wrong road"[2] and is misdirected into the senses of which she remains prisoner to the end. At this point the reader can look back to earlier moments in the novel when in her exasperation she dances in the streets of Rouen disguised, or when having relegated Charles to the second floor she locks herself in her room with "extravagant books in which there were orgiastic scenes wth bloody situations" (12:399). Léon finds "on that forehead covered with cold drops, on those babbling lips, in those wild pupils, in the embrace of those arms, something extreme, vague, and lugubrious" (12:391) which terrifies him. This powerful mixture of love, violence, and religion in her imagination stems from an inchoate and semiconscious exasperation at the imperfections of a world in which action and dream are irrevocably disjoined, and in which the "aspiration toward the infinite" (Baudelaire 2:421), that Baudelairean Romantic ingredient par excellence, is constantly frustrated.

In the suicide scene, we penetrate to the heart of Flaubert's irony which lies not just in the disproportion between desire and reality, and in the folly of thinking that the ideal can be made real. It resides rather in a vision of the world in which comedy and tragedy are not juxtaposed as in Hugo's dispiriting and inevitable antitheses, but indissolubly fused and synthesized. His irony is then the result and synthesis of the dialectical clash of the thesis tragedy upon the antithesis comedy. The ironic vision which is Flaubert's, and which he shares with many of the great writers of the century, does not allow the separation of the "grandeur" from the "misère" of his creations, anymore than does that of poets and artists from Baudelaire to Apollinaire and Rouault in the depiction of their fools, mountebanks, buffoons, pitres, pierrots, and Christ figures. The poet and painter celebrate a yearning which they know can have no outlet except in art; less lucid, but equally torn, Emma is duped by the illusion of the immanence of the ideal in reality.

The final text against which I should like briefly to test the theory is Zola's L'oeuvre. Does not the gruesome and essentially realist suicide by hanging of Claude Lantier point, in two very differing ways, to certain fundamental contradictions at the heart of Zola's thinking and novelistic universe? First, Claude appears most obviously as the victim of his own extravagant, mythologizing imagination in his impossible creation of the apotheosis of Paris, which is severely blamed by Sandoz, alter ego of Zola himself and voice of Naturalism, Impressionism, and perhaps above all of measure. Similar in many ways to le docteur Pascal,

Sandoz is clearly an incarnation of the author himself, sharing his aesthetic convictions together with all the correct attitudes towards work and a regular, bourgeois, settled existence, essential for creative endeavor. But one could also say that Claude represents the side of Zola which he would wish to suppress, the early Romanticism of La confession de Claude. It is possible that the shared christian name is significant. Sandoz explains that the trouble with Claude, the present generation, and indeed with Sandoz himself is to have been born "at the confluence of Hugo and Balzac" (Zola 1970, 5:43), a confluence of romantic exaggeration and realist observation, and much of the novel is taken up with a struggle to shake off the remnants of Romanticism, whether it be Hugo in literature or Delacroix in painting. Claude loses his battle and his painting is swallowed up by its own hyperbolic depiction of the mythical female representation of Paris. But one wonders to what extent Zola himself succeeds, when we see the mythical imagination at work in La faute de l'abbé Mouret, that extravagant and hyperbolic Naturalist rewriting of the myth of the Fall and the expulsion from Eden with the description of le Paradou with the awesome tree of life at its center. Myth is never excluded for long in Zola; indeed in Germinal and Le docteur Pascal it has the crucial and privileged function of resolving the contradictions within these novels. It is through the renovated myth of Cadmus and the modern revolutionary myth of germination that the optimistic vision of the final page of the former is conveyed, just as indeed in the latter the whole appalling and wretched Rougon-Macquart cycle ends with the greatest western myth of all, that of the redemption of the world through the birth of a child, in the description of Pascal and Clotilde, likened unto King David and Abishag, with their Christ-child offspring, "who was still nursing, his little arm in the air, raised like a flag calling to life" (Zola 6:655). In the light of this one wonders if the suicide is not that of Zola himself, or rather if it is not more like a murder of Zola the Romantic by Zola the Naturalist, as revealing about the artist as the killing of the poetic self by the social self in Baudelaire's "An heroic death," and involving an abortive attempt at purgation which, no doubt fortunately, does not extend beyond the novel itself.

Secondly, one wonders whether this extraordinary painting does not embody the ambivalence of Zola's attitude towards sexuality. It is clear from the first encounter with Christine that Claude's sexuality is at variance with his métier as a painter. His unease in front of the female nude stems from the sublimation of his sexuality; the real is abandoned for what appears on the canvas, and Christine in "Open air" is transformed into a kind of terrestrial Venus, "an Eve desired, rising from the earth, with her face, which was smiling, unseeing, her eyelids closed" (5:43). One of the reasons why the search for keys to his character (Manet, Cézanne, Monet or whoever) is dispiriting or misguided is that Zola had to depart from the originals in order to fit the paintings to the character of Claude and his obsessions. Reminiscent of Serge in *La faute de l'abbé Mouret* whose need to sublimate he shares, Claude in his extravagant painting of Paris confuses religion, art, and sex in a way which borders on the pornographic: "he painted the belly and thighs like a crazed visionary"; the thighs "became golden like tabernacle columns" (5:197); there is mention of "a monstrance-like nudity" and of the "mystical rose of her sex, between the precious columns of her thighs, under the sacred vault of the belly" (5:199). Claude is the victim of his own sexual neurosis; but above all the passage highlights more than anything Zola's own flawed vision, which ill becomes a believer in the power of nature and its vitality, since it combines outward praise for life and its force with a latent disgust and with the obscenity of the voyeur, an obscenity which extends beyond the depiction of the body and its functions to pervade his descriptions even of the natural world, as for example in the hyperbolic description of the tree of life and of the plants and animals of le Paradou during the coupling of Serge and Albine: "From the most remote corners, from the patches of sunlight, from the pockets of shadow, arose an animal odor, warm with universal rutting. All that teeming life had the shiver of childbirth. Under every leaf, an insect conceived; in each tuft of grass, a family grew; flies in the air, stuck together, did not wait to land to fertilize each other. The invisible bits of life which populate matter, the very atoms of matter, were loving, copulating, giving the ground a voluptuous movement, were making of the park one great fornication" (2:115). Clearly, the influence of Hugo, of whom there is here more than a hint, has not been exorcised, but much more disquietingly and pertinently there is a foretaste of that other kind of descriptive obscenity which we find in Sartre's description of a tree in another park, in *La nausée*. However that may be, the suicide of Claude Lantier brings out more dramatically and more explicitly than any other scene in the cycle the tensions in Zola's vision between myth and reality, and between the prestige of the natural and obscenity.

Much further research remains to be done, on the authors already mentioned and on the other great novelists of the period, in particular Balzac and Hugo, before the validity of the argument can be established with a satisfactory degree of certainty. I should like to conclude, provisionally, with a suggestion concerning philosophical suicide in the work of a more modern writer whose roots go deep into the nineteenth century, to such an extent that he has been called the Chateaubriand of the twentieth. Tchen in Malraux's *La condition humaine*, a mystic without God and who owes much to Dostoevski's Kirilov, wishes to make of terrorism a kind of religion, by indoctrinating his disciples to follow him and by striving to achieve in the instant of death a state of total self-possession and dominance over fate. His suicide not only gives substance to the idea, which in Romanticism rarely gets beyond posturing, that one kills onself in order to live; but much more importantly, it can be said to highlight the contradictions in Malraux's death-of-God philosophy by showing the "mal du siècle" of one who like a modern René seeks an impossible and unrealisable "unknown good, whose instinct pursues me" (Chateaubriand 1969, 128), who persists in the anguished and "meaningless" question: "What is to be done with a soul, if there is neither God nor Christ?" (Malraux 226), who in his metaphysical anguish is bent on being in a world of becoming, and who, like all men according to Gisors, the mouthpiece of Malraux himself, "dreams of being god" (Malraux 349).

Exeter College, Oxford

NOTES

1. Quoted in Sainte-Beuve 1861, 1.379: "In *René* Chateaubriand hid the poison under the religious idea; it is poisoning in a host."
2. Baudelaire 1975, 1.402: "it is a taste [for the infinite] which often takes the wrong road."

15

Barante's Historiography of Terror

PATRICIA A. WARD

PROSPER de Barante (1782–1866) represents a generation of history-makers and history-writers for whom the revolutions of 1789, 1830, and 1848 posed ongoing questions of personal identity, political alliance, and social responsibility. As a historian and political figure, he may be grouped with Guizot (1787–1874) and Lamartine (1790–1869). Guizot's *Essais sur l'histoire de la France* (1823) are part of the rebirth of history writing during the Restoration, as are the six volumes of his Sorbonne lectures (1828–30) on modern history. Lamartine's *Histoire des Girondins* (1847) figures among the important volumes on the Revolution of 1789 and appeared as Michelet's own account began to be published (six volumes, 1847–53). In the events up to 1848, Guizot represents social conservatism, for, as Minister of Foreign Affairs and the President of the Conseil, he refused all electoral reform. It is he whom that Revolution fells, and Lamartine the republican replaces him in the provisional government as Minister of Foreign Affairs.

For all three, history is literature in that its narrative structures and tropes render their writing figural as a natural part of the rhetorical tradition to which they belonged. Yet, Barante was much more intentional in his literary conception of history than Guizot or Lamartine, and the preface to his *Histoire des ducs de Bourgogne* (1824–26) is a manifesto. With at least eight editions, this history of the fifteenth century in France, Burgundy, and Flanders was as successful as the historical novels which inspired Barante. (*Quentin Durward* had been published in 1821.) Barante's achievement in writing medieval history won him entrance to the Académie Française and coincided with Romantic interest in historical process, local color, and the picturesque.

In his 1824 preface Barante calls for a renewal of historiography, decrying the abandonment of narrative, recommending the use of contemporary sources, the portrayal of the "customs and color of the time," and the effacement of the historian as moralist or partisan politician.

> One is tired of seeing history, like a docile and hired sophist, lend itself to all the proofs that everyone wants to draw from it. What we want from history are facts. Just as one observes, in its details, in its movements, this great drama of which we are all actors and witnesses, one wants to know what the life of nations and individuals was before us. We ask that they be evoked and brought back to life before our eyes: each person will then draw from them such judgment as pleases him or her, or even will not think of formulating any precise opinion from them. For there is nothing as impartial as the imagination: it has no need to draw conclusions; it only requires a painting of the truth.
>
> (Barante 1839, 1:21–22)

Stephen Bann has called Barante's method "a transgressive mode of representation" (Bann 15). The tension between the two signifying fields of this passage—between historical truth as fact and history as a drama—is evident in the impossible claim with which Barante concludes. "Nothing is as impartial as the imagination: it has no need to draw conclusions; it only requires a painting of the truth." A kind of catachresis results from these competing figures of historical reality and truthful historiography; at the same time, the imagination is assigned an unclear series of functions as a faculty of creative perception, judgment, or visualization for the reader examining the drama of the past.

Despite his claim that the historian can write a dramatic narrative, paint a period, and remain impartial, Barante is implicated in his story. His politics are a guiding force in his conception of the fifteenth century and, later, of the Convention. His version of the waning Middle Ages is one of four powerful dukes and of the disintegration of the dynasty of Bourgogne. Powerful, strong figures are cast in opposition to seditions and uprisings. Brutality and superstition coexist with feasts, festivals, and court life. "Public opinion" is the principal character in this story—"the thought and the voice of the people were already exercising an immense power" (1: 24). These issues are highlighted in the struggle between Charles-le-Téméraire and Louis XI: "the triumph of skill over violence, the beginning of more enlightened politics, and the better-advised ambition of princes who, having become absolute masters of their subjects, turn the new progress of civilization and of good order to their own advantage" (1: 23).

There are personal and public contexts for this view of history, one very like the theme of the obligations of the strong ruler to the *peuple* in Hugo during the late 1820s. In *Hernani* (4.2), for example, Don Carlos's vision of history includes the stirring of the masses. " . . . Kings! look below! / —Ah! the people!— ocean!—a constantly moving wave, / In which nothing is cast without placing everything in motion!"

The "liberals" of the Restoration saw in the 1814 Charter an affirmation of the inevitability of the Revolution and of its achievement in establishing the natural laws of liberty, justice, and representation. They rejected, however, its Jacobin extremism (Gérard 32, Mellon 50). Barante became a center-left *doctrinaire*, along with Royer-Collard, Guizot, de Broglie, and Charles de Rémusat. They "saw political life as a careful balancing of interests, and recognized no authority but that of law, or impartial reason, which however they tended to identify in practice with the interests of the socially dominant classes" (Cobban 2:78).

Born in the Auvergne in a family of the *noblesse de robe*, Barante remained there during the Revolution and recounts that it no longer was a place of refuge in the latter months of 1792. "Jacobism heated up; local authority was renewed, towns handed over to popular clubs, revolutionary committees instituted, loans and requisitions made mandatory, levy *en masse* required of all men capable of bearing arms, immediate departure for the army ordered for all young men between the ages of eighteen and twenty-five" (Barante 1890, 1:11). Barante's father was arrested and taken to Paris in 1793; his mother followed him to try to obtain his release. After an unsuccessful attempt to discuss the matter with Couthon, Robespierre's close ally and the representative of the Auvergne, Madame de Barante obtained her husband's release in the summer of 1794 through the intervention of Lacoste, the representative of the Dordogne.

A graduate of the Ecole Polytechnique, Prosper de Barante was always linked to the literary world. During the Empire, the family was well-connected to Napoléon and Barante's father was the *préfet* of the Léman when Prosper began to frequent Coppet. His tempestuous relationship with Madame de Staël between approximately 1805 and 1810 caused the family no end of worry due to the latter's troubled relations with the Emperor. Barante senior intervened, obtaining posts for his son with the Conseil d'Etat, the army, and then as a *sous-préfet* and *préfet*. Prosper became a public figure of moderate liberalism for his time, but he in no way questioned the power structures of society. During the July Monarchy, he had a brilliant diplomatic career as ambassador to Turin and then Saint Petersburg (Diesbach 363–64, 572, and passim).

The fall of Guizot and the events of 1848–1851 pushed Barante toward an increasingly conservative position, although he never was an active supporter of Louis Bonaparte. It is little known that Barante wrote a *Histoire de la Convention Nationale* in the aftermath of the turmoil of 1848. Readers of the six volumes, published both in Paris and Brussels between 1851 and 1853, could not help but view Barante's work as a gloss both on Michelet and on the constitutional issues of 1851.

In retrospect, however, the *Histoire de la Convention Nationale* is an allegory about the impossibility of the project which Barante had conceived in 1824—of writing narrative in which the authorial voice claims innocence and impartiality. It is a project which equates the representation of history with the fact of history. It is also a theory of confusing tropes in which history is drama and historiography, novel or picture.

In his 1851 preface, Barante repeats many of his earlier ideas, relating them to the problems of writing any history of the Revolution. Nothing, he says, can replace contemporary accounts in giving a lively and colorful impression of the scenes and characters of a period. The metaphors from theater reoccur, for Barante prefers history which is "the living drama of an epoch," contrasting it with history written from a providential, overriding view which guides the organization of events. "One may say that writers who thus envision history outside of the time in which the events occurred view it from above, that they do not participate in the incomplete judgments of their contemporaries, in their partiality, in their passions, in their prejudices" (Barante 1851–53, 1:2). Histories written from an overt point of view which is not truly philosophical result in "scenes [which] are a creation of the painter and not a portrait of reality" (1:3). (Again, the textual figures constitute a misleading layering of metaphors of representation. Reality is equated with a specific form of art, "le portrait," even as wrongly conceived historiography is equated with painting in general.)

To illustrate his historiographic theories, Barante contrasts two accounts of the Convention by Garat (who replaced Danton as Justice Minister and then Roland as Minister of the Interior). Garat's 1793 account vividly portrays "the insurrections of the city of Paris, the hate-filled struggles that absorbed all the attention of the Convention, the universal disorder, the absence of government."[1] In 1820, the "sincere historian" has disappeared, to be replaced by the "poet or artist."[2] The values of "social order, justice, and humanity" vanish in the "presence of grandeur and the poetry of chaos" (1:4). Barante comments, "the Creator brought the world out of chaos; it was not chaos which, by its own virtue, gave birth to the world" (1:5).

The glory of the Convention lay only in its defense of the territory of France; it left no legacy such as that of the generation of leaders in the Etats-Généraux or the Assemblée Nationale— "Equal rights, national representation, open debate on public matters." "A generation who wanted to make the exercise of power not a right but a duty; who proclaimed that sovereignty is called general interest" (2:6). In contrast, the leaders of the Convention "by ambition, by desire, by wild pride, worked to destroy a society in order to found another . . . [they] began their undertaking through insurrection in order to continue it by throat-cutting and scaffolds . . . led astray and deceived the working classes by showing a hypocritical sympathy for them . . . tried in vain to codify their political maxims, and to give a form of government to their passions" (1:7). Barante's own values could not be clearer in his two catalogues of positive and negative outcomes of the Revolution. These values clearly implicate him in his ensuing narrative, despite his insistence that his exact painting of the Convention is a copy of reality (1:9).

He continues to use Garat as a point of reference in attacking recent attempts to rehabilitate both the Convention and its major figures, such as Robespierre. (Gérard Walter indicates that Guillaume Lallement began this process for Robespierre in 1820, but that the apogee was Ernest Hamel's *Histoire de Robespierre,* 1865–67 [Michelet 1952, 2:1542]. And, in an inversion of Restoration liberalism, the Convention came to be seen in the 1840s as the expression of the true democratic spirit of the Revolution [Gérard 39].) Garat had originally described Robespierre as a "monster" and an "oratorical dictator." Later, he idealized this conception, comparing Robespierre to Jesus Christ.[3] Even Marat, whom contemporary documents portrayed as a "charlatan," has become a revolutionary hero (1.8).

In order to combat these sorts of inexact portrayals, Barante explains his use of a variety of sources and materials. First, if the leaders of the Convention have not been judged in recent years by their actions, perhaps readers will instead learn to know them by their speeches, reports, and discussions. "The history of an assembly takes place in large part at the tribune; speeches are often actions" (Barante 1851–53, 1:10). Barante has developed a certain ordering of facts and events. He has written the history of the parties, the customs, the struggle to divide power, the legislation, and the military administration of the Convention.

Finally, he sees the absolute power of the republicans of the Convention, who gained submission through fear, as "bearing death in its bosom" (1:13). Since reformers in 1851 are using these republicans as models, Barante sees a meaningful parallel. He would not have published his history had the February revolution not occurred. The public has been indifferent, but now, perhaps, it will accept the truth and recognize the symptoms of revolutionary illness and learn the lessons taught by the Convention. The principle of equal rights is irreversible; the issue in 1851 is not the maintenance of social order, but the mechanism of the constitution. Little did Barante know that a *coup d'état* was about to occur when he concluded, "The Republique of 1793 recognized that it was incompatible with French society; the republic of 1848 has not been long in admitting that the same is true for it; is it not then natural that one should place so little faith and hope in its future?" (1:17).

Barante organizes the ten books of his history in two ways—according to themes and major events. The themes are the expected: the Legislative Assembly, Paris Commune, War, Trial of the King, Girondins, Civil War, Terror, Reaction, Victory, Peace Treaties, and Constitution. The key events become markers or dramatic turning points of excess. The narrative is framed by 10 August 1792, the date of the attack on the Tuileries and the invitation to the French people to form a national convention; it ends on 5 October 1795 (le 13 Vendémiaire), the date of the suppression of the last Paris revolt and dissolution of the Convention. Other marker events include 2 September 1792 (the surrender of Verdun and the beginning of massacres), 21 January 1793 (the execution of Louis XVI), 31 March 1793 (Paris uprisings), le 9 Thermidor (27–28 July 1794—the fall of Robespierre), and le premier Prairial (20 May 1795, the suppression of the faubourg Saint-Antoine).

Barante's lexical choices in describing the role of the populace in these marker events are revealing. For example, of the assault on the Tuileries he says, "The Tuileries Palace, defiled by the massacre, was also handed over to banditry, to the savage entertainment of a crowd intoxicated with disorder and destruc-

tion. . . . It was the sack of a city taken by assault and put to the
fire and sword" (1:169). Or, in describing the assassins at the
Carmelite convent at the beginning of the September massacres,
he speaks of a ghoulish chase of the victims during which the
murderers "pursued these unfortunate priests from alley to alley,
from bower to bower, shooting at them, laughing when their shots
hit their mark, singing one of their cannibalistic songs: 'Dansez
la Carmagnole.'" (1:220). Later, during the Terror when the wor-
ship of Reason is instituted, Barante cites Mercier who describes
the crowd: "This people, suddenly freed of its political and religious yoke, was unrestrained, dancing in the sanctuary while
howling out the Carmagnole, and the dancers, almost without
breeches, neck and arms bare, stockings rolled down, were like
a whirlwind which precedes the ravages of a storm" (4:39).

The crowds are let loose in a fury of medieval, carnival-like
barbarism, harkening back to the fifteenth century. Terror for
Barante becomes, in the details of the text, a projection of personal terror. He indeed is implicated and his narrative is not
innocent. The excesses of the Convention are enactments of inversion; Barante's values of equal rights, popular representation,
and free discussion within the context of reason and social order,
all these values come crashing down. Of the atmosphere surrounding the revolutionary tribunal in late 1793, he comments,
"The revolutionary spirit was ouside the bounds of reason: it
had lost track of the real and the possible, it was living in an
atmosphere of grandiloquence, hyperbole, and lies" (4:9).

Robespierre is the dominant figure of the narrative, usually
linked to Saint-Just. "Robespierre was the sophist of the Reign
of Terror; Saint-Just was its apostle. Neither of them wanted nor
asked for anything other than tyranny, without explaining what
its aim and end would be" (4:189). Robespierre's ambition was
not to act or govern, but to elevate his station. The "festival of the
Supreme Being" represents this hubris brought to its extreme, as
Barante constructs this drama. "The airs of sovereign authority
that Robespierre took on" caused the public to perceive that he
thought that he was exercising complete power (4:263).

The downfall of Robespierre is that of a morality play. If the
Convention was his "battlefield" and speech was action there,
the refusal of the president to yield the tribune to him at the
critical moment of the action renders him impotent. Finally,
Robespierre and his allies are shown to the people of Paris "like
the wounded from a battle" (4:555). Barante enters the story with
this judgment: "In reading this bloody page of revolutionary his-

tory, we certainly applaud the day which put an end to the legal-
ized massacres and saved society from tyrannical anarchy; but
we feel a regret mixed with indignation in seeing this triumph
sullied with so much blood. Those defeated at Thermidor must
not have been surprised by their fate; they had made this sort of
victory customary" (4:357).

While the overthrow of Robespierre marks the beginning of
the end of the Terror, Barante brings it to closure in other ways.
As narrator and as dramatist, he enters his story precisely as he
said he would not, bringing judgment and order back to the scene
of chaos. In a different context, Hayden White has commented
that "narrativity in the representation of real events arises out of
a desire to have real events display the coherence, integrity, full-
ness, and closure of an image of life that is and can only be
imaginary" (White 24). Barante's desire for closure is the driving
force which sets his narrative at odds with the republicanism
of 1851 and, in a supreme irony, it marks the end of Romantic
historiography which the political values, so based in order, of
the Restoration and July Monarchy embody.

Vanderbilt University

NOTES

    1. Barante 1851–53, 1:3. Barante refers to Garat's defense when facing
charges from the Convention (Garat, an III).
    2. The reference here is to Garat 1820.
    3. Barante may have in mind here two remarkable passages in volume 2 of
Garat's 1820 *Mémoires*. First, Garat reaches a generalization about the Convention which, over time, "has come to be the most inconceivable and terrible
phenomenon in the entire historical corpus." He then concludes that our appropriate response before the Convention may be the same as that of Pascal, in
speculating about humanity: "What a novelty! what a chaos! what a contradictory subject! what a CHIMERA the Convention is! Judge of everything; stupid
earthworm; depository of truth; a mass of uncertainties; the glory and refuse
heap of the universe; if [the Convention] boasts, I humble it; if it humbles
itself, I praise it; keep on contradicting it until it understands that it is an
incomprehensible MONSTER" (334–35).
    A few pages later Garat, in speaking of Robespierre's origins and his moral
rectitude, compares him to Jesus. "Robespierre, whom Europe thinks it sees at
the head of the French nation, lives in the shop of a carpenter whose son he
aspires to be; and his morals are not only decent; without any affectation and
without any hypocritical self-supervision, they are as strict as the morals of
the God raised by a Judean carpenter" (339).

16

Terrorism and Terror in Balzac's *Histoire des Treize*

RICHARD B. GRANT

IF one is to deal with Balzac, terrorism, and terror from the vantage point of twentieth-century experience, what better point of departure than to quote from a justice of the Israeli Supreme Court, since Israelis—both on the receiving and on the giving end—have been intimately involved with the phenomenon of terrorism? Ochberg and Soskis cite Justice Shamgar, a specialist in international law, who has defined terrorism as "the use of murderous violence to achieve political ends that does not obey the rules of war" (2). The reference to war is understandable in the light of the history of Israel, but perhaps the most important word in his definition is the word *political*. In our day it has been just about impossible to think of terrorism without its political context or purpose, and in Balzac's day, thanks to the haunting memory of 1793, this was just as much the case.

If we turn now to Balzac's *Histoire des Treize*, with its three *nouvelles*, we must begin with the well-known tale, *La duchesse de Langeais*, precisely because of its political context. At first blush, however, the action may appear to be primarily personal, because informed readers are well aware that Balzac needed to avenge through the fantasy of literature his humiliating rejection at the hands of Mme de Castries. In *La duchesse*, he relived that experience but altered the outcome. His hero, Armand de Montriveau, furious (like Balzac) at having been toyed with and mocked by the frivolous Antoinette de Langeais, finally violates the law and (to modify Justice Shamgar's expression) the rules of war between the sexes. He kidnaps her and threatens her with facial branding so that other men will know her for the "tease" she really is. Whereas Mme de Castries never yielded to Balzac's entreaties, Montriveau's strong-armed action results in young

234

Antoinette's falling genuinely in love with her abductor, and later, thinking herself permanently rejected by him, she flees Paris and takes refuge as a nun in a convent off the Spanish coast, where her passionate love becomes spiritualized, blending love for Montriveau with love of God. Such was the fantasy of Balzac's revenge on Mme de Castries.

But, as Balzac makes clear, his tale transcends the personal. His narrative is also a political parable, almost an allegory of France under the Bourbon Restoration. France, Balzac informs his readers (Balzac 1976–81, 5:930), is a very feminine nation ("France, a capricious woman. . . . the most female country in the world"), and Antoinette is not only a perfect representative of her aristocratic class, by extension she incarnates the volatile qualities of the nation itself. As she toys with Montriveau's affections, she reveals herself as vain, self-centered, and pleasure-seeking, endowed, no doubt, with "fine feelings," but lacking "a thought which would coordinate them" (5:935). As a symbol of that aristocracy, she fails to realize the historical truth that the nobility must have a sense of obligation ("noblesse oblige"). It needs to realize that the nation calls upon it to lead, but it is not doing so. As Balzac puts it: "In every state, in whatever form the government takes, as soon as the patricians fail in their conditions of complete superiority, they become powerless and the people immediately overthrow them. The people always want to see fortune, power and action in the hands, heart, and head of patricians" (5:926). Balzac goes on to explain that in France of the Restoration the aristocracy has degenerated, becoming both an oligarchy and a gerontocracy, too self-centered, too tired, too lacking in understanding of what is needed even to include in the government young noblemen, intelligent and eager, who could revive their class and then the nation. Instead, aristocrats, young or old, squander their energy on fancy dress balls.

The hero, Armand de Montriveau, on the other hand, is very different. An orphan, raised under Napoleon and an admirer of the Emperor's energy, he is gifted to the point of genius, modest, ascetic, and hard-working. In Balzac's mind, he represents the type of leader that France badly needs. Furthermore, as there was under the monarchy no electoral system that could permit the ouster of the tired patricians, Balzac has set up a situation in which Justice Shamgar's "violence against the rules" is actually justified. In having Montriveau kidnap and threaten to brand Antoinette, Balzac was implicitly justifying a violent overthrow of the government, and it might be possible to see his hero, there-

fore, as a kind of political terrorist. But here a distinction must
be made, because everything depends on point of view. When
serious frustrations arise at the inequities in the social order,
there develops a strong sense of in-group/out-group opposition.
The in-group fears the threat from the out-group and, condemn-
ing its illegal, hence immoral status, brands its members as terrorists. But, conversely, the out-group sees itself not only as
justified morally, but even as saviors. It rejects a system in which
it claims that the deck is stacked, and operates in the name of
"true" justice or some higher law. As Ochberg and Soskis conclude (115–16), its members do not see themselves as terrorists
at all.

As if obscurely aware that Montriveau, an outsider to his class,
even though actually of noble birth, is justified in seeking revenge, Antoinette begins to feel terror even before her kidnapping, as Montriveau tells her that she should not have played
with fire. Actually, his words were "Don't touch the axe" (5:989),
which suggest if not the guillotine, at least some royal beheading,
especially that of Marie-Antoinette, during the Reign of Terror.
Thus it is that "despite her apparent disdain for Armand's dark
predictions, the duchess was stricken by a real terror" (5:990),
and after her abduction she cannot keep from crying out in fear.

The nature of her terror needs to be understood with some
precision. It is based on guilt. She knows that as an individual
she has toyed with a man's sincere affection, and as a symbol of
France's ruling class she knows too that she has been irrespon-
sible and frivolous. Thus punishment is deserved, and atone-
ment is required. Because she knows that she has done wrong,
she is more than ready, psychologically speaking, to embrace
her abductor. As an individual, she falls genuinely in love with
Montriveau, an anticipation, if one will, of the famous Stockholm
syndrome, in which hostage victims identified with the bank
robbers rather than with the police. As a symbol of her class,
once she has been released by Armand, Antoinette abandons her
peers and turns to the strong man who has seized her. She flouts
the codes of her class by openly compromising herself with him.
All this is Balzac's way of saying that if only a more modern
Napoleonic figure would appear, one whose values were based
on intellectual genius, like Montriveau, rather than on the martial genius of a Bonaparte, he would be the perfect leader for the
nation, and "feminine" France would respond eagerly.

Balzac was not afraid to express his feelings in language that
might well make feminists wince: "Most women want to feel

their moral being violated" (5:962). Balzac was scornful of democracy, and in the Armand-Antoinette duel, he gives the victory to the moral man of genius who can bend the nation to his will. In this way is terrorism justified, or to put it better, it constitutes salvation for the nation and not terrorism at all.

Yet there is a problematic aspect to Balzac's admiration of the power of the individual, whether personal or political. In *La fille aux yeux d'or* and in *Ferragus*, the other two stories of the trilogy, the members of the "Treize," who are above the law and revel in their quasi-divine status, can and do cause immense harm to the innocent. In *La fille aux yeux d'or*, Henri de Marsay and his half-sister (the latter is not a member of the Thirteen, but is certainly someone worthy of inclusion) combine to exploit and even bring about the death of the innocent Paquita Valdès. In *Ferragus*, a jealous father inflicts far more damage and death than can reasonably be justified. To cause a young man a slow, horrible death by poisoning just because he has been attracted by the mystery of a woman whose actions intrigue him and has sought to penetrate that mystery is surely Balzac's way of warning against the abuse of total power, whether personal or by implication political. Balzac is never quite simplistic.

Leaving direct political considerations, something resembling terrorism can occur in the form of powerful social pressures that can instill fear in an individual. But it is perhaps wiser to abandon the term *terrorism* for that of *terror*, because terror is individual, and it is the individual who is normally threatened by society's condemnation, not society (or a class) as a whole. Now Antoinette de Langeais is not affected by that pressure once she has truly fallen in love with Armand. She violates all the codes of her caste, even sending her carriage to spend the night at his door, despite his refusal to see her. Her family is appalled at her action and pressures her to be discreet, calling her imprudent and hot-headed, but to no avail.

But if we move to *Ferragus*, we see that terror socially inflicted can be a grim reality, especially in the case where one's place in society is not assured by aristocratic birth. For those not familiar with this less well-known story of *Histoire des Treize*, the central female figure, Clémence Desmarets, is married to a decent man, but he is unaware of her true origins. Her father, Ferragus, one of the Thirteen, is a criminal a bit in the manner of Vautrin, and her birth is illegitimate to boot. Fearful that her husband's love might be affected should he learn of her socially unacceptable origins, she is stricken with terror when the young man, Auguste de Maulincour, tries to penetrate her secret. Later, questioned by her husband, who has been tipped off by Auguste that there is something irregular about her life, she says, "I will tell you, Jules; but it will not be without terror" (5:837), but she manages to avoid telling him the full truth, and because she lies clumsily, her husband's doubts only become more acute. The stress becomes so great that she dies at the end, worn out by the tension and fear.

But whether in a given case Balzac's preoccupation is with the political or the social, we have not yet penetrated to the heart of his concerns. Macauley and Berkowitz cite the psychologist Melvin Lerner, who argues persuasively that people desperately need to believe in a just world, and even blame themselves when, as in the case of rape, no blame exists, so that they may continue to believe that cause and effect govern the world and therefore that the world is just. This "just world theory," however, is only the façade that cloaks an even more fundamental need: to believe in an orderly world and universe. If the concept of justice has strong political overtones, the idea of an orderly universe raises the subject to the level of metaphysics.

Which leads us to consider Balzac's own vision of his world or universe. For many years, scholars stressed Balzac's desire to create a unified vision to his vast Comédie humaine, but more recently, there has emerged a revisionist attitude. As Allan Pasco has observed (4–6), many scholars, including Pierre Macherey (287), Pierre Barbéris (215), and especially Lucien Dällenbach, have noted that while Balzac claimed that he wrote out of a unitary vision, in their eyes his universe was fragmented, full of holes or empty spaces, and therefore ultimately discontinuous. Dällenbach has even gone so far as to assert that this very lack of unity in La Comédie humaine is what makes it fascinating for modern readers. Because, he argues, the Balzacian corpus is more scriptible than lisible, the reader is encouraged to create his own "text," to fill in the admittedly numerous blank spaces that create gaps in the Human Comedy.[1]

Balzac's own characters, however, experience no creative joy at the thought of living in a discontinuous universe, one in which there is not only no justice, but one in which the patterns of cause and effect seem violated. In La fille aux yeux d'or, young Paquita Valdès, like a victim in a Gothic novel and sequestered by her lesbian lover, lives in almost constant terror as a prisoner of forces that she cannot comprehend. In the case of Auguste de Maulincour of Ferragus, I indicated earlier that the young man begins to pry into the affairs of an apparently proper lady for whom he had a secret longing. His curiosity had been piqued because he saw her by chance one day acting furtively as she walked along a street in a seedy neighborhood. As a result of what he considered normal, understandable curiosity, terrifying events take place. A huge stone topples from a building and almost crushes him and does kill his valet. This was terror enough for Auguste to take to his bed for a few days. Soon afterwards the axle on his carriage breaks, and again he is nearly killed. This time he learns that the axle had been cleverly sabotaged. His life is in danger because of Ferragus's fanatical desire to protect his daughter's reputation, but Auguste, unaware of this fact, can discern no cause, no guilt sufficient to justify attempted murder. Hence the terror: the law of cause and effect no longer seems to be operating. His old mentor, a *vidame*, explains that going to the police is of no use, because one can only reasonably ask of them to seek out the causes of an event (5:826), and what is happening seems to defy any obvious rational pattern. Finally Auguste is poisoned by a deadly slow-acting toxin that little by little destroys his body and his mind. Bewildered, but in order to bring back stability to his tottering universe, the young man decides that his curiosity must have been a serious crime (although it really was not), and thus he justifies through guilt what has happened to him. His aristocratic code permitted him to pursue a married woman who had, he thought, at least one affair underway, and if one, why not another, that is, with himself? But he had to abandon his code and assume guilt if he was to avoid suffering the feeling of dying meaninglessly in an absurd universe.

In this respect, Auguste feels as did Balzac, and indeed the nineteenth century as a whole. As Pasco concluded: "No one—neither Balzac nor his readers—doubted that reality was unified. It never occurred to authors that readers might not seek the principles that give order, coherence, unity to their works. . . . In short, . . . nineteenth-century readers lived within the convention of wholeness and unity [even if] certain modern critics resist closure and seek fragmentation and chaos" (6).

Thus it is that in *Histoire des Treize* we find Balzac almost obsessed with the values of order, coherence, and harmony. If Ferragus lives in a disorderly apartment, with objects scattered about in random fashion, it is because he represents something diabolical, something opposed to God's true order. If Paquita Valdès of *La fille aux yeux d'or* dies in terror, it is because she did not have the opportunity to understand the forces controlling her world. Conversely, in *La duchesse de Langeais*, Balzac gives the reader his vision of life's true harmony, as he describes Antoinette's convent perched on a rocky island off the Spanish coast. It had been spared the upheavals of the French Revolution (5:905), and now the convent glories in a setting of natural beauty, which is in harmony with the music that she plays on the chapel organ, and this harmony is itself only a reflection of the harmony and unity created by the fusion of exalted human love with divine love, as Antoinette, now a nun, celebrates on this spiritual instrument France, her love for Montriveau, and God. As Balzac puts it: "Are not Religion, Love, and Music the triple expression of the same thing, the need for expansion by which every noble soul is tormented?" (5:914)? In Balzac's day—*Histoire des Treize* dates from 1833 to 1835—the dis-unity, the dis-harmony of 1793 was still a haunting memory. Terrorism had to be reckoned as an ever-present political danger, and the chance of an individual's feeling terror is of course a constant of the human condition. But Balzac's political message in his trilogy is that it may be possible, despite the potential for abuse of power, for strong swift action by a bold leader to mean not terrorism but harmony for a nation. On the individual level, despite the ever-present threat of personal terror, behind and beyond all the apparent discontinuities and seemingly arbitrary events, Balzac gives his readers the distinct impression that he wishes to reassure them that, as Antoinette de Langeais discovered in her convent, they can rejoice in the harmony and meaning of life if they will only spiritualize their desires.

But Balzac cannot be reduced to such a simplistic vision. After all, ambivalence was inherent in this monarchist who castigated the monarchy, this Roman Catholic who often was harsh on the Church, and this capitalist who exposed its many cruelties. At the end of *Ferragus* we find yet another example of this ambivalence. When Clémence Desmarets dies, a solemn funeral mass is held, and Balzac goes out of his way to emphasize the rite as a "hymn of despair," which generates "Those cries which overwhelm souls," "that religious dread which terrifies." It is true that he goes on to mention that the ceremony closes with a "song of hope," but this brief allusion to hope (only a few words) is all but lost in his emotional description of the "fears" and the "cries of terror" of the *Dies irae*. Given the human condition, terror can never be truly overcome once and for all, despite the Church and any belief in God. In short, there is no seamless fabric of logic or coherence that can contain Balzac. If Pasco is correct in his awareness that Balzac and indeed his century sought that "dark and profound unity" of which Baudelaire wrote in "Correspondances," Dällenbach and the others are also correct that the discontinuities and contradictions in Balzac's vision cannot lightly be dismissed. It was not just the haunting memory of 1793 that unnerved him and his generation. Balzac had also sensed the fear underlying the easy complacency of a century too optimistic in its belief in continuing moral, as well as social and technological progress, and the deeper, abiding terror caused by the knowledge of our inevitable death.

University of Texas

NOTES

1. For more detail see Pasco (4–6), to whom I am greatly indebted.

17

Balzac: Tenebrous Affairs and Necessary Explications

ARMINE KOTIN MORTIMER

This style does not suggest, does not reflect: it explains.
—Marcel Proust

IN *Une ténébreuse affaire,* Balzac postures as the one who knows
the answer to the question his novel poses—"what really happened and why?"—for if ever an *explication* was *nécessaire,* it
is in this "impure fiction."[1] The kidnapping of the senator Dominique Clément de Ris in 1800 underlies Balzac's story, a murky
business of multiple royalist and republican conspiracies set in
three moments of the Consulate and early Empire. History thus
apparently comes first, but Balzac claims to prove what happened by retelling the story in fiction. In its relation to history,
the novel engages in hysteron proteron, which is not only a figure
of speech in which natural or rational order is reversed, but also a
figure in logic: the fallacy of assuming as a premise a proposition
following something yet to be proved.[2]

A striking reversal in the title strategically controls meaning
and direction. Prosaic word order would call for "Une affaire
ténébreuse," two anapests with the accented syllables at regular
intervals. Instead, the adjective placed abnormally before the
noun forces equal accentuation on the three syllables of "ténébreuse." Thus stressed, "ténébreuse" alerts the reader to a potential for mystification and intrigue, which naturally provokes
the desire to find out the truth. Richly signifying, "ténébreux"
means dark, sinister, gloomy, dismal; secret, hidden, covered, obscure, mysterious, impenetrable, difficult to elucidate;[3] perfidious, unavowable, dishonest ("doing harm in a covert manner;
hiding, plotting under cover," according to the *Robert*); melan-

cholic. In the novel, "ténébreuse" occasionally alludes to the atmosphere both meteorological and moral; the obscure and impenetrable, in sum, become perfidious. Such is the "tenebrosity" of the political story told by the fiction that the reader, confused and distressed, also craves explication.

For the question the novel poses on behalf of the reader—what really happened and why?—authorizes us to ask *about the novel:* "what *really* really happened?" In other words, it is pertinent to comment on Balzac's narrative strategies. *Une ténébreuse affaire* has the advantage of including in its mimetic narrative a model for each of the terms or limits between which the novel lies, tenebrosity and explication. The *cachot* or prison-hiding place in the impenetrable center of the forest of Nodesme figures its tenebrous affairs, while the interpretive reading of the *procès politique* or political trial gives consistency to necessary explications. I suggest the novel also illustrates the precarious posture of all Balzacian narratives between tenebrous affairs and necessary explications. The outer limits of any narration are the secrecy of its affairs and the necessity of unfolding them.

Balzac believed he alone could tell the real story because he had inside information from his father and from Mme de Berny. He presumes to correct mistakes in other accounts, such as the *Mémoires* of the duchesse d'Abrantès, which had already added a layer of mediation between story and event. (The duchess retells the history because she also thinks she can "correct" it.) In a long preface later suppressed, Balzac claims that his novel resolves a question that remains unanswered to this day about the historical events of the kidnapping: who did it? The novel would play the historian's role on the stage of real history. (As Marthe Robert writes, "it is not the politicians, *but Balzac's characters* who created the country's History.")[4]

What Balzac "knows" and tells us is that his character Malin de Gondreville or the real senator Clément de Ris acted in concert with a secret party born of the Revolution opposed to Bonaparte and conspiring to create a new government. In Balzac's account, Talleyrand, Fouché, Sieyès, and Carnot, joined by Malin as factotum, plot against the Premier Consul on the eve of the battle of Marengo, on 13 June 1800. If Napoleon is defeated, the conspirators intend to exploit popular disappointment to take power; if victorious, they will rally round the Consulate. Fouché has forced Malin to print and stockpile the documents needed for the "new government" in sufficient quantities for distribution.[5] When news of Napoleon's decisive victory reaches Paris,

Malin hastens to conceal the compromising papers in his chateau at Gondreville, a "national property" filched from the Simeuse family, and returns to Paris in time to congratulate the
Premier Consul. Six years later, the distrustful Fouché, to bury
the conspiracy more surely, secretly sends his police to Gondreville, led by Corentin, to seek and destroy any evidence. To cover
their actions, five policemen disguised as four noblemen, the
Simeuse and d'Hauteserre brothers, and their faithful follower
Michu, kidnap and sequester the senator. Fouché pretends to
investigate the kidnapping and has the four aristocrats and Michu arrested; they are tried and convicted. Thus is consummated
an official crime, in which the guilty punish the innocent. As
S.-J. Bérard writes, "Balzac thought he knew that in the real affair,
agents authorized by Fouché and the secretary of the prefecture
himself, Sénéchal, had aided, organized the judicial error and
had not backed away from the irreparable: the death penalty"
(8:1456). So convinced was Balzac of the truth of his story that
he told it a second time, as part of the muddy past of the character du Bousquier in La vieille fille.

Let us be clear about this: the answer Balzac gives may or may
not be the truth of history. Taken with respect to facts, the story
of the novel stands in an awkward and uncertain relation as to
revealing or hiding. It may darken or eclipse the story of Clément
de Ris, in altering it for fiction's purposes, or reveal something
hitherto unknown about it.

The change of title from the first draft's "Une affaire secrète"
(8:1495) concisely indexes how what was merely secret became
tenebrous. The draft began by portraying the five conspirators in
dialogue in a certain boudoir, thus telling the cause of the events
the novel was to recount. Between the first draft and the later
manuscript version, a major reordering of the novel's parts re-
sulted in a tenebrous reading effect: Balzac moved these necessary explications to the last few pages (making at the same time
several smaller changes which contribute to entenebrating
causes).[6] Hysteron proteron begins to overtake narrative logic:
the telling of the cause now follows the telling of its complex
effects. Chapter 22 of the Souverain edition of 1842, retained in
the Folio edition, is called "Darkness Dissipated," an apt name
for the place of necessary explanations; but would the sky have
been so dark if the explanations had come in chapter 1? The life
of the plot now depends on the final scene of explication without
which the story would remain entenebrated. Yet, instead of one
of those assertive, informative, airless explanations by the famil-

iar, all-knowing narrator, the one Proust chided for striking but
disharmonious images (Proust 1971, 270), the "secret of the affair" (Balzac 1973, 238) comes mediated by a secondary narration. Now an aged Henri de Marsay tells the story at a classic
gathering of duchesses and princesses in 1833, decades after the
event, to reveal why the comtesse Laurence de Cinq-Cygne leaves
in a huff of *ancien régime* disdain when the comte—*d'Empire*—
Malin de Gondreville arrives. This genteel mediation necessi-
tates, as a trait of verisimilitude, the frequent use of phrases such
as "I believe" or "he must have said" and several other markers
of hearsay knowledge—and of taking a safe political distance.

Putting the necessary explication after the tenebrous affair
mirrors the psychological effect that receivers of the event experience; the story remains inexplicable until all the facts are
in. While we read the cause in the last chapter, we must mentally
retell everything that has been recounted, not unlike those who
would interpret evidence for the trial. Intelligence comes only
when the novel is done and chronology whole. Having forced us
to seek explanations, the novel turns the reader into something
like the Proustian character, one who says "later I understood."
This characteristic choice for complication defines *Une ténébreuse affaire* and the character Malin: "one of those characters who have so many faces and so much depth under each face
that they are impenetrable at the moment they act and can only
be explained long after the game is over."[7] Complication precedes explication. The premise according to which personal or
small history unfolds from prior cause to later result reigns, mi-
croscopically, in the narrative of the hatreds and alliances among
the characters Malin, Marion, Michu, Laurence de Cinq-Cygne,
the Simeuse twins, and others. What Balzac's necessary explications do the novel proposes to do: explaining or unfolding personal history replicates, in small, the macroscopic unfolding of
past causes in history.[8] Speaking of himself in an almost pomp-
ous third person, Balzac writes: "He has changed the location,
changed the interests, while preserving the political point of
departure; he has, finally, literarily speaking, made the impossible true" (8:493). So much and no less does the fiction claim
for itself; making real history into literary fiction, he has made
it "true." In retelling the story, Balzac's hysteron proteron makes
it possible to "know" much more about history than his suppressed preface recounted, for the fabulation in *Une ténébreuse
affaire* retells a "secret" deeper and greater than the truth about
the kidnapping.

* * *

The *cachot* in the Nodesme forest is also a *cachette* ("hiding
place"); it is plurivalent and expressive, natural and symbolic.
Hard to find, difficult to get to, invisible from the outside, the
prison suggests a crypt that protects the aristocrats but also situates danger. It emblematizes tenebrosity. It represents the heart
of darkness of the story as it lies in the heart of the dense forest,
unknown, implausibly, to Laurence de Cinq-Cygne who spends
entire days riding in the woods. The space of this hiding place
defines its location in a historic past as the secret prison of a
monastery eight centuries old, for the relation of space to time
is archeological (93). Of the five avenues that once led to the
monastery, several are nearly effaced, symbolizing incomplete
and difficult access to the secret. The "inaccessible edges" and
the "impenetrable bushes" that surround the cave naturalize the
allegory (92, 93). In telling how Michu guides Laurence to the
cachot, "by making detours, doubling back, cutting his own trail
across clearings to cover his tracks" (91), Balzac provides a fine
metaphor for how the characters experience events and for how
knowledge is encrypted in his narrative. Once inside, characters
are in the dark, figuratively and literally (50), for people in the
midst of actions do not know what they mean: "Marthe, ex-
hausted, trembling, expected some sort of outcome after such a
run. What purpose was it to serve? a good deed or a crime?"
(57). If the notion of a dénouement implies seeing clear, with
the characters, in the meantime actions are enshrouded in tenebrosity. By the same logic an essential element of the power of the
police lies in avoiding darkness, for instance by reconnoitering
hiding places: "Corentin received from Fouché the order to explore the chateau of Gondreville, to etch a plan of it in his memory, and to reconnoitre its smallest hiding places."[9]

While de Marsay eventually explains the conspiracy that secretly initiated the entire sequence of events in the novel, not
all of its proliferating tenebrosity is assigned to revelation by a
knowledgeable informer. Laurence de Cinq-Cygne, bearer of all
past generations of her family's history including its political
secrets, reinvents herself in the text in a way that keeps intact
her secret stance and throws up obstacles to revisions of her
history. Her behavior and speech are determined by what Esther
Rashkin has called a phantom: her unstinting devotion to the
legitimist cause. So adamant is her refusal to recognize any but
ancien régime royalty that well into the July Monarchy she con-

tinues to refer to Louis-Philippe as "monseigneur le duc d'Orléans" (228). All the aristocrats are too unyielding in their
pretentions based on inheritance and a dead past ("We are true
knights of the Middle Ages," says the elder Simeuse [155]); they
are the victims of "their pride of feeling" (210). Laurence, however, not only appears in the story as the exemplary heroine of
chivalric romance, she "covers" another archeological figure and
its secrets. In tandem with this "secret" of the old aristocracy,
which is meant to be found out just as the police must find the
cachot for the story to go forward, the novel unfolds another
secret. When de Marsay explains what happened, at the end, he
clears a path, in our later retelling, to a tenebrosity of the highest
stature, which the novel encodes. It is Napoleon's secret that the
novel tells and repeats, a secret preserved in the family of France
in the generations preceding the July Monarchy.

The cachot provides a seductive model for writing or en-
crypting the story, which remains in a state of tension with the
reading or decrypting exemplified in the judicial trial.[10] Like the
model of composition in "Le chef-d'oeuvre inconnu," the trial
would create "truth" by addition, fabricating it out of the fragments of evidence—the "remains" or "fossils." Tiny details in
the writing lend convincing complication to the story; variants
reveal, moreover, that to revise is to complicate (see 8:1569). The
notion of a proof is the very meat of a trial, and of an interpretation; a proof bolsters. One reasons on the basis of testimony and
evidence; "reasoning" leads to the truth (184). Reasoning, however, may fail; proofs may be absent or incomplete; they may lie;
they may even be manufactured to suit a political interest: the
five disguised men contrived by the police are taken as "proof,"
a duplication that prevents the introduction of accurate evidence.
For although in principle a judicial trial tests guilt by uncovering
the truth, in Balzac's emplotment formulating the events for the
retelling during the trial primarily puts into question credibility.
As elsewhere, Balzac here deploys his intrigue to speculate on
the paradoxical relation between "the true" and "the plausible,"
and, once again, the truth is not plausible.

The defense attorney Bordin gives a fascinating performance
as a reader. After listening to the defendants recounting the
events we know from Balzac's narration, the attorney interprets
them according to the plausible. Bordin demonstrates how "justice," which will not be just (181–82), will badly explain actions.
The "truth of nature"—the fact that the aristocrats had spent
the day in the forest recovering their secret treasure—would be

"implausible," and on no account should the jury be told such a truth, Bordin holds. Either it would be laughed out of court, or it would condemn them more surely. The truth would convince the jury (and the public) that the cousins are lying, since they would be seen as having resorted to inventing such an implausible story to support their claim. Or it would make them appear guilty of a theft, because no one would believe the preposterous reality: that Michu, whom everyone takes for a revolutionary, had protected the Simeuse treasure during the years of their emigration. Three times Balzac tells us that people habitually judge events "under a presumption that has reached the level of certainty" (160, 164, 177). Public accuser, jury, judges, audience, and all France would "know" with the certitude of presumption that the Simeuse brothers had kidnapped Malin to steal his money. Balzac chooses a most paradoxical way of saying the truth may cause the greatest harm: "Taking the accusation as it now stands, the matter is not clear; but, in its pure truth, it would become *limpid;* the jurors would explain by the robbery all the tenebrous parts" (182; emphasis added). Among the acts and words that the jury would unfailingly interpret to condemn the accused, Bordin lists "the words said to Beauvisage," a farmer (153–54), and "the words spoken in the courtyard," overheard by a man from the village (150). Bordin's reading thus forces us to remember these details where they occurred in the story, or, failing that, to seek out the sentences in which the events were narrated; the call to memory resembles the tenebrous effect that putting the cause last has on the reading. No surprise, then, that the text explicitly compares the trial to all the dynamics at play in *reading a novel:* "Innocence must make a clear and plausible account of its actions. The duty of the defense is therefore to oppose a probable novel to the improbable novel of the prosecution, [which] becomes a fable" (195). The facts be damned. Plausible lies told by the defendants during the trial, the "probable novel," nearly bring their acquittal (an example concerns their use of the plaster [196–98]). As the narrator observes, "If, in law, truth often resembles a fable, the fable also very much resembles truth" (196)—in a nutshell, the credo of the realistic author.[11]

In all, the trial suggests that explication saves, while inexplicability, or the failure to explicate, is fatal, for the noblemen's inability to explain how they spent the day of the crime causes their condemnation. Not all complication admits explication. Implausibility requires them to keep it a secret that they were digging up their own money—eleven hundred thousand francs buried seven feet deep at the foot of eleven old oak trees scattered in an obscure part of the forest, their locations indicated by a ciphered map (97). Innocence means clarity (179), and "With time, the innocent can clarify matters" (183), but the "inexplicable circumstances," the "mysterious parts" (204) make victims, for this "case" remains "indecipherable," "inexplicable," for the accused and accusers, for justice and the public (183, 185, 204). The crime seems obscure, the outcome of the trial muddy at best, and above all, the true story cannot be unfolded for justice; it is tenebrous. Yet, if the "real" true story is saved at all, it is because Balzac recasts it into his fiction.

The historical "truth" that Balzac writes, obeying the "duty of a historian" (92), is embedded in the complex verisimilitude of the plot: it is Fouché himself, he claims, who ordered the kidnapping and framed the noblemen by disguising five men as the accused. As history, this is not credible—it is a fable; yet it stands in the structural position of history, and that is how we are intended to read it. Verisimilitude mediates between history and the reader, to whom is granted that safe political distance that the story's tenebrosity vouchsafes. The text would force the reader to follow in the great explicator's wake and to use plausibility to explicate tenebrosity, to pursue our trial reading into deeper crypts.

A broader perspective connects the narrow story of the kidnapping to the general history of France during the Consulate and the start of the Empire. The political history underlying the story implies that the author may not monkey with the relation between causes and effects, but Balzac plays fast and loose.[12] Hysteron proteron in the narrative logic shows that it is fallacious to assume as a premise that a cause can be uncovered for the puzzling events the characters undergo (and for the incoherences of the narrative). It is not simply that the cause remains untold until the end, it also remains to be proved what did indeed cause the events. And Balzac did much to obscure the relation to history when he suppressed his preface with its parallel account of the historical events: pulling a "coup," he effaced the pathways. He thus acted on his premise that Malin represents a "type" and his claim that he had transposed a most implausible event into "a true setting," the transposition being the only true story.[13]

In effect, the stance of the novel in the face of the historical event is tenebrous. As a "reader" of the tenebrous affair of the trial, Napoleon holds the key to its explication. With a single stunning sentence, the third in the novel, Balzac had inaugurated a governing metaphor which connects sunshine dissipating darkness to Napoleon's prestige in bringing prosperity to France: "Then the people were beginning to establish between the sky and Bonaparte, then declared consul for life, an entente to which this man owed one of his prestigious powers; and, strange to say, the day when, in 1812, the sun failed him, his prosperity ceased" (23).[14] The suggestion that a mystique hovers about this "entente," placing Napoleon above mere mortals, contributes to the mystical comprehension of history ("strange to say") that Balzac proposes in this novel. Folding the time of the writing, the July Monarchy, onto the epoch of the events, the era of Napoleon, in a narrative that oscillates between entenebration and explication, Balzac teaches that the connections between facts or events—the causes—and their "atmospheric" effects are obscure, concealed, mysterious. He gives us to understand that the tenebrosity Napoleon most feared is represented by Fouché, described twice as possessing a "tenebrous genius" and as a "singular genius who struck Napoleon with a sort of terror" (79, 80, 234). "To be sure," writes Balzac, "Napoleon's excessive pride is one of the thousand reasons for his fall, which moreover has cruelly expiated his wrongs. In this mistrustful sovereign could be found a jealousy of his young power which influenced his actions as much as his secret hatred of skillful men, the precious legacy of the Revolution" (80). The minister of police acting behind the scenes insures that what is (merely) obscure, impenetrable, or secret becomes perfidious; that the hidden is also the evil. Fouché is the only character in the action who stands to explicate the story better than the narrator can: "Fouché thus reserved for himself a large part of the secret knowledge he discovered, and carved out for himself a power over people that was greater than Bonaparte's" (81); he plans "absolutely like" Napoleon at Austerlitz; he is the Napoleon of police. In the chapter of "darkness dissipated," de Marsay observes about Fouché, Masséna, and Talleyrand, with some exaggeration: "if Napoleon had freely associated them with his mission, there would no longer be a Europe, but a vast French empire" (234).

Hence, on a deeper level, the ultimate tenebrous affair explicated only for a genial reader is that Napoleon's fear of Fouché represents the central Balzacian theme of the harm caused by mediocrities and the failure of government to make a place for capable men. In an uncanny repetition, this huge defect of France since the July Monarchy, in Balzac's analysis, stems from Napoleon's tenebrosity and undermines the potential of France for greatness since his fall. Napoleon's "secret" defect has played out over time and several governments, as if a germ has spread from one to many, from the unique to the general.

What the great explicator unfolds therefore has stature, not only as a reading out of history but also in bolstering the fundamental stance of La comédie humaine as both social document and narrative model. The flaw that Napoleon expiated in exile, a secret fear of superiorities, is the very defect that permanently undermined the July Monarchy and that had such a large role in the existence of La comédie humaine.[15] This archeological "family secret" of a nation motivates Balzac's political writing (however the novels are classified); it is the well-known secret of the Balzacian novel, a motive force that makes stories happen.[16]

Politics imposes a way to run the country; it represents order, meaning, and direction, in both senses (to direct the country, to go in a certain direction); power invested in authority; a use of history dependent on knowledge thereof; the march of time to the future; progress. As Ned Lukacher writes, Bonapartism reintroduced hierarchy reversing anarchic republicanism (266), and therein lay its value and its harm. According to Une ténébreuse affaire, Balzac's assessment of Napoleon remains dark, hidden, or contradictory, the verity of his pro-Napoleonic sentiment apparently conflicting with the verisimilitude of his monarchical intention. If the four ancien régime aristocrats (but not Michu) are saved from condemnation, it is only because Napoleon grants them amnesty. Heaping paradox upon paradox, Balzac gives us to understand that the figure of a lost aristocracy whose nobility is yet unperishable (also illustrated by the Chouans who are serving both sides in the affair) stands in apparent conflict but secret affinity with Napoleon the Emperor. When the plausible fables recounted by the accused noblemen fail to prevent their conviction, only the majesty of Napoleon's nobility and grace saves them. The grandeur of the accord Laurence wins, in the memorable scene at Napoleon's bivouac at Iéna, plays out and projects onto the metonymic narrative line a metaphoric replication of the old and the new aristocracies.[17] "Do you understand what the French empire must be? . . . ," the emperor asks. "Ah! at this moment I understand only the Emperor, she said, vanquished by the humanity with which the man of destiny had spoken those words which allowed her to anticipate a pardon" (222). The novel displays at once the arrogance of telling the *real* story and the assurance that it is impossible to do so except by narrating the plausible. As Michel Butor has put it, "to make us understand reality, Balzac tells stories that have not taken place" (89). Following the plausible, the "it-must-have-been-this-way," Balzac's narrative eschews hierarchy, ascribing no certain historical cause; it buries sense and direction, disseminates the power of authority; it looks backward to an archeological present-in-the-past.

What makes this novel especially compelling is that the tensions between hiding and revealing exemplify those of realistic writing in general. In other words, not only does the novel include in its story the structure of its own semiotic processes, the strategies by which it makes meaning and guides the reader, it can also stand as a general reader's guide to Balzac. The processes of the events that entenebrated history, on the referential level, and the narrative events that entenebrate the story, which constitute the mimetic level, are analogous. This is not surprising; it is the common business of mimesis to pretend to imitate, in a narrative, what "happened" in the world, even if it does so by convention. That is, although we know that mimesis is a *composition*, not a *reflection*, of "reality," we agree that in mimesis narrative imitates reality. It is less of a common business that a further analogy governs the hiding that happens in the story and the structure of Balzac's writing, which creates and hides secret motivation. The events of the writing, on the semiotic level, replicate those of the story, the mimetic level. Everywhere there are "mechanisms of concealment and dissembling that thwart readability" (Rashkin 33)—which are in fact the essential strategy for awakening and sustaining interest. Although Balzac most characteristically fulfills his mission to describe when he obeys what Genette has called his "démon explicatif" (1969, 79), paintings that obscure the message abound in *La comédie humaine*. To paint is to cover over as well as to depict; in "Le chef-d'oeuvre inconnu," the creation of the masterpiece obscures what it intends to show; it reveals instead an unintended message (there are messages loaded with death, like "Le message," as Ross Chambers has shown in a brilliant reading). A writer cannot show too little, or understanding fails; or too much, for then interest flags; as Lucien Dällenbach writes, the text that fills all the holes loses interest (1979, 430). The ideal would lie somewhere between tenebrous affairs and necessary explications—

the equilibrium also struck in this novel between noble sentiment and base dealings. One may thus take *Une ténébreuse affaire* as a model for many other novels and especially for a certain kind of reading that Balzac's novels require of us. Reading is an affair of genius, and it is significant that "the genius of evil," the police who incarnate evil, read according to the political process of the trial. Describing the devious policemen Corentin and Peyrade as "impénétrables," Balzac compares them to reasoning canines: "But for anyone who had followed the effects of the moral flair of those two hounds on the trail of *unknown and hidden facts*, for anyone who had understood the movements of canine agility that led them to discover the *true* by means of a rapid examination of the *probabilities*, there was something to tremble about. How and why were these men of genius so low when they could be so high?"[18] When Corentin and Peyrade find the *cachot*, the heart of darkness, they guide the reader to the Kurtz-like evil of Fouché. It is the reading of the probabilities, the plausible in the domain of fiction, and not the real facts, that uncovers the secret horror in this history. Reading is "a political trial," fraught with murkiness, fringing the horrible. Balzac's preposterous claim that the truth would not "save" the story, that he tells the "plausible" because the truth would not be convincing, deviously lends an excessive degree of truth to the truth when mediated by his narration, and only then. Explication, finally, constitutes Balzac's greatest presumption to an aristocracy of writing.

University of Illinois at Urbana-Champaign

NOTES

1. According to Genette's *Seuils*, an impure fiction has strong referentiality to history, or philosophical reflection (1987, 305).

2. Lukacher's discussion in *Primal Scenes* (262) prompts my consideration of hysteron proteron.

3. The *Petit Robert* cites Balzac's title for the sense "obscure for the mind."

4. Robert 258. An additional layer of "correction" is added by the editors of the novel in the Pléiade edition (volume 8), Suzanne-J. Bérard and Pierre-Georges Castex, who cite archives that disagree with contemporary written accounts.

5. The expression "new government" comes from *Une vieille fille* (Balzac 1976–81, 8:1501). Page numbers preceded by the volume number refer to the Pléiade edition of *Une ténébreuse affaire* in volume 8; otherwise, page numbers in parentheses refer to the Folio edition.

6. While the first version immediately identifies Talleyrand, the second

resorts to various enigmatic but colorful periphrases, such as "The one who walked with difficulty."

7. 1973, 47. Another example of this delay in the ability to understand: "The presence [of the duc d'Enghien] on the territory of Baden . . . *later* gave weight to these suppositions" (64; emphasis added).

8. A typical introduction of a necessary explication reads: "Perhaps it will not be useless to recount the circumstances . . ." (43).

9. 1973, 81. The novel also develops the "buried treasure" theme (à la Poe). A text indexes the location of the aristocrats' fortune which Michu buried in the forest (97). As in "The Gold Bug," one has to know how to interpret a coded map in order to arrive at wealth, happiness, and possibly marriage.

10. Christopher Prendergast's useful term "extended structural metonymy" applies well to the function of this part of the story in the narrative discourse (90).

11. Balzac's preface recounted in passionate detail the visit of the judge who presided at the first trial of Clément de Ris's kidnappers, one Viriot, who claims to have learned "the secret of the mystery," Balzac triumphantly reports, from the prepublication of his novel in *Le Commerce* (8:499). The novel as creator of truth . . . or was Balzac still writing fiction?

12. "Style so marks the transformation that the writer's thought imposes on ˙reality that, in Balzac, there is not strictly speaking a style" (1971, 269). Was Proust so coopted by the reality claims of the Balzacian text that he failed to see in what multiple ways Balzac does impose style on reality?

13. 8:492–93. Balzac writes in his abolished preface about "the type": "a character who condenses in himself the traits characteristic of all those who more or less resemble him" (250).

14. Max Andréoli, in a detailed commentary on these opening lines, points out the miracle accompanying this alliance; he also underscores the contrast of the sun with the significance of obscurity throughout the novel. Interestingly, justices of the peace were required as of 1796 to display a symbol of their policing authority consisting of an eye surrounded by rays, poetically suggesting the clarity that comes with seeing well in sunshine, as if in an equation: eye plus sun equals power (8:1505–06). And might one suggest that the resetting of the events in the department of *Aube* is poetically justified?

15. Many have noted the insistence of this theme, but no one has put it better, I think, than Nicole Mozet: "As for Louis-Philippe, on the other hand, one might well ask if he did not involuntarily make a very fine gift to the writer, for, by blocking his future, he forced him to imagine and to create in the present. Closed off by a revolution more trenchant than a guillotine blade, the indecisive and fluid period of the Restoration suddenly furnished a past both very recent and still quite alive, which Balzac will very quickly transform into a kingdom of causes. In other words, thanks to the Revolution of 1830, he found himself definitively liberated from the dead weight of the historical novel under which the prose fiction of the last years of the Restoration was becoming mired, after having found renewal in it."

"1830 was for Balzac a sort of death of the father—both a mourning and a liberation" (239, 241).

16. Scarcely has one opened the book when a Balzac family secret parades before our eyes: Jean de Margonne, to whom the novel is dedicated, was Mme Balzac's lover and the father of younger brother Henri. More overt than covert, like a perverse secret that reveals by hiding, and like many supposedly secret

details of the Clément de Ris affair, Mme Balzac's adultery can qualify as tenebrous in its effects on our author. Proust alludes to causes of which Balzac the explainer has never spoken: "In his writing, under the visible action of the drama, there circulate mysterious laws of the flesh and feeling" (1971, 277–78). If it is virtually certain that Proust had homosexuality in mind, it is also possible to think about the relation of revealing and concealing in writing a narrative. Perhaps the quality of Mme Balzac's secret was particularly on Balzac's mind, as he wrote Une ténébreuse affaire, because in October 1840 he was moving from les Jardies to Paris, and his mother was to move in with him in November. Was the absent father, dead since 1829 but the source of the writer's exceptional "knowledge" about the historical tenebrous affair, to be enveloped in darkness?

17. Balzac added the bivouac scene on proofs.

18. 108–09; emphasis added. I am reminded of the last words Balzac added in the Furne edition to "Les secrets de la princesse de Cadignan": "Is this an ending? Yes, for the intelligent; no, for those who want to know everything" (6:1005).

Works Cited

Adamson, Donald. "The Priest in Balzac's Fiction: Secular and Sacred Aspects of the Church." In *Ideology and Religion in French Literature. Essays in Honour of Brian Juden*. Edited by Harry Cockerham and Esther Ehrman. Camberley, Surrey: Porphyrogenitus, 1989.

Adler, Laure. *A l'aube du féminisme: les premières journalistes 1830–1850*. Paris: Payot, 1979.

Aikin, Susan Hardy. "Dinesen's 'Sorrow-acre': Tracing the Woman's Line." *Contemporary Literature* 25 (Summer 1984): 156–86.

Ancelot, François. *Louis IX, tragédie en cinq actes*. Paris: J.-N. Barba, 1819.

Andréoli, Max. "Sur le début d'un roman de Balzac, *Une ténébreuse affaire*." *L'Année Balzacienne* (1975): 89–123.

Antosh, Ruth B. "The Role of Painting in Three Novels by J.-K. Huysmans." *Nineteenth-Century French Studies* 12 (1984): 131–46.

Aynesworth, Donald. "Anonymity, Identity, and Narrative: Sovereignty in *Quatrevingt-treize*." *Kentucky Romance Quarterly* 29 (1982), no. 2: 201–13.

Baldick, Robert. *The Life of J.-K. Huysmans*. Oxford: Clarendon, 1955.

Ballanche, Pierre-Simon. "Essai sur la propriété littéraire." Edited by William Paulson. *Romantisme* 47 (1985): 10–16.

———. *L'homme sans nom*. Edited by Agnès Kettler. Paris: Editions France-Empire, 1989.

———. *Oeuvres*. Paris: Bureau de l'Encyclopédie des Connaissances Utiles, 1833.

———. *Le vieillard et le jeune homme*. Edited by Arlette Michel. Paris: Garnier, 1981.

Balzac, Honoré de. *La comédie humaine*. 12 vols. Paris: Gallimard/Bibliothèque de la Pléiade, 1976–81.

———. *La cousine Bette. La comédie humaine*. Vol. 6. Paris: Gallimard/Bibliothèque de la Pléiade, 1950.

———. *Une ténébreuse affaire*. Edited by René Guise. Paris: Gallimard/Folio, 1973.

———. "Traité de la vie élégante." *Oeuvres diverses 1830–1835*. Vol. 2 (1938). Paris: Conard. 152–85.

Bann, Stephen. *The Clothing of Clio. A Study of the Representation of History in Nineteenth-Century Britain and France*. Cambridge, London, and New York: Cambridge University Press, 1984.

Baptiste-Marrey. Lecture. *Une ténébreuse affaire*. By Honoré de Balzac. Arles: Actes Sud, 1991. 295–314.

Barante, M. de. *Histoire de la Convention Nationale*. 6 vols. Bruxelles: Meline, Cans, 1851–1853.

———. *Histoire des ducs de Bourgogne et de la maison de Valois, 1364–1477*. 10 vols. Bruxelles: Grégoire, Wout, 1839.

————. *Souvenirs du baron de Barante.* Edited by Claude de Barante. Vol. 1. Paris: Calmann Lévy, 1890.

Barbéris, Pierre. Préface. *La duchesse de Langeais suivi de La fille au yeux d'or.* Paris: Livre de Poche, 1972.

Barbey d'Aurevilly, Jules. *Du dandysme et de George Brummell.* 1843. Edited by Marie-Christine Natta. Paris: Plein Chant, 1989.

Barrès, Maurice. *Du sang, de la volupté, de la mort.* Paris: Plon, 1903.

Barry, Joseph. *The Infamous Woman: The Life of George Sand.* Garden City, NY: Anchor Press, 1978.

Barthes, Roland. "Le dandysme et la mode." *Le mythe du dandy.* Paris: Colin, 1971.

————. "Langage et vêtement." *Critique* 142 (mars 1959): 242–52.

————. "Rhétorique de l'image." *Communications* 4 (1964): 25–42.

Baudelaire, Charles. *Oeuvres complètes.* 2 vols. Paris: Gallimard/Bibliothèque de la Pléiade, 1975, 1976.

————. *Oeuvres.* Paris: Gallimard/Bibliothèque de la Pléiade, 1958.

————. "Réflexions sur quelques-uns de mes contemporains." *Oeuvres complètes.* Paris: Gallimard/Bibliothèque de la Pléiade, 1961.

Beaumont, Barbara, ed. and tr. *The Road from Decadence: From Brothel to Cloister: Selected Letters of J.-K. Huysmans.* Columbus: Ohio State University Press, 1989.

Beauvoir, Simone de. *Le deuxième sexe.* 2 vols. Paris: Folio, 1949, 1976.

Beecher, Jonathan. *Charles Fourier: The Visionary and his World.* Berkeley: University of California Press, 1986.

Beizer, Janet. *Family Plots. Balzac's Narrative Generations.* New Haven and London: Yale University Press, 1986.

Bem, Jeanne. *Châtiments ou l'histoire de France, comme enchaînement de parricides. Victor Hugo 1.* Paris: Lettres Modernes/Minard, 1984.

Bérard, Suzanne-J., éd. Introduction. *Une ténébreuse affaire.* By Honoré de Balzac. *La comédie humaine.* 8:453–81.

Bernard, Claudie. *Le Chouan romanesque. Balzac, Barbey d'Aurevilly, Hugo.* Paris: Presses Universitaires de France, 1989.

Berthier, Philippe. *Lamiel ou la boîte de Pandore.* Paris: Presses Universitaires de France, 1994.

Besnard, Micheline. "Ecritures d'un lieu commun: Constantinople (Théophile Gautier, Pierre Loti)." *Australian Journal of French Studies* 30 (1993): 40–62.

Blanchot, Maurice. *La part du feu.* 1949. Paris: Gallimard, 1972.

Bossuat, André, ed. *Les chroniqueurs français du moyen age.* Vol.1. Paris: Larousse, 1936.

Bowman, Frank P. "Religion, Politics and Utopia in French Romanticism." *Australian Journal of French Studies* 11 (1974), no. 3: 307–24.

Breton, André. *L'anthologie de l'humour noir.* Paris: Pauvert, 1966.

Brombert, Victor. *Stendhal: Fiction and the Themes of Freedom.* New York: Random House, 1968.

————. *Victor Hugo and the Visionary Novel.* Cambridge: Harvard University Press, 1984.

Bronfen, Elisabeth. "From Omphalos to Phallus: Cultural Representations of Feminity and Death." *Women. A Cultural Review* 3 (1992): 145–58.

Brosman, Catharine Savage. *Art as Testimony: The Work of Jules Roy.* Gainesville: University of Florida Press, 1989.

———. "Living with Vichy in Algeria: The Experience of Jules Roy." *CELFAN Review* 9 (1996).

———. "Telling the Wars: 1815, 1870, 1914." American Association of Teachers of French, 1992. Unpublished paper.

———. "Theories of Collectivities in Sartre and Rousseau." *South Central Review* 2, no. 1 (Spring 1985): 25–41.

Burton, Richard D.E. "'Le sacrifice du bourreau': Capital Punishment and the Nineteenth-Century French Imagination, 1815–1848." Paper presented at the Colloquium in Nineteenth-Century French Studies, Binghamton, 1992.

Butler, Ronnie. "Balzac et Louis XVIII." *L'Année Balzacienne* (1991): 111–34.

———. "Balzac et Talleyrand." *L'Année Balzacienne* (1985): 119–36.

Butor, Michel. "Balzac et la réalité." *Répertoire I.* Paris: Minuit, 1960.

Camus, Albert. *L'homme révolté.* Paris: Gallimard, 1951.

Canovas, Frédéric. "This Is Not a Dream: Drawing the Line between Dream and Text." *The Journal of Narrative Technique* 24 (1994): 114–26.

Carassus, Emilien. *Le mythe du dandy.* Paris: Colin, 1971.

Carlyle, Thomas. "The Dandiacal Body." *Sartor Resartus.* 1883. New York: Funk and Wagnalls, n.d.

Carmignani-Dupont, Françoise. "Fonction romanesque du récit de rêve: l'exemple d'*A rebours.*" *Littérature* 43 (1981): 57–74.

Carpenter, Scott. "Splitting Hairs and Chopping Heads in Balzac's *César Birotteau.*" Paper presented at the Colloquium in Nineteenth-Century French Studies, Binghamton, 1992.

Cate, Curtis. *George Sand.* Boston: Houghton Mifflin, 1975.

Céline, Louis-Ferdinand. *Voyage au bout de la nuit.* Paris, 1932; reprinted. Paris: Gallimard, 1952.

Chaitin, Gilbert D. *The Unhappy Few: A Psychological Study of Stendhal's Novels.* Bloomington: Indiana University Press, 1972.

Chamberlin, Wells F. "Genèse et structure d'*Une ténébreuse affaire.*" Dissertation. University of Chicago, 1956.

Chambers, Ross. "Reading and the Voice of Death: Balzac's 'Le message.'" *Nineteenth-Century French Studies* 18 (1990): 408–23.

Chapon, François. *Le peintre et le livre.* Paris: Flammarion, 1987.

Chateaubriand, François René de. *Essai sur les révolutions, Génie du christianisme.* Paris: Gallimard/Bibliothèque de la Pléiade, 1978.

———. *Oeuvres romanesques et voyages.* Tome 1. Edited by Maurice Regard. Paris: Gallimard/Bibliothèque de la Pléiade, 1969.

Chollet, Roland. "Trophée de têtes chez Balzac." *L'Année Balzacienne* (1990): 257–72.

Cobban, Alfred. *A History of France.* Vol. 2. 1799–1871. Second Edition. London: Penguin, 1965.

Coblence, Françoise. *Le dandysme: obligation d'incertitude.* Paris: Presses Universitaires de France, 1988.

_____. "Disraëli: Du style dandy en politique." *Critique* 405–406 (février-mars 1988): 276–99.

Cogny, Pierre. *J.-K. Huysmans: De l'Ecriture à l'écriture*. Paris: Téqui, 1987.

Collomb, Michel. "Le cauchemar de des Esseintes." *Romantisme* 19 (1978): 79–89.

Crow, Thomas. *Painters and Public Life in Eighteenth-Century Paris*. New Haven: Yale University Press, 1985.

Cummings, Frederick. "Painting under Louis XVI, 1774–1789." *French Painting, 1774–1830: The Age of Revolution*. Detroit: Detroit Institute of Art, 1975.

Dällenbach, Lucien. "Du fragment au cosmos (*La comédie humaine* et l'opération de lecture I)." *Poétique* 40 (1979): 420–31.

_____. "Le tout en morceaux: *La comédie humaine* et l'opération de lecture II." *Poétique* 42 (1980): 156–69.

Davies, Gardner. *Les "Tombeaux" de Mallarmé: Essai d'exégèse raisonnée*. Paris: Corti, 1950.

Davis, Grady Scott. *Warcraft and the Fragility of Virtue: An Essay in Aristotelian Ethics*. Moscow: University of Idaho Press, 1992.

De Palacio, Jean. "Ecriture romanesque et écriture critique: Huysmans et Léon Bloy juges de Gustave Guiches." *Figures et formes de la Décadence*. Paris: Séguier, 1994.

_____. "La postérité d'*A rebours* ou le livre dans le livre." *Figures et formes de la Décadence*, 1994.

Delevoy, Robert L. *Le Symbolisme*. Genève: Skira, 1982.

Delon, Michel. "Nodier et les mythes révolutionnaires." *Europe* 614–15 (juin-juillet 1980): 31–42.

Derrida, Jacques. *Cinders / Feu la cendre*. Translated and edited by Ned Lukacher. Lincoln: University of Nebraska Press, 1991.

Des Pres, Terrence. *Praises and Dispraises: Poetry and Politics, the 20th Century*. New York: Penguin, 1988.

Desanti, Dominique. "Flora . . . messie du temps des prophètes ou messie parce que femme?" *Un fabuleux destin*. Edited by Stéphane Michaud. Dijon: Editions de l'université de Dijon. 1984.

_____. *Flora Tristan la femme révoltée*. Paris: Hachette, 1972.

Didier, Béatrice. "Ophélie dans les chaînes: Etude de quelques thèmes d'*Indiana*." *Hommage à George Sand*. Edited by L. Cellier. Paris: Presses Universitaires de France, 1969.

_____. Préface. *Indiana*. Paris: Folio, 1984.

Diesbach, Ghislain de. *Madame de Staël*. Paris: Perrin, 1984.

The Doctrine of Saint-Simon: An Exposition. Translated by Georg G. Iggers; preface by G.D.H. Cole. Boston: Beacon Press, 1958.

Dommanget, Maurice, et al. *Babeuf et les problèmes du babouvisme*. Paris: Editions Sociales, 1963.

Donaldson-Evans, Mary. "Huysmans's *roman-abattoir: En ménage*." *Stanford French Review* 13 (1989): 193–210.

Du Camp, Maxime. *Mémoires d'un suicidé*. Paris: Librairie Nouvelle, 1855.

Dumas, Alexandre. *Impressions de voyage*. Paris: Michel Lévy Frères, 1862.

Dunn, Susan. "Louis XVI and His Executioners." *L'Esprit Créateur* 27 (1987): 42–55.

Eigeldinger, Marc. "Huysmans découvreur d'Odilon Redon." *Revue des Sciences Humaines* 43 (1978): 207–16.

Eksteins, Modris. *Rites of Spring: The Great War and the Birth of the Modern Age*. Boston: Houghton Mifflin, 1989.

Explication des ouvrages de peinture, sculpture, gravure, lithographie et architecture des artistes vivans, exposés au Musée royal des arts, le 4 novembre 1827. [1827] Reprint, New York: Garland, 1977.

Favardin, Patrick, et Laurent Boüexière. *Le dandysme*. Paris: La Manufacture, 1988.

Flaubert, Gustave. *Oeuvres complètes*. 21 vols. Paris: Conard, 1923–54.

Fleishman, Avrom. *Figures of Autobiography*. Berkeley: University of California Press, 1983.

Fletcher, John. Henry de Montherlant. *French Novelists, 1930–1960*. Edited by Catharine Savage Brosman. *Dictionary of Literary Biography* 72. Detroit: Gale, 1988.

Fortassier, Rose. "Le récit de rêve dans *En rade*." *Huysmans. Une esthétique de la décadence*. Genève: Slatkine, 1987. 303–11.

Fourier, Charles. *Oeuvres complètes*. 12 vols. N.p.: Editions Anthropos, 1966.

Frappier-Mazur, Lucienne. "Les fous de Nodier et la catégorie de l'excentricité." *French Forum* 4 (1979): 32–54.

French Painting, 1774–1830: The Age of Revolution. Exhibition catalogue. Detroit: Detroit Institute of Arts, 1975.

Furet, François. "The Tyranny of Revolutionary Memory." *Fictions of the French Revolution*. Edited by Bernadette Fort. Evanston: Northwestern University Press, 1991.

Gallie, W.B. *Philosophers of Peace and War*. Cambridge: Cambridge University Press, 1978.

Garat, Dominique-Joseph. *Mémoires historiques sur la vie de M. Suard, sur ses écrits, et sur le XVIIIe siècle*. 2 vols. Paris: A. Belin, 1820.

———. *Mémoires sur la Révolution, ou Exposé de ma conduite dans les affaires et dans les fonctions publiques*. Paris: J.-J. Smits, An III.

Gat, Azar. *The Origins of Military Thought from the Enlightenment to Clausewitz*. Oxford: Clarendon, 1989.

Gay, Peter. *Voltaire's Politics*. Princeton: Princeton University Press, 1959.

Genette, Gérard. *Mimologiques: Voyages en Cratylie*. Paris: Seuil, 1976.

———. *Seuils*. Paris: Seuil, 1987.

———. "Vraisemblance et motivation." *Figures II*. Paris: Seuil, 1969.

Gérard, Alice. *La Révolution française, mythes et interprétations (1789–1970)*. Collection Questions d'histoire. Paris: Flammarion, 1970.

Girard, René. *Deceit, Desire and the Novel: Self and Other in Literary Structure*. Translated by Yvonne Freccero. Baltimore: Johns Hopkins University Press, 1965.

———. *La violence et le sacré*. Paris: Grasset, 1972.

Glenn, John D., Jr. "Philosophy and the 'Truth' of War." Mellon seminar, Tulane University (Fall 1990.). Unpublished paper.

Godechot, Jacques, éd. *Les constitutions de la France depuis 1789*. Paris: Garnier-Flammarion, 1979.

Goethe, Johann Wolfgang von. *Gedichte*. Edited by E. Trunz. Munich: Beck, 1978.

Goodman, John. "A History of Artistic Practice and the Monarchy's Crisis of Representation at the End of the Old Regime." Ph.D. diss., New York University, 1990.

Gracq, Julien. *En lisant En écrivant*. Paris: Corti, 1980.

The Graphic Works of Odilon Redon. Intro. Alfred Werner. New York: Dover Publications, Inc, 1969.

Greimas, Algirdas Julien. *Maupassant: La sémiotique du texte, exercices pratiques*. Paris: Editions du Seuil, 1976.

Guibert, Jacques-Antoine-Hippolyte, comte de. *Essai général de tactique*. London: Libraires associés, 1772.

Gutwirth, Madelyn. "The Rights and Wrongs of Woman: The Defeat of Feminist Rhetoric by Revolutionary Allegory." *Representing the French Revolution: Literature, Historiography, and Art*. Edited by James A. W. Heffernan. Hanover: University Press of New England, 1992.

Gutwirth, Madelyn, Avriel Goldberger, and Karyna Szmurlo. *Germaine de Staël: Crossing the Borders*. New Brunswick: Rutgers Uniersity Press, 1991.

Haig, Stirling. "The Circular Room of George Sand's *Indiana*." *The Madame Bovary Blues: The Pursuit of Illusion in Nineteenth-Century French Fiction*. Baton Rouge: Louisiana State University Press, 1987.

———. "The Grand Illusion: Vigny's *Servitude et grandeur militaires*." *The Madame Bovary Blues*. 1987.

Hamon, Philippe. *Introduction à l'analyse du descriptif*. Paris: Hachette, 1981.

Hautecoeur, Louis. *Littérature et peinture en France du dix-septième siècle au vingtième siècle*. Paris: Colin, 1963.

Heathcote, Owen. "The Engendering of Violence and the Violation of Gender in Honoré de Balzac's *La fille aux yeux d'or*. *Romance Studies* 22 (Autumn 1993): 99–112.

———. "The Representation of Violence and the Violence of Representation: Balzac, Mishima, Wittig, Chedid." *New Comparison* 14 (Autumn 1992): 202–09.

Hemmings, F. W. J. "A propos de la nouvelle édition de *Lamiel*. Les deux *Lamiel*. Nouveaux aperçus sur les procédés de composition de Stendhal romancier." *Stendhal Club* 15 (1973): 287–315.

Heraclitus. *Fragments*. Text and translation, with commentary by M.T. Robinson. Toronto: University of Toronto Press, 1987.

Hertz, Neil. "Medusa's Head: Male Hysteria under Political Pressure (and Responses from Catherine Gallagher and Joel Fineman)." *The End of the Line: Essays on Psychoanalysis and the Sublime*. New York: Columbia University Press, 1985.

Hobbes, Thomas. *Leviathan*. Edited by C. B. Macpherson. Baltimore: Penguin Books, 1968.

Hoog, Marie-Jacques. "George Sand Reader of Stendhal ou *Le défi sandien*." *George Sand: Collected Essays*. Edited by Janis Glasgow. Troy, NY: Whitson, 1985.

Hugo, Victor. *Oeuvres complètes*. Poésie 4. Paris: Laffont, 1986.

———. *Quatrevingt-treize*. Ed. Jean Boudout. Paris: Garnier, 1963.

Hunt, Lynn. *The Family Romance of the French Revolution*. Berkeley: University of California Press, London: Routledge, 1992.

Huysmans, Joris-Karl. *La cathédrale*. Paris: Plon, 1930.

———. *Là-bas*. Paris: Plon, Livre de poche, 1908.

———. "Le nouvel album d'Odilon Redon." *La Revue Indépendante* (février 1885): 291–96.

———. *Oeuvres complètes*. 18 vols. Paris: Crès, 1928–34.

Jal, Auguste. *Esquisses, croquis, pochades, ou Tout ce qu'on voudra, sur le Salon de 1827*. Paris: A. Dupont, 1828.

Johnson, James Turner. *Ideology, Reason, and the Limitation of War: Religious and Secular Concepts, 1200–1740*. Princeton: Princeton University Press, 1975.

Kahn, Annette. *J.-K. Huysmans: Novelist, Poet and Art Critic*. Ann Arbor: UMI Research Press, Studies in the Fine Arts: Criticism, 1982, 1987.

———. *J.-K. Huysmans: Novelist, Poet, and Art Critic*. Ann Arbor: UMI, 1981.

Kant, Immanuel. *Critique of Judgment*. Translated by J. H. Bernard. New York: Hafner, 1951.

———. *Kant's Political Writings*. Edited by H. Reiss. Cambridge: Cambridge University Press, 1970.

Keats, John. "Ode to a Nightingale." *The Poems of John Keats*. Edited by de Sélincourt. London: Methuen, 1907.

Kempf, Roger. *Dandies: Baudelaire et Cie*. Paris: Seuil, 1977.

Kingcaid, Renée A. "Amazing Grace: A Rebours Twenty Years After." *L'Esprit Créateur* 23 (1987), no. 3: 68–78.

———. "With a Knickknack on his Back: Huysmans's 'Sac au dos' ['Backpack'] and the Comfy Object." *Studies in Psychoanalytic Theory* 2, no. 2 (1993): 93–106.

Krafft, Maurice. *Volcanoes: Fire from the Earth*. Translated by Paul G. Bahn. New York: Harry N. Abrams, Inc., 1993.

Labouret, Mireille. "Le sublime de la terreur dans *Les Chouans* et *Une ténébreuse affaire*." *L'Année Balzacienne* (1990): 317–27.

Lambert, Pierre. "Le carnet secret de J.-K. Huysmans." *Le Figaro Littéraire* 950 (2 juillet 1964): 1.

Landes, Joan B. *Women and the Public Sphere in the Age of the French Revolution*. Ithaca: Cornell University Press, 1988.

Laurent, Jacques, éd. *Lamiel, suivi de La fin de Lamiel*. Paris: 10/18—Union Générale d'Editions, 1966.

Lebrun, Richard A. *Joseph de Maistre: An Intellectual Militant*. Kingston and Montreal: McGill-Queen's University Press, 1988.

Lemaire, Michel. *Le dandysme de Baudelaire à Mallarmé*. Montréal: Presses Universitaires de Montréal, 1978.

Lemaître, Jules. *Les contemporains*. Paris: Lecène et Oudin, 1889.

Léonardi, Ch. "Le Conseil d'état sous la restauration." Doctoral diss., Université de Paris, 1909.

Leroy, Claude. "L'écrivain en habit dandy." Revue des Sciences Humaines 38, no. 150 (avril-juin 1973): 261–76.

Leys, Simon. La forêt en feu: Essais sur la culture et la politique chinoises. Paris: Hermann, 1983.

Lhoste, Pierre. "Jules Roy: Mes mots de passe." Nouvelles Littéraires 2201 (17 November 1969): 1, 7.

Ligne, Prince de. Oeuvres choisies du Prince de Ligne. Edited by Basil Guy. Saratoga, CA: Anma Libri, 1978.

Lowrie, Joyce O. The Violent Mystique: Thematics of Retribution and Expiation in Balzac, Barbey d'Aurevilly, Bloy, and Huysmans. Geneva: Droz, 1974.

Lukacher, Ned. Primal Scenes: Literature, Philosophy, Psychoanalysis. Ithaca: Cornell University Press, 1986.

Macauley, J., and L. Berkowitz. "The Desire for Justice and the Reactions to Victims." Altruism and Helping Behavior. New York: Academic Press, 1974.

Macherey, Pierre. Pour une théorie de la production littéraire. Paris: François Maspero, 1966.

Maigron, Louis. Le romantisme et les moeurs. Paris: Champion, 1919.

Maistre, Joseph de. Oeuvres complètes. Vol. 5. Lyon: Librairie Générale Catholique et Classique, 1892.

Mallarmé, Stéphane. Oeuvres complètes. Edited by Henri Mondor et G. Jean-Aubry. Paris: Gallimard/Bibliothèque de la Pléiade, 1945.

Malraux, André. Romans. Paris: Gallimard/Bibliothèque de la Pléiade, 1947.

Marand-Fouquet, Catherine. La femme au temps de la Révolution. Paris: Stock, 1989.

Marcoin, Francis. "Mutisme de Maupassant." Maupassant miroir de la nouvelle. Edited by Jacques Lecarme and Bruno Vercier. Saint-Denis: Presses Universitaires de Vincennes.

Marrinan, Michael. Painting Politics for Louis-Philippe: Art and Ideology in Orléanist France, 1830–1848. New Haven: Yale University Press, 1988.

Martineau, Henri, éd. Lamiel. By Stendhal. Paris: Gallimard/Bibliothèque de la Pléiade, 1933.

Massardier-Kennedy, Françoise. "Indiana: Lieux et personnages féminins." Nineteenth-Century French Studies 19 (1990): 65–72.

Maupassant, Guy de. Contes et nouvelles. Vol. 1. Edited by Louis Forestier. Paris: Gallimard/Bibliothèque de la Pléiade, 1974.

Maurice, Jacques. "La transposition topographique dans Une ténébreuse affaire." L'Année Balzacienne (1965): 233–38.

Meininger, Anne-Marie, éd. Préface. Lamiel. By Stendhal. Paris: Gallimard/Folio, 1983.

Mellerio, André. "Odilon Redon (1840–1920)." La Gazette des Beaux Arts (août-septembre 1920): 137–56.

Mellon, Stanley. The Political Uses of History. A Study of Historians in the French Restoration. Stanford: Stanford University Press, 1958.

Merlant, Joachim. De Montaigne à Vauvenargues. Genève: Slatkine, 1969.

Metz, Christian. "Au-delà de l'analogie, l'image." Communications 15 (1970): 1–11.

Meyer, Henry. *Voltaire on War and Peace. Studies on Voltaire and the Eighteenth Century,* 144. Banbury, Oxfordshire: Voltaire Foundation, 1976.

Michel, Arlette. "Une femme devant l'histoire: Laurence de Cinq-Cygne ou la fidélité." *L'Année Balzacienne* (1977): 51–70.

Michelet, Jules. *Histoire de la Révolution française.* Edited by Gérard Walter. 2 vols. Paris: Gallimard/Bibliothèque de la Pléiade, 1952.

Milner, Max. "L'écrivain et le désir de voir." *Littérature* 90 (mai 1993): 8–20.

Monluc, Blaise de. *Commentaires.* Edited by Paul Courteault. Paris: Gallimard/ Bibliothèque de la Pléiade, 1964.

———. *The Hapsburg-Valois Wars and the French Wars of Religion.* Edited by Ian Roy. Hamden, CT: Archon Books, 1972.

Montesquieu, Charles-Louis Secondat de. *Oeuvres complètes.* 2 vols. Paris: Gallimard/Bibliothèque de la Pléiade, 1949, 1951.

Montherlant, Henry de. *Le songe.* Paris: Grasset, 1922.

Moses, Claire Goldberg. *French Feminism in the Nineteenth Century.* Albany: State University of New York Press, 1984.

Moses, Claire Goldberg, and Leslie Wahl Rabine. *Feminism, Socialism and French Romanticism.* Bloomington: Indiana University Press, 1993.

Mozet, Nicole. "Temps historique et écriture romanesque: '1830 a consommé l'oeuvre de 1793'." *L'Année Balzacienne* (1990): 233–41.

———. *La ville de province dans l'oeuvre de Balzac.* Paris: SEDES/CDU, 1982.

Mugnier, l'abbé. *Journal (1879–1939).* Edited by M. Billot. Paris: Mercure de France, 1985.

Musset, Alfred de. *La confession d'un enfant du siècle. Oeuvres complètes en prose.* Paris: Gallimard/Bibliothèque de la Pléiade, 1960.

Nerval, Gérard de. *Oeuvres complètes.* Edited by Jean Guillaume and Claude Pichois. Vol. 2. Paris: Gallimard/Bibliothèque de la Pléiade, 1984.

Nesci, Catherine. *La femme mode d'emploi. Balzac, de la Physiologie du mariage à La comédie humaine.* Lexington, KY: French Forum, 1992.

Nietzsche, Friedrich. *Thus Spoke Zarathustra. The Portable Nietzsche.* Translated by Walter Kaufmann. New York: Viking, 1954.

Nodier, Charles. *Contes.* Edited by Pierre-Georges Castex. Paris: Garnier, 1961.

———. *Souvenirs de la Révolution et de l'Empire.* Nouvelle édition. Vol. 1. Paris: Charpentier, 1872.

O'Connor, John R. *Balzac's Soluble Fish.* Madrid: José Porrúa Turanzas, 1977.

Ochberg, Frank M., and David A. Soskis. "Concepts of Terrorist Victimization." *Victims of Terrorism.* Boulder, CO: Westview Press, 1962.

Olivier-Martin, Bernard. "Le Conseil d'état de la restauration." Doctoral diss., Université de Paris, 1941.

Ormesson, Jean. "Arrivisme, snobisme, dandysme." *Revue de Métaphysique et de Morale* 4 (oct-déc 1963): 443–59.

Orr, Linda. *Headless History. Nineteenth-Century French Historiography of the Revolution.* Ithaca and London: Cornell University Press, 1990.

Outram, Dorinda. "Le langage mâle de la vertu: Women and the Discourse of the French Revolution." *The Social History of Language.* Edited by Peter Burke. Cambridge: Cambridge University Press, 1987.

Pasco, Allan. *Balzacian Montage: Configuring* La comédie humaine. Toronto: University of Toronto Press, 1991.

Paulhan, Jean. *Les fleurs de Tarbes ou la terreur dans les lettres.* Edited by Jean-Claude Zylberstein. Paris: Gallimard/Folio, 1990.

Paulson, William. "Fragment et autobiographie dans l'oeuvre de Ballanche: Etude et textes inédits." *Nineteenth-Century French Studies* 15 (1987): 14–32.

Pécile, Marie-Jeanne. "George Sand's Literary Encounters." *The George Sand Papers: Conference Proceedings, 1976.* New York: AMS, 1976.

Perkins, Merle L. *Voltaire's Concept of International Order. Studies on Voltaire and the Eighteenth Century,* no. 36. Geneva: Institut et Musée Voltaire, 1965.

Petrey, Sandy. "George and Georgina Sand: Realist Gender in *Indiana.*" *Textuality and Sexuality: Reading Theories and Practices.* Edited by Judith Still and Michael Worton. Manchester: Manchester University Press, 1993.

Pizzorusso, Arnaldo. "Le due stesure di *Lamiel.*" *Saggi e ricerche di letteratura francese* nouvelle série 20 (1981): 127–56.

Planté, Christine. "Les féministes saint-simoniennes: Possibilités et limites d'un mouvement féministe en France au lendemain de 1830." *Regards sur les Saint-Simoniens.* Edited by J. R. Derré. Lyon: Presses Universitaires de Lyon, 1986.

Plutarch. "Alcibiades." *Lives of the Noble Grecians.* Edited by Edmund Fuller. New York: Dell, 1959.

Popper, K. R. "Utopia and Violence." *Hibbert Journal* 46.2 (January 1948): 97–116.

Powell, David. *George Sand.* Boston: Twayne, 1990.

Praz, Mario. *The Romantic Agony.* London: Collins, 1960.

Prendergast, Christopher. *The Order of Mimesis: Balzac, Stendhal, Nerval, Flaubert.* Cambridge: Cambridge University Press, 1986.

Proust, Marcel. *A la recherche du temps perdu.* Edited by Jean-Yves Tadié. 4 vols. Paris: Gallimard/Bibliothèque de la Pléiade, 1987–1989.

———. *Contre Sainte-Beuve.* Edited by Pierre Clarac and Yves Sandré. Paris: Gallimard/Bibliothèque de la Pléiade, 1971.

Queffélec, Lise. "La figure du bourreau dans l'oeuvre de Balzac." *L'Année Balzacienne* (1990): 273–89.

Rashkin, Esther. *Family Secrets and the Psychoanalysis of Narrative.* Princeton: Princeton University Press, 1992.

Réboul, Pierre. "*Peuple Enfant, Peuple Roi* ou Nodier, mélodrame et révolution." *Revue des Sciences Humaines* 162 (1976): 247–56.

Redon, Odilon. *A Edgar Poe.* Paris: G. Fischbacher, 1882.

———. *A Gustave Flaubert: La tentation de Saint Antoine* (deuxième série). Bruxelles: Edmond Deman, 1889.

———. *A soi-même.* Paris: H. Floury, 1922.

———. *Un coup de dés.* [1898]. Unpublished.

———. *Les fleurs du mal.* Bruxelles: Edmond Deman, 1890.

———. *Hommage à Goya.* Paris: L. Dumont, 1885.

———. *La tentation de saint Antoine* (première série). Bruxelles: Edmond Deman, 1888.

————. *La tentation de Saint Antoine* (troisième série). Paris: at author's expense, 1896; Paris: Ambroise Vollard, 1909.

Renan, Ary. "Gustave Moreau." *La Gazette des Beaux Arts* (juillet 1886), 377–94.

Réveil, Etienne Achile. *Musée de peinture et de sculpture, ou Recueil des principaux tableaux, statues et bas-reliefs des collections publiques et particulières de l'Europe. Dessiné et gravé à l'eau forte par Réveil, avec des notices descriptives, critiques et historiques par Duschesne aîné.* Vol. 4. Paris: Audot, 1829.

Rhodes, S. A. "Baudelaire's Philosophy of Dandyism." *Sewanee Review* 36 (1928): 387–404.

Ribner, Jonathan P. *Broken Tablets: The Cult of the Law in French Art from David to Delacroix.* Berkeley: University of California Press, 1993.

Richer, Jean. *Nerval, expérience et création.* Paris: Hachette, 1963.

Robert, Marthe. *Roman des origines et origines du roman.* Paris: Gallimard/Tel, 1972.

Roger, Jacques. *Les sciences de la vie dans la pensée française du XVIIIe siècle: La génération des animaux de Descartes à l'Encyclopédie.* 1963; réédition Paris: Albin Michel, 1993.

Rogers, Nancy E. "George Sand and Honoré de Balzac: Stylistic Similarities." *The George Sand Papers: Conference Proceedings, 1978.* New York: AMS, 1978.

————. "Slavery as Metaphor in the Writings of George Sand." *French Review* 53 (1979): 29–35.

Rosenblum, Robert, and H.W. Janson. *Nineteenth-Century Art.* New York: Abrams, 1984.

Rousseau, Jean-Jacques. *Oeuvres complètes.* Vol. 3. Paris: Gallimard/Bibliothèque de la Pléiade, 1964.

Rousset, Jean. *Forme et signification.* Paris: Corti, 1963.

Roy, Jules. *Le métier des armes.* Paris: Gallimard, 1948.

Russo, Elena. "*Le rouge et le noir:* Jeux de l'autorité." *Nineteenth-Century French Studies* 16 (1987–1988): 1–14.

Sainte-Beuve, Charles Augustin. *Chateaubriand et son groupe littéraire.* Vol. 1. Paris: Garnier, 1861.

Sand, George. *Indiana.* Paris: Gallimard/Folio, 1984.

Sartre, Jean-Paul. *Baudelaire.* Paris: Gallimard, 1947.

————. *La nausée.* Paris: Gallimard, 1938.

————. *Situations IX.* Paris: Gallimard, 1972.

Schaeffer, Gérald. *Une double lecture de Gérard de Nerval:* Les illuminés et Les filles du feu. Neuchâtel: Editions de la Baconnière, 1977.

Schor, Naomi. "Unwriting *Lamiel.*" *Breaking the Chain: Women, Theory and French Realist Fiction.* New York: Columbia University Press, 1985.

Schuerewegen, Franc. "*Un épisode sous la Terreur:* une lecture expiatoire." *L'Année Balzacienne* (1985): 247–63.

————. "*Une ténébreuse affaire* ou l'histoire et le jeu." *L'Année Balzacienne* (1990): 375–88.

Schwartz, Lucy M. "Persuasion and Resistance: Human Relations in George

Sand's Novels, *Indiana* and *Lélia.*" *The George Sand Papers: Conference Proceedings, 1978.* New York: AMS, 1978.

Seltzer, Mark. "Serial Killers (1)." *Differences* 5 (1993), no. 1: 92–128.

Setbon, Raymond. "Un détracteur 'progressiste' de la Révolution: Charles Nodier." *Lettres Romanes* 32 (1978): 52–77.

Simons, Madeleine Anjubault. *Sémiotisme de Stendhal.* Genève: Droz, 1980.

Smith, Sidonie. *A Poetics of Women's Autobiography.* Bloomington: Indiana University Press, 1987.

Sontag, Susan. "Notes on 'Camp' (1964)." *Against Interpretation.* New York: Anchor, 1990.

Staël, Germaine de. *An Extraordinary Woman: Selected Writings of Germaine de Staël.* Translated by and with an Introduction by Vivian Folkenflik. New York: Columbia University Press, 1987.

———. *Madame de Staël on Politics, Literature, and National Character.* Translated and edited by and with an Introduction by Morroe Berger. Garden City, NY: Doubleday, 1964.

———. *De l'influence des passions.* Paris: Treutel et Wurtz, 1832.

Stanton, Domna. *The Aristocrat as Art.* New York: Columbia University Press, 1980.

Starobinski, Jean. *Portrait de l'artiste en saltimbanque.* Genève: Skira, 1970.

Stendhal. *Armance.* Paris: Garnier, 1962.

———. *La chartreuse de Parme.* Paris: A. Dupont, 1839.

———. *Lamiel.* Edited by Victor Del Litto. Vol. 44 of *Oeuvres complètes.* Genève: Cercle du Bibliophile, 1971.

———. *Oeuvres intimes.* Edited by Henri Martineau. Paris: Gallimard/Bibliothèque de la Pléiade, 1955.

———. *Le rouge et le noir.* Paris: Garnier-Flammarion, 1964.

Stryienski, Casimir, éd. *Lamiel.* By Stendhal. Paris: Librairie Moderne, 1889.

Le Symbolisme dans les collections du Petit-Palais. Paris: Paris-Musées, 1988.

Taylor, Françoise M. "Mythe des origines et société dans *Une ténébreuse affaire* de Balzac." *Nineteenth-Century French Studies* 14 (1985–86): 1–18.

Thompson, J. M. *Robespierre.* Oxford: Basil Blackwell, 1988.

Thomson, David. *Europe Since Napoleon.* London: Longmans, 1957.

Tristan, Flora. *Pérégrinations d'une paria.* 2 vols. Paris: Arthus Bertrand, 1838.

Tulard, Jean. "Fouché dans *La comédie humaine.*" *L'Année Balzacienne* (1990): 7–12.

Vadé, Yves. "Onirisme et symbolique: d'*En rade* à *La cathédrale.*" *Revue des Sciences Humaines* 43 (1978): 244–53.

Valéry, Paul. "Souvenir de J.-K. Huysmans." *Oeuvres.* Tome 1. Paris: Gallimard/Bibliothèque de la Pléiade, 1960.

Vanoncini, André. *Figures de la modernité. Essai d'épistémologie sur l'invention du discours balzacien.* Paris: Corti, 1984.

Vasquez, John A. *The War Puzzle.* Cambridge: Cambridge University Press, 1993.

Vauvenargues, Luc de Clapiers, marquis de. *Oeuvres.* Edited by D.-L. Gilbert. Paris: Furne, 1857.

Vest, James M. "Dreams and the Romance Tradition in George Sand's *Indiana*." *French Forum* 3 (1978): 35–47.

Vigny, Alfred de. *Oeuvres complètes*. Edited by Fernand Baldensperger. 2 vols. Paris: Conard, 1935.

———. *Oeuvres complètes*. Edited by Fernand Baldensperger. Vol. 2. Paris: Gallimard/Bibliothèque de la Pléiade, 1948.

———. *Servitude et grandeur militaires*. Edited by Auguste Dorchain. Paris: Garnier, 1955.

———. *Stello; Daphné*. Edited by Annie Prassoloff. Paris: Gallimard, 1986.

Villiers de L'Isle-Adam, Auguste, comte de. *Axël*. Paris: Quantin, 1890.

Voltaire. *Essai sur les moeurs*. Edited by René Pomeau. Vol. 2. Paris: Garnier, 1963.

———. *Mélanges*. Edited by Emmanuel Berl. Paris: Gallimard/Bibliothèque de la Pléiade, 1961:

———. *Oeuvres complètes*. Vol. 48. Oxford: Voltaire Foundation, 1984.

Vouilloux, Bernard. "La description du tableau: la peinture et l'innommable." *Littérature* 73 (février 1989): 61–82.

Wahl, Pauline. "Stendhal's *Lamiel*: Observations on Pygmalionism." *Pre-text / Text / Context: Essays on Nineteenth-Century French Literature*. Edited by Robert L. Mitchell. Columbus: Ohio State University Press, 1980.

Weil, Kari. "A Woman's Place in the Utopian Home." *Home and Its Dislocations*. Edited by Suzanne Nash. Albany: State University of New York Press, 1993.

White, Hayden. *The Content of the Form. Narrative Discourse and Historical Representation*. Baltimore and London: Johns Hopkins University Press, 1987.

Wilde, Oscar. *The Complete Works of Oscar Wilde*. New York: Harper and Row, 1989.

Wilkinson, Lynn R. "Gender and Class in Stendhal's *Lamiel*." *Romanic Review* 80 (1989): 57–74.

Winchell, James. "Capital and Cephalic Oil: Annointment, Sacrifice and Foundation in *César Birotteau*." Paper presented at the NCFS Colloquium, Binghamton, 1992.

Wingard, Kristina. 1983. "Thèmes et techniques narratives chez George Sand d'*Indiana* (1832) aux *Maîtres sonneurs* (1853)." *Actes du VIIIe Congrès des Romanistes Scandinaves*. Odense University Press, 1983.

Wordsworth, William. "Resolution and Independence." *The Poetical Works of William Wordsworth*. Edited by E. de Sélincourt. Oxford: Clarendon Press, 1944.

Zaragoza, Georges. *Charles Nodier: Le dériseur sensé*. Paris: Klincksieck, 1992.

Ziff, Norman D. *Paul Delaroche: A Study in Nineteenth-Century French History Painting*. New York: Garland, 1977.

Zola, Emile. *Les Rougon-Macquart*. 6 vols. Paris: Seuil/Intégrale, 1969–70.

———. *Salons*. Genève: Droz, 1959.

Index